S0-ALI-609

THE
AQUARIUM FISH
SURVIVAL MANUAL

THE
AQUARIUM FISH
SURVIVAL MANUAL

NEW
BURLINGTON
BOOKS

A QUARTO BOOK

This edition published 1989 by
New Burlington Books
6 Blundell Street
London N7 9BH

© Quill Publishing Limited 1985

All rights reserved
No part of this publication may be reproduced,
stored in a retrieval system, or transmitted, in any form or by any means,
electronic, mechanical, photocopying, recording
or otherwise, without the permission of the
copyright holder.

ISBN 1 85348 173 4

This book was designed and produced by
Quarto Publishing plc
The Old Brewery, 6 Blundell Street
London N7 9BH

Senior editor Patricia Webster
Project editor Paul Barnett
Editors Jane Laing Emma Foa
Designer Ian Hunt
Photographer John Heseltine
Illustrators Ray Brown Fraser Newman
Indexer Richard Bird
Also thanks to Stewart Larking

Art director Nigel Osborne
Editorial director Jim Miles

Quill would like to extend special thanks to
the British Marine Aquarists' Association;
Rosalind Everett, Anglo Aquarium Plant;
and the author would like to thank Eileen Gascoigne.

Typeset by Leaper & Gard Ltd, Bristol, England
Colour origination by Hong Kong Graphic Arts Limited, Hong Kong
Printed and bound by Leefung-Asco Printers Limited, Hong Kong

CONTENTS

INTRODUCTION

ABOVE: *The type of aquarium kept by most tropical fish hobbyists is the community tank. It contains a mixture of compatible fish, which live together peacefully. This tank is well planted and also acts as a decorative feature of the room.*

ABOVE: *The Paradise fish,* Macropodus opercularis *was probably the first tropical fish to be seen in Western Europe. An extremely hardy fish, it can withstand low temperatures and poor conditions.*

Many people feel that keeping tropical fish is complicated and difficult, but very often these same people own pet goldfish, which are in fact very much harder to keep looking attractive and clean, and much less likely to thrive in the home.

Tropical fish are beautiful, fascinating and relaxing to watch. They enhance any home, and require the minimum of care. If you want to treat them as more than just living decoration, there are many species you can breed and whose young you can then raise. If you are ambitious and prepared to put even more effort into your hobby, you can enhance your home with what is, in effect, a section of a tropical coral reef complete with some of the most dazzlingly coloured living creatures on Earth.

The practice of keeping fish as pets, and of breeding them, goes back thousands of years. Fish-keeping was raised to a fine art by the ancient Chinese, and later the Japanese took over, developing the goldfish in all its forms and colours by breeding selectively from close relatives of the common Crucian carp. True tropical fish have likewise been widely kept over many centuries. In the Far East, Siamese fighting fish (*Betta splendens*) and the Halfbeak (*Dermogenys pusillus*) have traditionally been bred for fighting — a practice which continues today. They command high prices, and heavy bets are placed on the fights. Other fish are, of course, kept in Asia for more pacific reasons.

The Paradise fish (*Macropodus opercularis*) was probably the first tropical fish to be kept successfully in Europe, having been brought in by mariners. This fish is unusual among 'tropicals' in that it can survive in unheated water at normal room temperatures. A fish described by Samuel Pepys in 1665 may well have been a Paradise fish, although by about that time the goldfish, too, had been introduced into England.

It was not until the nineteenth century that fish-keeping became popular in Europe, with the construction of a number of public aquaria. Since then the hobby has enjoyed several booms, first in the 1930s, then in the years following World War II, and again more recently. Today the emphasis seems to be changing towards keeping the more spectacular marine fish, although most tropical species kept in the home are still freshwater, since they are hardy and need little attention, and do not require the use of a great deal of specialized equipment.

There are of course many thousands of species of freshwater fish, and even more of marine fish, to be found in the wild. However, only a few of these are kept in the home. Most wild fish are neither particularly attractive nor notably interesting in their behaviour, and so are rarely bred. Many other species are highly

ABOVE: *The Siamese fighting fish,* Betta splendens, *is a well-known and popular aquarium fish. It bears little resemblance to its wild, drab relation of Southeast Asia, which for centuries has been bred to fight. Wagers are still placed on the outcome of vicious battles between the male fish. The modern, domesticated form has been bred to produce bright colours and flowing finnage.*

specialized for the habitats which they occupy, so that it is extremely difficult to create conditions in the aquarium suitable for them to thrive. Indeed, while you can adjust water conditions in your aquarium, albeit often with some difficulty, most aquarists compromise by accepting water conditions in which a wide range of the readily available species will succeed. These species are the hardiest, capable of adapting to water changes, unnatural lighting and the stresses of captivity.

If the conditions in the aquarium are sufficiently agreeable to the fish, they will breed, and this is one of the most fascinating aspects of the hobby. A few fish breed in the presence of other species in the common aquarium, but these are rare. More commonly, the presence of other fishes disturbs or interferes with any attempts to breed, and almost always leads to the eggs or young offspring being eaten. In a densely planted aquarium, however, some of the young may escape this fate by hiding in the plants, and standard aquarium fishes like Guppies (*Poecilia reticulata*), Platies (*Xiphophorus variatus*) and Swordtails (*X. helleri*) often breed in community tanks in this way.

For most fish to breed in captivity, though, they must have peace and quiet and some understanding of their breeding require-

ments on the part of the aquarist. A special tank for each species — or sometimes even for each breeding pair — is necessary. You must practise careful aquarium hygiene in order to protect the vulnerable spawn or fry, and pay painstaking attention to the provision of food for the young.

Freshwater fish are generally easier to breed than the marine varieties, which with a few exceptions are not bred in the aquarium.

Difficult though it may sometimes be, there is every incentive to breed tropical fish either in the home or in commercial fish hatcheries, as importing them is very expensive. Fish bred in captivity are well acclimatized, and are generally healthier than wild stock, which can be diseased. In addition, they can be bred selectively to produce improved colouring, larger fins and other changes which have given rise to the wide range of brilliantly attractive fish freely and cheaply available today.

However, you may not want to go to the trouble of breeding your own fish. In this case, the best possible instruction is: keep it simple. An aquarium can be set up and maintained without undue complication, needing minimal attention for years. Most fish live for years, too, and if chosen properly will not outgrow the tank or

LEFT: *Most aquarists keep tropical marine fish for their beautiful colours and bizarre shapes.*

TOP AND ABOVE: Botia macracantha *has a large spine beneath its eye. The Black neon,* Hyphessobrycon herbertaxelrodi, *bears the name of its discoverer.*

BELOW: *This delicate marine Angelfish cannot be bred in the aquarium and is expensive to buy.*

dine on their fellow-occupants. It doesn't cost much to set up a tank of Guppies or other common freshwater fishes. Alternatively, at a rather greater cost, you can concentrate your attention on some more specialized type of fish.

Whatever your level of interest, however, the keeping of an aquarium is an extremely rewarding hobby, which will amply repay your investment of time and money.

THE TYPES OF FISH

To a person first starting to keep fish as a hobby, the taxonomic (Latin) names can be distinctly offputting. However, these names have a very real and important function. Although every aquarist knows exactly what a Guppy, Swordtail or Neon is, these popular names become less useful when you are dealing with the less common types — some of which have no popular name at all. In particular, popular names are least reliable when applied to newly imported varieties, where the dealer usually makes up some imposing-sounding name — anything that comes to mind and 'looks good'. In the case of marine fishes, the diversity of types is so huge that the use of taxonomic names is imperative.

So how do these names work? They have two parts. The first is the generic name; it describes a particular group or single type of fish. Generally speaking, fish within the same genus will be quite similar in size, appearance and behaviour, but may vary considerably in their colours. The genus name starts with a capital letter, as in *Barbus* or *Rasbora*.

The second part of the name is the specific name; that is, it denotes the species to which the fish belongs. By convention, the name is always given with an initial letter in lower-case. For example, the Clown loach is technically called *Botia macracantha*. It belongs to the genus *Botia*, but there are several species in this genus. The specific name *macracantha* means that this particular fish carries a large spine (in this fish, the spine is beneath the eye). A similar and related fish is *B. pulchripinnis*, something of whose appearance can be deduced from the fact that *pulchripinnis* means 'pretty-finned'.

Sometimes, as in these examples, the names are useful and descriptive to those with even the lightest smattering of Latin, but often they are abitrary and would make a scholar flinch, being merely a Latinization of the discoverer's name: *Hyphessobrycon herbertaxelrodi* is the classic example. Moreover, it is the convention that spelling errors in the Latin used by the discoverer and namer of a new species are preserved: had the Clown loach been christened *B. mocrocontho* by some dyslexic discoverer, the name would inevitably have stuck.

A further complication is that the system is not so cut-and-dried as it may sound. The earliest description of a fish (or any other organism) always takes priority, unless the original classification

Aplocheilus lineatus

Pseudotropheus auratus

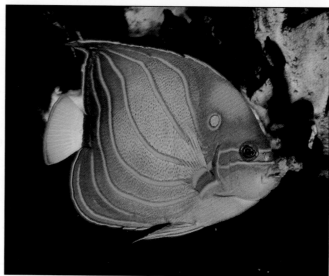

Pomacanthus annularis

Symphyosodon aequifasciata haraldi

Cichlasoma octofasciatum

TOP FAR LEFT: *The second or specific part of the name* Aplocheilus lineatus *refers to the lines or bars which can be seen on the side of the fish.*
BELOW FAR LEFT: *Sometimes a subspecies or minor variant of a fish is precisely described by the addition of a further name, as in the case of this Discus,* Symphysodon aequifasciata haraldi.
TOP LEFT: *The specific name of the Cichlid,* Pseudotropheus auratus, *refers to its golden-yellow colouring.*
MIDDLE LEFT: *The small ring, or annulus, on the shoulder of* Pomacanthus annularis *gives the fish its specific name.*
BOTTOM LEFT: *As its name reveals,* Cichlasoma octofasciatum *has eight bars running along its side.*

put the creature in quite the wrong genus; for example, there were many early attempts to put the Orangutan in the genus *Homo*. More importantly from our point of view, it is quite often discovered that a fish whose taxonomic name has become well established is in fact identical with one which was described and differently named some while before; all the textbooks have therefore to be changed. Another possibility is that biologists may decide to alter the groupings for technical reasons — usually because two species hitherto ascribed to different genera are discovered to be very closely related on the evolutionary tree. Before evolution was fully appreciated, scientists, for obvious reasons, classified lifeforms according to their shapes and structures (morphologies), which meant that many misleading classifications appeared. Even today, morphological considerations may lead biologists to temporarily classify newly discovered species into quite the wrong genera. In due course such mistakes are corrected, so that the universally recognized *Barbus* overnight may become *Puntius*, or *Molliensia* become *Poecilia*.

The whole system of taxonomic nomenclature is, therefore, something of a labyrinth — and one whose walls are quite frequently being moved. For this reason, I have decided in this book to make no attempt to keep up with every latest variant name, but in all cases to avoid confusion by using the most commonly accepted taxonomic name — with alternatives listed where appropriate. (Consult the index for a complete cross-reference.)

But there is more to the taxonomic story than a fish's specific and generic names. Each genus falls into a broader grouping called a family, and so on up to the broadest grouping of all, the kingdom (fish obviously fall into the kingdom Animalia). In ascending order up the evolutionary tree, these higher taxa are family, order, subclass, class, superclass, subphylum, phylum and, finally, kingdom. In practice, and certainly for the purposes of this book, there is little point in carrying the classification beyond the level of the family, except in a very few cases.

HOW TO USE THIS BOOK

This book is divided into three parts. The first concerns itself with the sort of general knowledge with which any successful aquarist should be at least vaguely acquainted: the biological functions of fish and the general provisions which should be made for the home aquarium.

Part Two concentrates on the freshwater aquarium, and contains an extensive directory of the various freshwater species which you might wish to own. Part Three performs the same function for the marine (saltwater) aquarium.

Finally, you will find a comprehensive index, subdivided into three sections: Index of fish, General index and Index of plants. Use the index to locate individual species and topics quickly and easily.

PART ONE
GENERAL KNOWLEDGE

The gaily coloured tropical fish you can see in the dealer's tanks, or in public aquaria, can be maintained in your own home with very little fuss or bother, and at a surprisingly modest cost. If you take the trouble to understand these exotic creatures and the way they survive in the wild, you will find it relatively easy to provide an environment in which they will live for a long time, and even breed, if conditions are really to their liking.

You must remember that aquarium fish come from almost all parts of the tropics and, particularly in the case of freshwater varieties, from a very wide range of specialized habitats; it is, therefore, not always possible to provide suitable accommodation in a single tank for all the types of fish you may wish to keep. Some may require different water conditions; others may be too aggressive with their tank-mates, to the extent that some must be kept singly, or only with others of their own kind. If in doubt as to the suitability of a particular type of fish, don't buy it.

When starting an aquarium, it is always best to find a reliable dealer who can give you the advice you need. Look for a dealer whose tanks are spotlessly clean and all of whose fish look alert and healthy.

LEFT: *Some small but spectacular fish, such as* Aphyosemion australe, *require a knowledge of their natural habitat and careful attention to their special requirements if they are to thrive in the aquarium.*

FISH AND HOW THEY WORK

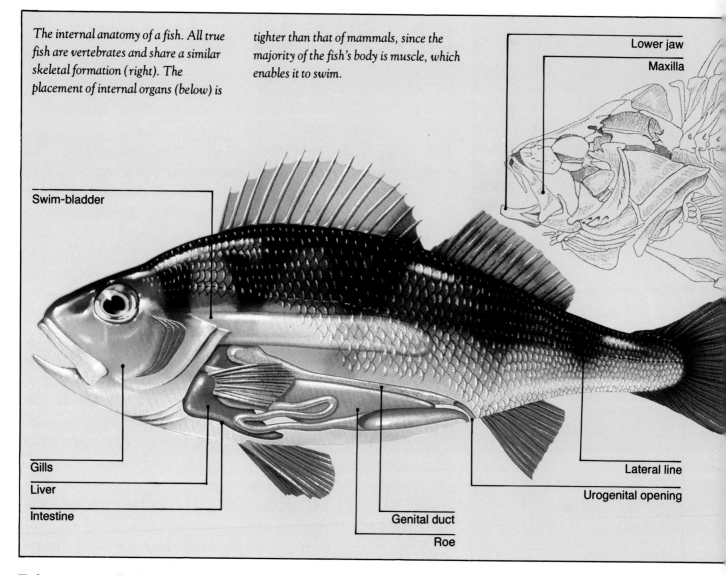

The internal anatomy of a fish. All true fish are vertebrates and share a similar skeletal formation (right). The placement of internal organs (below) is tighter than that of mammals, since the majority of the fish's body is muscle, which enables it to swim.

Lower jaw

Maxilla

Swim-bladder

Gills

Liver

Intestine

Genital duct

Roe

Lateral line

Urogenital opening

Fish come in all shapes and sizes. The Whale shark is the largest, up to 20m (66ft) in length, while others are less than 1cm (½in) long, but all fish are constructed to roughly the same general plan, with the same types of structure and organs. This applies even to very oddly shaped fish; although their bodies are distorted and adapted for some specific function, they nevertheless have all the basic organs common to other fish.

Fish have skeletons to support their muscles and allow them to swim: those of sharks and rays are rubbery, but fish kept in the aquarium normally have bony skeletons. Like other higher animals, fish have a skull protecting the brain, and a long spinal column, made of vertebrae jointed together. (In everyday speech we often talk about invertebrate marine creatures, such as shellfish, as 'fish', but strictly speaking the word should be applied only to vertebrates.)

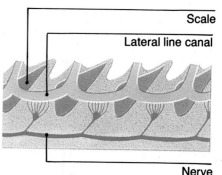

Scale

Lateral line canal

Nerve

A vertical section through the lateral line. This unique sensory organ, clearly visible on many species, detects variations in water pressure around the fish.

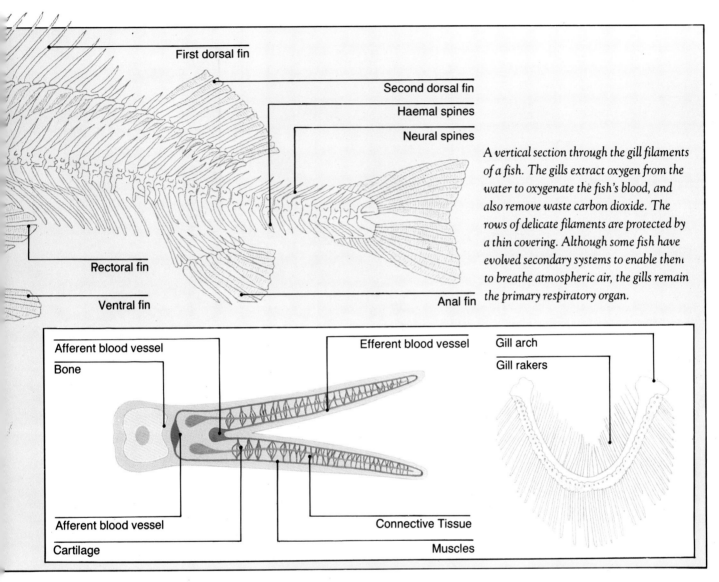

First dorsal fin

Second dorsal fin

Haemal spines

Neural spines

Rectoral fin

Ventral fin

Anal fin

A vertical section through the gill filaments of a fish. The gills extract oxygen from the water to oxygenate the fish's blood, and also remove waste carbon dioxide. The rows of delicate filaments are protected by a thin covering. Although some fish have evolved secondary systems to enable them to breathe atmospheric air, the gills remain the primary respiratory organ.

Afferent blood vessel

Bone

Efferent blood vessel

Gill arch

Gill rakers

Afferent blood vessel

Cartilage

Connective Tissue

Muscles

By far the greatest part of a fish's bulk is made up of muscle. The other internal organs are packed into what is, by comparison with mammals, a very small space. The muscles of a fish drive it forwards through the water by flexing its spine from side to side.

The fins assist in swimming, and in stabilizing the fish. The tail, or caudal, fin at the end of the body works like an oar, to help propel the fish forwards. The dorsal fin, on the back of the fish, stops it rolling from side to side, as do the small pelvic or ventral fins and the anal fin. Towards the front of the body, corresponding to a mammal's front legs, are the pectoral fins. These are not generally used while swimming at speed, but are, together with the pelvic fins, extended for braking. The pectoral fins are used also to manoeuvre the fish slowly, acting as paddles. The fins have further functions, such as for sexual display and threatening other fish. Fins may be modified, or even missing, but there is always some

ABOVE: *The fish's scales overlap to form a flexible 'armour' that streamlines and protects the body.*

Pomacanthus imperator, *the Imperial angelfish, easily slips through small gaps.*

Zanclus cornutus, *the Moorish idol, is easy to recognize.*

Derivations of one species

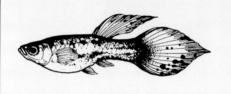

Male guppies clearly illustrate the effects of selective breeding over many years. TOP LEFT: *The wild fish is small and has only a slightly larger tail fin than the female.*

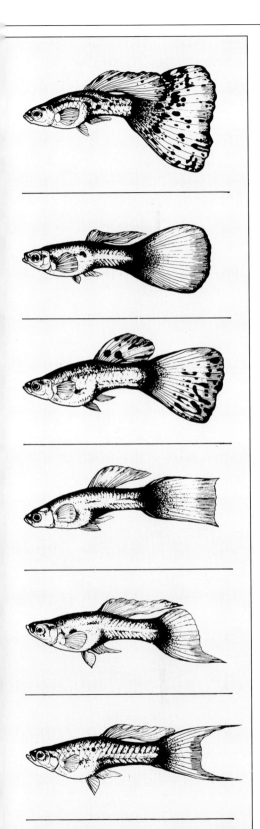

The domesticated forms have developed enormously enlarged tails of varying shapes, which can be found in a wide range of colours.

The slender Marine catfish, Plotosus lineatus, can enter tiny holes.

specific reason for such departures from the basic plan.

One of the most important organs is the swim bladder, which acts as a buoyancy tank to control the position of the fish in the water. Like a submarine's tanks, it can be filled or emptied to keep the fish stationary at any depth. It is of significance to the aquarist only when it goes wrong, with the result that the fish either becomes too buoyant or sinks. The swim bladder is sometimes used like a resonator, with the fish making grunting or clicking noises which can be clearly heard outside the tank. Some bottom-living fish have no swim bladders, and must swim hard to leave the bottom.

By use of their gills, fish obtain oxygen from the water in which they swim. The gills are a series of branching, delicate organs in which thin (capillary) blood vessels are each surrounded by a thin membrane. They are contained in gill chambers, which lie at the back of the fish's mouth. Water is taken in through the fish's mouth and forced through gill slits over the gills; oxygen is absorbed from the water through the thin membrane and into the capillaries, while carbon dioxide is expelled.

Not all fish obtain oxygen solely through use of their gills. Some, which live in water deficient in oxygen, supplement their supplies by gulping air from the surface into specialized organs. Labyrinth fish take air into a lung-like chamber in the head, while some Catfish swallow air bubbles into the gut, the oxygen being then absorbed through the gut walls.

The bizarre shape of Pterois volitans *acts as both camouflage and warning.*

The mouth and jaws of fish are specially modified according to their diet. Fish are incapable of chewing, although a few can grind up food in their throats: most simply gulp their food in one piece. They may have small teeth to help them grip their prey, and a few types, including the famous Piranha, have sharp teeth which can cut through their prey's flesh.

The kidneys of fish are proportionately very much larger than those of mammals. Being surrounded by water, the tissues of a fish could easily become waterlogged, so the kidneys must work hard to maintain the proper water balance. Some fish, such as the Scat, Malay angel and Archerfish, which can live in either fresh, brackish or pure seawater, have kidneys specially adapted to help them cope with these varying conditions.

Fish have some special senses which we do not possess. Along each side of a fish is a line called the lateral line, running from just behind the gill covers to the tail. It may be straight, but is more often curved. The lateral line consists of a fine tube, connected to the surface at intervals, and containing large numbers of tiny sense organs. These can detect movements in the surrounding water very accurately, and are used as a form of radar. Fish which swim closely together in schools position themselves by means of the signals received through the lateral line, and many species hunt their food by detecting movements in the same way.

Some fish have very well developed organs of smell; these may be in pits on the head, as in Eels, or on long sensitive whiskers, as

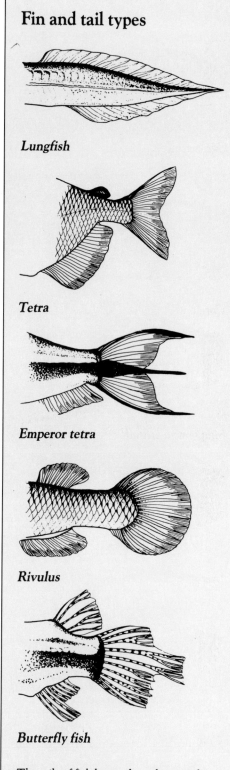

Fin and tail types

Lungfish

Tetra

Emperor tetra

Rivulus

Butterfly fish

The tails of fish have adapted to suit their differing ways of life. The sluggish Lungfish has an eel-like tail, which allows it to swim deep into muddy reed banks, while the short, rounded tail of the Rivulus allows it to make powerful leaps at its prey. Frequently, the tails of male

in Catfish. These fish are able to find food even in dark turbid water where their eyes are useless. A few extraordinary fish generate electric fields with which they can sense their surroundings; they, too, are found in dark muddy waters.

The skin of most fish is covered with scales — thin bony plates which protect and streamline the body. Scales may be large and silvery or brightly coloured, or can be very tiny and sunk into the skin, as in some Catfish. The colours of fish are produced by living cells containing pigment, which expand or contract according to mood or emotion: as a result, many fish are able to change their colour quickly and completely. A newly purchased fish is usually disappointingly dull-looking until it has settled down and resumed its normal coloration. Similarly, a sick fish often shows its ill-health either by looking pale or, alternatively, by turning almost black.

The whole body of the fish is covered by a slimy layer which both helps to protect it from skin parasites and, by improving its streamlining, enables it to slip more easily through the water.

BREEDING

For fish to breed successfully in the aquarium, they must be healthy and feel that all conditions are right. Generally, it is difficult to breed fish caught in the wild, as they are much more demanding in their requirements, but usually even the most awkward types can be bred by expert aquarists. After the first few generations have been bred, further breeding is progressively less

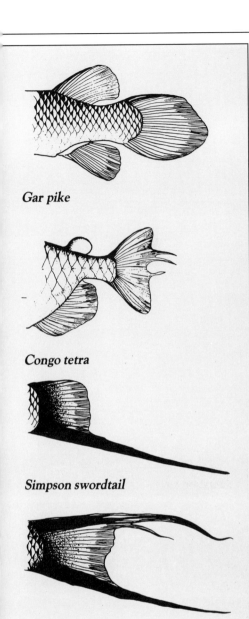

Gar pike

Congo tetra

Simpson swordtail

Lyre swordtail

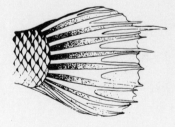

Comb-tail paradise fish

fish are part of their sexual display, as in the case of the Swordtail and the Emperor tetra. For some reason, the elongated tail and any other fins do not always develop in tank-bred fish; this is probably due to a dietary deficiency of some kind.

Cheirodon axelrodi *is spawned in huge numbers commercially.*

19

difficult, as the 'easy breeders' become selected out from the population. Thus fish which, when first imported, commanded very high prices become quite cheap once the principles of breeding have been mastered. For example, the Neon and the Cardinal were originally very expensive and bred only — and with great difficulty — by the specialist, but now both are standard aquarium fishes, available everywhere at moderate prices, and easily bred.

Among the species which cannot be bred easily are those which become very large, and in which only the immature fish are kept in the aquarium. Some African Catfish fall into this category, as do many marine fish. Usually, however, breeding can be accomplished once the environment and biology of the fish are completely understood.

One curious factor in breeding is that, although the breeder can often select out natural mutations with unusual colours or long trailing fins, and develop new strains, sometimes the general quality deteriorates in captivity. For example, it is seldom possible to preserve the huge dorsal fin on the Sailfin molly or the bright colours of the Cichlid *Apistogramma ramirezi* when these fish are bred in captivity. Wild stock are larger, more robust and more brightly coloured.

Breeding considerations have given rise to much of the interesting behaviour of fish. Even colouring can be traced back to breeding needs. Often male and female fish are coloured quite differently, and male fish may be brightly coloured both to attract females and to frighten off rival males.

Most fish do not breed continually. The experienced eye can pick out fish which are pairing off as they reach peak condition for breeding. The sides of the fish fill out, and females, packed with eggs, become especially plump. Colouring becomes generally more intense, and males may display to the females with rigidly outstretched fins. When spawning is imminent, there is often a change in the fishes' behaviour: they tend to become very active and to explore possible spawning sites.

The sexual organs of fish are relatively simple, consisting of paired, elongated organs lying along the abdominal cavity — these organs produce either eggs or sperm (milt). Nearly all fish shed both eggs and milt together into the water, where fertilization takes place. However, a few are live-bearers; that is, the male introduces his milt into the female, who retains the fertilized eggs and gives birth to live young. The Guppy is the best known of these fish.

Fish eggs are thin-walled and delicate, and are eaten greedily by most species, many consuming even their own spawn. Various special techniques have been evolved to ensure the survival of fishes' eggs — or, at least, of enough of them to ensure the continuation of the species. Indeed, the method evolved by most fishes is to produce such huge quantities of eggs that *some* are bound to survive. These egg-scatterers are usually shoaling fish, which spawn in a group. Our common river fish are of this type, and so are their exotic relatives which are kept in the aquarium. Fishes

The fry of the Discus, Symphysodon aequifasciata, *feed on the slime on the parents' bodies.*

like Barbs, Danios and Rasboras all scatter their eggs among plants. Sometimes the eggs are sticky, and become attached to the plants; others simply drop to the bottom. The spawning fish and others promptly eat as many of the eggs as they can find, but some will normally survive, hidden among the leaves of plants or in cracks between the gravel.

In the aquarium, the survival rate can be improved by using a breeding tank. The parent fish are placed in the tank when ready to breed, and removed as soon as spawning is complete, so that the fry can be safely raised. The type of breeding tank used depends on the type of fish involved (details are given on pages 72-129). For fish which naturally spawn on gravel it is usual to cover the tank bottom with glass marbles or glass rods: scattered eggs fall between the marbles or rods, and the parent fish are unable to reach them.

A slightly different set-up is needed for fish which spawn among plants. You can place fine-leaved plants like *Myriophyllum* (see page 65) in the breeding tank but, although these may look more natural to us, fish do not discriminate between them and the more hygienic option, a bunch of nylon wool, which will not carry any disease organisms to attack the eggs or fry. Spawning fish will dive with equal enthusiasm into either plants or wool tufts to deposit their eggs.

Not all fish are such profligate egg-scatterers. Egg-laying tooth-carps attach their eggs individually or in clusters to the plants. As would be expected, more eggs survive so fewer need be laid. Other members of the same group bury their eggs, diving down into the mud on the pool bottom and releasing their spawn. Here it is protected from predators and can survive for long periods — even if the water dries up completely. For some species, the drying-up is essential, and eggs will hatch only after a prolonged period of drying followed by normal aquatic conditions. Since these are the conditions they experience in their normal habitat, the breeder must imitate them (see pages 50-1).

Many fish look after their spawn and their young. This behaviour is typical of the freshwater Cichlids, many marine fish such as Damsels and Clownfish, and various other types. Since parental care provides the best guarantee of survival of the young, these fish are not generally as prolific as egg-scatterers.

The egg-guardians have developed complicated rituals for pairing off and spawning. Most are territorial, which means that once a pair has established itself it drives away all other fish from the selected spawning area, being especially aggressive towards other fish of its own species. These are the species in which the most dazzling courtship displays take place. Often a pair will wrestle or mock-fight and carry out complicated courtship rituals before spawning.

A spawning site is selected — this may be a stone, a leaf, or the tank bottom. Small fish of this type often spawn in a little cave; in the aquarium they will spawn inside an overturned flowerpot. The spawning site is carefully cleaned, and the eggs are fertilized

21

immediately after having been laid. Usually both fish guard the spawning site, driving off intruders and removing any fungussed eggs. The parent fish normally fan the eggs with their fins, and may pick up eggs to clean them with their mouths. When the fry hatch, they are gathered into a group by the parents, who guard them until they are large enough to lead an independent life.

In the breeding tank, egg-guardians are for obvious reasons strictly separated from other fish. However, even the parents may still panic and eat their eggs or fry if disturbed, or if conditions are not quite right.

Some species have modified their spawning behaviour to the point where the eggs are carried in the mouth, completely protected. Usually the female scoops up her eggs as they are laid, then picks at coloured spots on the anal fin of the male which closely resemble the eggs. As she does so, the male releases a cloud of milt, fertilizing the eggs within her mouth. With these mouth-breeders, the fry are gathered back into the mother's mouth when danger threatens.

Another type of protective behaviour is seen in the Labyrinth fishes. In fish of this group, the male constructs a bubble nest from mucus. The bubbles are strong, and form a clump on the water surface. The female is enticed to the nest and, after courtship, the male wraps himself about her and squeezes her so that she sheds her eggs. After fertilization, he catches the eggs in his mouth and 'spits' them into the nest. He then guards the nest from all intruders until the eggs hatch.

The ultimate form of care of the young is found among the live-bearers, such as Guppies, Mollies, Swordtails and Halfbeaks. These are the easiest fish to breed, as they tend to ignore the presence of other fish in the community aquarium. They produce relatively few young, but these are well developed and able to swim actively and feed as soon as they are born.

Male live-bearers have their anal fin modified into a special organ, the gonopodium, which is used to deposit sperm inside the female. The male courts the much larger female, pursuing her until she is receptive. When the female is ready, the male swims alongside and extends his gonopodium sideways, introducing a packet of sperm (a spermatophore) into her vent. Some of these sperms are used directly to fertilize the eggs, but most are stored to fertilize further quantities of eggs at later dates. The young fish are quite large when born — up to 1cm (½in) in length.

This group of fish is unusual in that sex-changes are not uncommon; a female fish may give birth to young fish and then change to become a normal breeding male. In addition, some types of these fish are thought all to be females, producing young by virgin birth (parthogenesis) without the intervention of males.

Once fish have bred, the task of the aquarist is more difficult. Scrupulous cleanliness is necessary in order to prevent eggs or fry being attacked by parasites or predators. The fry are very vulnerable in the early stages. Fish eggs contain yolk, which nourishes

ABOVE: *The Damselfish,* Dascyllus melanurus, *is one of the few marine fish that frequently breeds in the aquarium. Like the freshwater Cichlids, it spawns on rocks or any solid surface and stays close by to guard the eggs. Unfortunately, the fry are very difficult to raise.*

the newly hatched fry for a short time, and this yolk is contained in a large sac which weighs down the newly hatched fish so that it is unable to swim. For the first few days after hatching, therefore, the fry lie helplessly on the tank bottom, or sometimes attached to the sides or stones. They gradually become mobile as the yolk sac is absorbed, and begin to feed. This is the critical time. They must be fed on precisely the right type of food, supplied in the proper size; they will then grow rapidly. Nevertheless, there is usually a high mortality rate among such young fish.

Anableps anableps *can see both above and below the surface.*

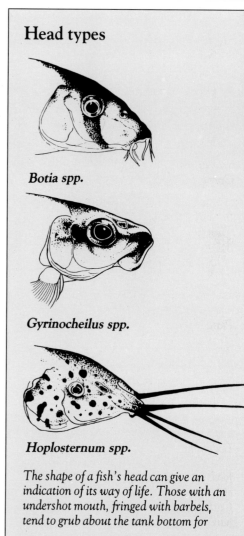

Head types

Botia spp.

Gyrinocheilus spp.

Hoplosternum spp.

The shape of a fish's head can give an indication of its way of life. Those with an undershot mouth, fringed with barbels, tend to grub about the tank bottom for

FISH, THEIR HABITATS AND THEIR ADAPTATIONS

Thanks to the process of evolution, fish — and other organisms — have become adapted to suit the specific types of environment in which they live.

The minimum amount of modification is seen in fish of large, moderately fast-running rivers and of the open seas. Fish living in these habitats are usually elongated, and have no exceptional changes to their fins or body-shapes. Some of the Barbs and fish like the Herring are typical of this type; unless they are brightly coloured, they seldom make interesting aquarium inhabitants.

Fishes may be adapted to feed on insects floating on the surface, in which case they will normally have an upturned mouth, and the upper surface of their bodies will be flattened so that they can lie with their head and body close to the surface. The Hatchetfish and Archerfish are adapted in this way. For feeding on the bottom, the reverse is true, so that the fish's underside is flattened and its mouth undershot, as in *Corydoras* (Catfish). Often the mouth of bottom-feeders is fringed with sensory whiskers (barbels) to help them find food while grubbing about in the mud. Some more ordinary-shaped fish get over the problem of bottom-feeding by having swimming habits which allow them literally to stand on their heads (*Chilodus, Anostomus* and *Leporinus*).

The snake-like Catfish, Clarias batrachus.

24

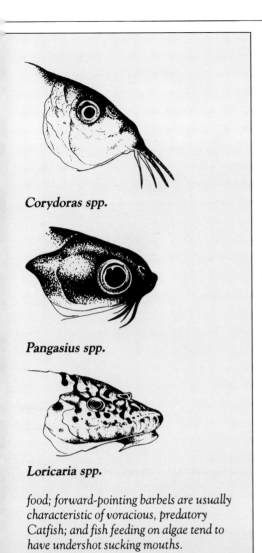

Corydoras spp.

Pangasius spp.

Loricaria spp.

food; forward-pointing barbels are usually characteristic of voracious, predatory Catfish; and fish feeding on algae tend to have undershot sucking mouths.

In the wild, the bright colours of the Betta *attract a mate and warn off enemies.*

The degree of local water movement, or its lack, can also be responsible for modifications, over the generations, in the appearance of fish. Fish adapted for fast-flowing streams are often elongated, rapid movers, like the Trout, and are restless swimmers in the aquarium. In addition, they have very high oxygen requirements, and so may not be ideal inhabitants of a crowded tank. Alternatively, fish adapted to such habitats may be flattened bottom-livers, able to cling to the stream-bed to avoid being swept away. Several Loaches and Catfish are of this type.

In still or slow-flowing waters, water movement is not a major influence on fish adaptation, and other considerations come into play. Camouflage, warning colouring, special feeding techniques and courtship can all affect the development of interesting characteristics. For example, while the Angelfish's shortened and compressed body makes it highly distinctive in the aquarium, it becomes almost invisible in its natural habitat, among reed stems, the vertical stripes adding to its effective camouflage.

The colouring of fish is a balance between two opposing biological principles. A fish must be camouflaged to blend with its surroundings and protect it from predators, but at the same time it may need bright colouring or large fins to attract a mate and scare off possible rivals. In general, the brightest colours are found in fish able to defend themselves against predators (such as the Cichlids), or which can move swiftly to escape predators (like Danios and many Barbs), or which hide among dense vegetation.

THE HOME AQUARIUM

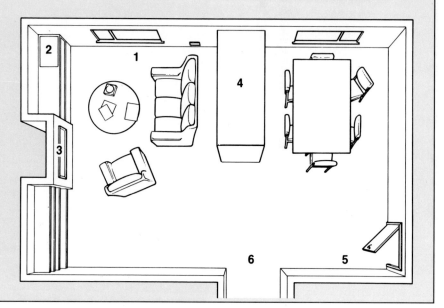

Locating the aquarium

1 Never place an aquarium in direct sunlight or close to an open fire.

2 A large aquarium can be neatly tucked away in an alcove, provided that the floorboards and joists beneath are strong enough to bear its weight.

3 Aquaria can be attractively located in a natural recess, such as a disused fireplace or serving hatch.

4 Aquaria make unusual room dividers, but you must ensure that the tank is located close to a double electrical socket.

5 Never place an aquarium in a draught from an open door or window.

6 Avoid siting a tank in a busy thoroughfare, to protect it from knocks and vibrations.

Before embarking on keeping tropical fish, first consider where you are going to keep them. An aquarium is a large rectangular box which takes up a lot of space — but even more space is taken up by the stand, for it is best to set the aquarium 0.5-1m (20-40in) from the floor, so that you can see the fish without bending down. Even a moderate-sized aquarium is *very* heavy — probably 400kg (nearly 8cwt) or more — and so cannot be put on top of any ordinary piece of furniture.

You will need at least a double socket for the exclusive use of your tank and its equipment. It is no good sharing the socket with the vacuum cleaner, as sooner or later someone will forget to put the aquarium plug back in after doing the housework.

So what is the ideal position for an aquarium? You need a place where the floor is adequately strong — no weak floorboards. Sometimes an alcove or a knocked-out fireplace provides a suitable site for an aquarium, which can be built-in so that the associated plumbing and cables are concealed behind panelling. Aquaria have also been successfully built into disused serving hatches between rooms; and specially made tanks, if they are sufficiently tall, can be used as room dividers.

There are several important 'don'ts' when planning a position for an aquarium. **Don't** put it in a sunlit spot. If you do, algae will grow over the glass and spoil the appearance of the tank. You can have better control of the lighting by switching the tank lights on and off at the proper times of day, and you can also thereby regulate the lighting so that algae will not thrive. **Don't** position the

ABOVE: *Positioning an aquarium requires careful consideration, as it is difficult to rectify mistakes later. Positions in direct sunlight or severe draughts are best avoided, as are corridors or throughways. Factors to bear in mind when planning the position of your aquarium are the availability of an exclusive double power socket; the strength of the flooring, or the presence of a supporting joist; the possibility of utilising an existing fitment, such as an alcove, a disused fireplace, or a serving hatch or room divider.*

ABOVE RIGHT: *Setting your aquarium in an alcove, so that no light shines through from behind, ensures that the colours in the tank appear especially vibrant.*
RIGHT AND FAR RIGHT: *Favourable positions for an aquarium: out of the way of direct sunlight and draughts, and against a wall.*

Types of tank

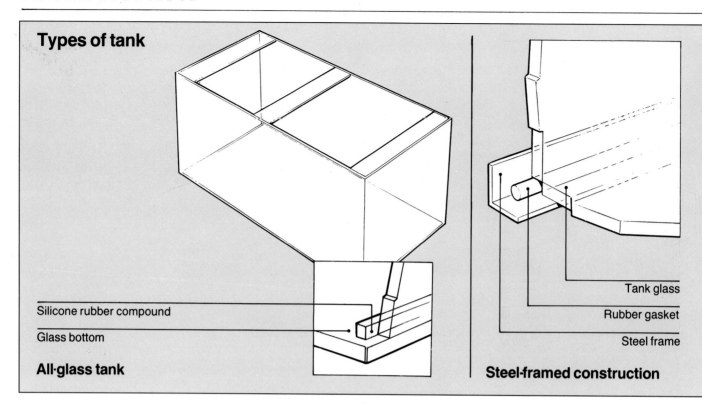

Silicone rubber compound

Glass bottom

All·glass tank

Tank glass

Rubber gasket

Steel frame

Steel-framed construction

Fish tank sizes/weights

The weight of a fish tank is an important consideration — tanks can be surprisingly heavy. The weight of the water itself is a major factor, although the tank, stand and contents can add up, too; the larger the tank, of course, the more it weighs. Small glass tanks are often cast in a piece and are useful for breeding, as they are easy to clean; the drawbacks are that casting makes the glass slightly opaque and it cracks easily. The maximum size for such tanks is about 36×26×24cm (14×10×9in), which gives a capacity of 20l (4.5gal), weighing 20kg (44lb). Plastic is rapidly replacing glass for tanks of this size, as it is lighter and easier to handle.

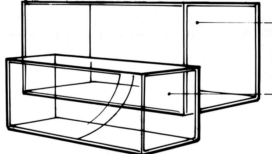

SIZE	100x40x50cm
CAPACITY	200l
WEIGHT	200kg

SIZE	80x26x38cm
CAPACITY	c80l
WEIGHT	c80kg

RIGHT: *The diagram illustrates how weight increases dramatically with only quite a small increase in dimensions.*

BELOW RIGHT: *Bear in mind that any rocks, gravel and so forth added to the tank will increase the overall weight, sometimes quite noticeably.*

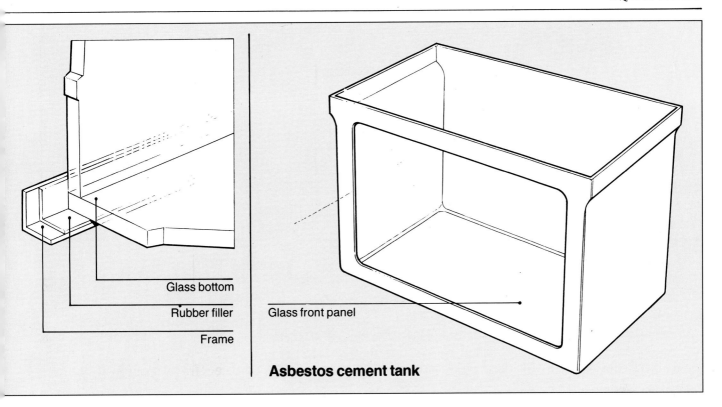

Glass bottom

Rubber filler

Frame

Glass front panel

Asbestos cement tank

ABOVE: *The modern, all-glass aquarium is now almost universally used, as it is durable, attractive, and reasonably priced. Older types with steel frames, or frames constructed from concrete or asbestos, can sometimes be acquired very cheaply, and may be worth refurbishing.*

tank in a draughty hall. These are *tropical* fish, and should be treated accordingly. And **Don't** position the tank where people will constantly be pushing past it, or where it could be knocked during the housework. Aquaria are extremely strong, but a sharp accidental blow can shatter the glass when it has the full weight of the water pressing against it. Moreover, the fish will be disturbed by constant movement around the tank.

EQUIPMENT

Types of Tank: The type of tank you buy depends to some extent on the sort of fish-keeping you intend to pursue. Generally speaking, it is a false economy to buy a small tank, for a number of important reasons. Firstly, a small tank will almost inevitably be a *too* small tank — ie, it is likely to be overstocked — and this is dangerous to the fish. More important, the larger the tank, the more stable it is as an environment, and the more the whole system is able to resist changes which could damage the fish. Beginners, who often start out with a small tank, are also the least able to anticipate problems and head them off at an early stage. So always buy the largest tank you can afford and can safely accommodate. Although many fish will live in small tanks, it is best to start with one of at least 90 l (20 gal) capacity. This will be approximately 60 cm long, 30 cm in breadth, and 37.5 cm in depth (24×12×15 in), and will weigh about 90 kg (200 lb). For reasons discussed later (see page 134), marine fish require even larger tanks than freshwater fish.

The capacity of a tank is determined by multiplying the length by the depth by the breadth, then dividing the result by 1000 (metric) or 280 (imperial).

For many years, steel-frame aquaria were the rule, but these have now been generally superseded by all-glass tanks. These are made from five sections of plate glass, bonded along their edges with very tough silicone rubber, and are extremely strong. They have the added advantage that they avoid the unsightly frame of the older type of tank. But remember that, the larger the tank, the thicker the glass has to be: for a giant tank of 1m (40in) depth, the side would need to be of at least 13mm (½in) plate glass, and the bottom nearly 2cm (¾in) thick. For the average aquarist, therefore, such giant tanks are not really practicable. However, due to the simplicity of the construction, aquarium manufacturers can rapidly make up a tank of any special size to fit a particular corner or alcove you may have.

Bonded-glass tanks of this type have many advantages over the traditional variety. The seal is slightly flexible, and will not leak if the tank shifts slightly. The tanks are comparatively light and are cheaper to make; and, having no internal gaps around the edges, they are easy to clean and will not allow contaminants to seep into the water.

Small tanks do have their place — for breeding purposes, or as quarantine or hospital tanks. Small metal- or plastic-framed tanks can be used for these purposes, but *must never be used for marine fish*. Not only is saltwater much more proficient at corroding metal than is fresh, but these fish are very sensitive to dissolved metals or other substances in the water. So use only all-glass or all-plastic tanks.

You may be offered an old metal-framed aquarium for renovation for freshwater use. If you want to use it, first strip it down. Remove or knock out the old glass (it is almost impossible to remove it without breaking it). Chip out the dried putty or mastic, and sandpaper all the rust off the frame. Paint the whole frame with rust-proofing primer as used for cars, followed by a layer of non-toxic gloss paint, which must be allowed to dry thoroughly.

BELOW: *The ideal position for the light is directly above the tank.*
BELOW RIGHT: *If a small reflector is placed towards the front, the back of the tank is left in shadow.*
RIGHT: *Lights towards the front of the tank and a medium-sized reflector give good all-round illumination.*

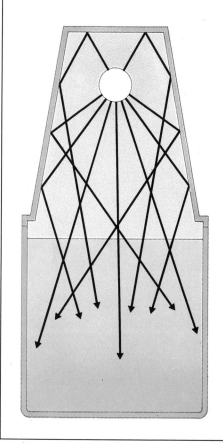

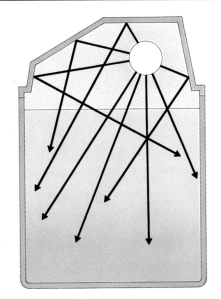

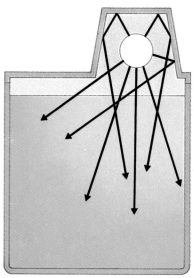

LEFT: *An arrangement of waterworn rock and waterlogged wood can be very attractive if properly planned. Usually these materials must be cemented in place with silicone adhesive to prevent the fish dislodging them. Purchase such materials from a reputable dealer, as using the wrong one could have a devastating effect on water conditions.*

The glass must then be sealed in using special aquarium putty or, preferably, aquarium mastic. Neither substance dries out completely, so you obtain a slightly flexible seal. Start off by running a strip of mastic around the bottom edge of the frame, then seat the bottom glass (this can be wired glass, for extra strength). Add the sides, pressing the glass carefully against the mastic to bed it in well. Stand the tank on a flat surface and fill it cautiously; excess mastic will be pressed out and can be trimmed off tidily. Leave the tank filled with water for at least a week, and then empty and clean it thoroughly before setting it up with fish and plants.

Covers and Lights

All aquaria need some form of cover. Without one, many fish will be able to jump out and be killed. In addition, the rates of evaporation and heat-loss from the water surface will both be very high.

Special plastic clips are available to suspend a sheet of glass just below the top edge of the tank so that condensation can drip back into the tank and the need for frequent topping-up be reduced. A small gap is left around the edges for air lines and electrical cables.

Artificial lighting is required, and must be in the form of miniature fluorescent tubes; these produce very little excess heat, unlike ordinary light bulbs. However, the colour of light they produce can be rather unnatural. It is best to buy special tubes manufactured for horticultural use: these produce a purplish-coloured light which both enhances the colours of fish and stimulates plant growth. You can buy a plastic or metal hood to contain the lights; this simply stands on the glass cover. As with all aquarium electrics, it is absolutely essential that this is properly earthed, and connected by a fused plug.

Tank size length × width × height	No.	Fluorescent Tubes required
60 × 25 × 40cm (24 × 10 × 16in)	1 1	20W Horticultural-type 20W Universal white
80 × 26 × 38cm (32 × 10 × 15in)	1 1	20W Horticultural-type 20W Universal white
80 × 10 × 50cm (32 × 16 × 20in)	1 1 1	20W Horticultural-type 20W Universal white 20W Warm tone de luxe
100 × 30 × 40cm (40 × 12 × 16in)	1 1 1	20W Horticultural-type 20W Universal white 20W Warm tone de luxe
100 × 40 × 50cm (40 × 16 × 20in)	1 1 1	20W Horticultural-type 25W Universal white 25W Warm tone de luxe
130 × 50 × 50cm (52 × 20 × 20in)	1 1 1	40W Horticultural-type 20W Warm tone de luxe 40W Universal white

Temperature conversion

°C	°F
[1] 100	212
95	203
90	194
85	185
80	176
75	167
70	158
65	149
60	140
55	131
50	122
45	113
40	104
35	95
30	86
[2] 25	77
20	68
15	59
10	50
5	41
[3] 0	32

[1] Water boils
[2] Normal tank temperature for tropical fish
[3] Water freezes

Five Centigrade degrees are equal to nine Fahrenheit degrees.
Simple formulae for conversion are:

$$((°C \times 9) \div 5) + 32 = °F$$
$$((°F - 32) \times 5) \div 9 = °C$$

Heating and Thermostats

In our climate, tropical fish tanks need permanent heating under thermostatic control. The thermostat will normally be set at around 25°C (77°F), depending on the type of fish, so in hot weather or in centrally heated homes the heater will not always be in operation, having been switched off automatically. The whole system is left on all of the time, and works completely automatically. The equipment for controlling the heating of a tropical aquarium is very simple and economical, and extremely reliable.

In its basic form, used for smaller tanks, it consists of a submerged unit combining a heater and a thermostat. The heater is a large glass test-tube with a sealed rubber stopper, containing a heater wire coiled around a ceramic former. A simple mechanical thermostat operates by the bending of a metal strip at various preset temperatures, so that the current is cut in or out, switching the heater coil on or off, and thus the temperature is kept constant to within a couple of degrees. A heat- and waterproof cable runs from the rubber seal out of the tank, and off to the power supply, via a fuse and earth, of course. Both heater and thermostat are always operated completely submerged; indeed, heaters switched on out of the water will quickly overheat and may burst.

For larger set-ups separate heater (or heaters) and thermostat are used, with connections made outside the tank via a terminal block, which must be protected from drips. Obviously, the larger the tank, the greater the capacity the heater(s) must have. Usually, for a 90l (20gal) tank, a 100W unit is sufficient; 200W for a 200l (45gal) tank. Specific details are provided by the manufacturers, but remember that, the higher the capacity or wattage of the heater, the greater must be the capacity of the thermostat which controls it.

Some aquarists prefer to use two or more heaters in a large tank. This system provides better heat distribution than a single heater, and also gives a greater degree of 'fail-safe' in the unlikely event of heater failure. And some aquarists prefer to use external thermostats glued onto the outside of the glass. These can be simply adjusted to vary the temperature and easily removed for maintenance — that is, cleaning the contacts, which become burned after years of use. It is best to replace both heaters and thermostats every few years rather than risk failure and the possibility of the consequent death of your fish.

Checking the Temperature

A thermometer is essential to provide a check on the conditions within your tank. This can be the traditional liquid-filled glass type, attached to the inside of the tank with a plastic sucker, or a dial-type stuck on the outside. Most aquarists now prefer a plastic strip containing liquid crystals: this is cheap and unobtrusive. It is stuck on the side of the tank, and indicates temperature by changing colours.

Generally, a temperature between 24 and 28°C (75-82°F) suits

most tropical fish. At temperatures lower than 20°C (68°F) most fish show signs of discomfort, and chilling may result. This can weaken the fish and make them susceptible to infection.

Air Pumps and Aeration

Fish use oxygen dissolved in the water, and excrete waste carbon dioxide back into the water. In the aquarium, there is very little scope for changes in the amounts of these substances. Decaying food generates extra carbon dioxide, which can eventually suffocate the fish. Overcrowding and excess heat both reduce oxygen levels, and this too can kill the fish. Tight-fitting lids to the tank restrict the movement of air and reduce the amount of oxygen dissolving in the water.

ABOVE: *Subtle and sometimes subdued lighting may be necessary to bring out the colours of some fish.* Nannacara anomala, *here in a courtship mock battle, looks drab and pale under harsh lighting.*

33

ABOVE: *The beautiful Congo tetra,* Phenacogrammus interruptus, *is one species which has specialized water requirements. However, it is worth taking the trouble to provide it with the conditions it prefers, if you wish to grow such magnificent specimens, with irridescent colours and flowing finnage.*

So, to avoid all these problems, air must be forced through the water. Done properly, aeration serves some important functions:

○ it increases the levels of dissolved oxygen
○ excess carbon dioxide is removed
○ the movement of air causes water circulation which eliminates 'cold spots' within the tank
○ many fish benefit from water movement, which approximates to the flowing water of their natural habitats

Aeration is carried out by forcing air through a submerged diffuser. This is a porous plastic or synthetic-stone material which releases a stream of tiny air bubbles — the smaller the better. Air is pumped electrically into the diffuser along a thin and inconspicuous plastic pipe.

The pump can be of one of several types. The simplest and cheapest is a vibratory pump, in which the alternating current of the mains electrical supply vibrates a tiny rubber pump mechanism up and down to produce an airstream. Such pumps are long-lasting and need little maintenance, but have a restricted flow rate and may not generate enough pressure to force air to the bottom of a very deep tank. Their main drawback is a loud and irritating hum which is difficult to muffle. More powerful and very quiet are pumps in which an electric motor drives a piston pump or, sometimes, a high-output rotary pump. These can provide sufficient air for several tanks as well as to operate filters. They do, however, need proper lubrication and maintenance.

Remember that the pump draws its air supply from its surroundings. Smoke, paint fumes, aerosols and other material in the air will all be transported into the aquarium. Although the pump will be fitted with a filter (which should be changed regularly) to prevent the entry of dust, other materials can be kept out only by ensuring that the surrounding air is clean. There is no reason why the aerator pump should not be placed well away from the tank, or even in another room where there is cleaner air.

Remember also that, although artificial aeration minimizes some of the bad effects of overcrowding, it is no substitute for proper aquarium management and hygiene.

WATER CONDITIONS

pH and Water Hardness: Natural water contains a variety of dissolved substances which affect its characteristics, and these in turn can have a drastic effect on the fish living in it.

Water hardness is a measure of the amount of dissolved lime and other minerals. Tap water from limestone areas is normally very hard: as it evaporates it leaves white lime deposits. Where water is drawn from granite areas it is very soft; that is, it has very little dissolved lime. Such water is sometimes amber-coloured, having filtered through peat beds. Each type of water has a place in the freshwater aquarium and, if necessary, the aquarist can make adjustments. Domestic water softeners should be used with caution, as they sometimes introduce other materials.

pH is a measure of the acidity or alkalinity of water. The neutral point on the pH scale is 7; waters registering below 7 are acid, while those above 7 are alkaline. Usually tap water has a pH between 6.5 and 7.5, and most fish can live happily under these conditions. A few specific types need very acid water, and these are described later under the relevant entries in the freshwater directory.

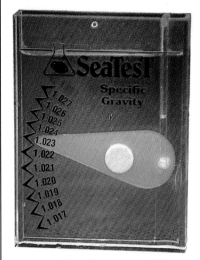

ABOVE: *Specific gravity or SG is a measure of the amount of salt dissolved in sea-water; SG is measured with a hydrometer.*

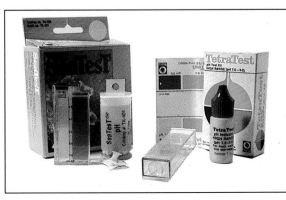

LEFT: *To set up and maintain a healthy marine environment, you will require several test kits to measure pH, nitrate level, and water hardness. There are many excellent proprietary test kits available.*

ABOVE: *The Pufferfish, Tetraodon, is typical of the freshwater fish that have specialized water requirements. If kept in untreated fresh water it usually suffers from fungus diseases, but the addition of a small amount of salt to the water will keep the fish healthy. It is found naturally in estuaries, where there is a mixture of fresh and salt water.*

You can buy simple, cheap test kits which check the pH by means of dyes which change colour under differing degrees of acidity or alkalinity. The pH can then be adjusted by adding solutions of sodium bicarbonate, to increase the pH, or of phosphoric acid, to decrease it (freshwater tanks only). This procedure is seldom necessary, however, unless one of the more sensitive types of fish is being bred.

The Freshwater Tank

Within the restricted environment of the aquarium there take place several complex processes which need to work efficiently if the tank is to remain healthy. Both fish and plants have some specific requirements, as shown in the diagrams, and the tank must be set up in accordance with these.

The fishes' waste products, uneaten food and dead plant material are all broken down by bacteria. The fishes' urine contains ammonia, an extremely poisonous substance, but the bacteria swarming in the tank quickly convert this to less toxic nitrites. These are in turn broken down again by bacteria to relatively harmless nitrates, which are used by and encourage the growth of plants. The breakdown of other wastes proceeds in the same way, and the plants form an important 'buffer' against the build-up of minerals which could otherwise cause problems. 'Old' or matured water does vary in these constituents from fresh water, however, and it is wise to change a proportion of the aquarium water occasionally (say, 20 per cent every three months). Fully matured water often has a yellow tinge due to the build-up of certain organic materials. Some types of fish prefer these conditions, as described in the Directories.

ABOVE: *The aquarist can achieve a reasonable chemical water balance in a community aquarium, with plants thriving on the breakdown products of the fish wastes. This depends on good aquarium hygiene: all uneaten food and any dead fish must be removed promptly.*

Filtration for the Freshwater Aquarium

Fish faeces, uneaten food, decaying plant material and living and dead micro-organisms form a thick sediment called mulm, which settles to the bottom of the tank and accumulates in corners and behind plants. More bacteria breed in this mulm, which is constantly stirred up as Catfish, Loaches and other fish grub about in search for food. Not only is mulm unsightly, it can also be a source of health problems if it builds up to high levels, when bacterial decay may deplete oxygen.

The mulm can be removed, and the water kept sparklingly clear, by using simple filters powered by the air supply from the aerator pump. Air-powered filters all depend on a simple principle: as air bubbles rise to the surface, they carry a flow of water with them. If the bubbles are confined in a vertical tube, they can lift the water above the tank surface. This simple device is called a bubble airlift. In its simplest form, the bubble lift can be used to remove coarse mulm and surplus dried food from the tank, by

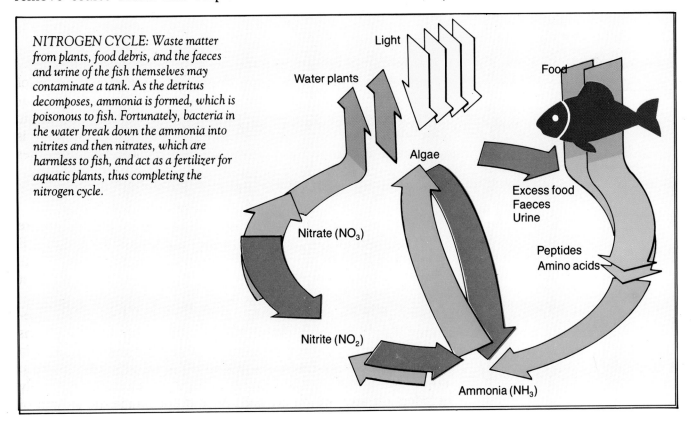

NITROGEN CYCLE: Waste matter from plants, food debris, and the faeces and urine of the fish themselves may contaminate a tank. As the detritus decomposes, ammonia is formed, which is poisonous to fish. Fortunately, bacteria in the water break down the ammonia into nitrites and then nitrates, which are harmless to fish, and act as a fertilizer for aquatic plants, thus completing the nitrogen cycle.

Light

Water plants

Food

Algae

Excess food
Faeces
Urine

Peptides
Amino acids

Nitrate (NO_3)

Nitrite (NO_2)

Ammonia (NH_3)

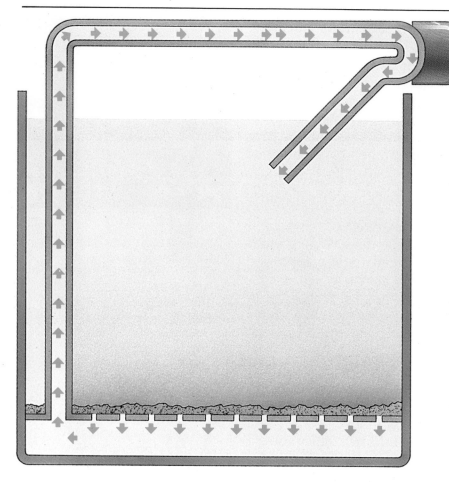

Biological or sub-gravel filters are very popular, requiring little maintenance and operating smoothly for long periods.
ABOVE: The usual type of filter consists of a perforated plate covered with at least 7.5cm (3in) of gravel; and a bubble airlift, which causes water to be drawn down into the gravel, where large solids are filtered out and bacteria break down unwanted chemical wastes.
FAR RIGHT: In the reverse flow type, water is drawn through a mechanical filter, then pumped down beneath the gravel, where bacterial breakdown can take place.

drawing the water through a filter medium.

Cheapest and simplest is the corner filter, a small plastic box which sits on the surface of the aquarium gravel and has a bubble airlift protruding from its upper surface. The lower part of the box is perforated, and it is packed with fine terylene fibres which act as a filter medium. (Never use glass fibre for this purpose. It can be a serious health hazard.) As the bubble airlift operates, it draws water in through the perforations in the box and so traps suspended waste materials in the filter medium. The corner filter operates continuously, and needs cleaning only every few weeks, when it is removed and the filter medium replaced. As with other filters using the bubble airlift, this one has the advantage of helping aeration and maintaining good water circulation. It is, however, large and unsightly, and if possible should be hidden behind plants or rocks.

This problem is overcome by using an outside filter, which hangs over the side or rear of the tank. The airlift draws water and sediment from the bottom of the tank through an inconspicuous plastic tube, lifting it out of the tank and into a plastic box containing filter medium. Cleaned water then returns to the tank through a short syphon tube. This type of filter has some important advantages, chief of which is that it can be cleaned out with a minimum of disturbance of tank or fish. In addition, the filter chamber can be quite large, and so needs less frequent cleaning.

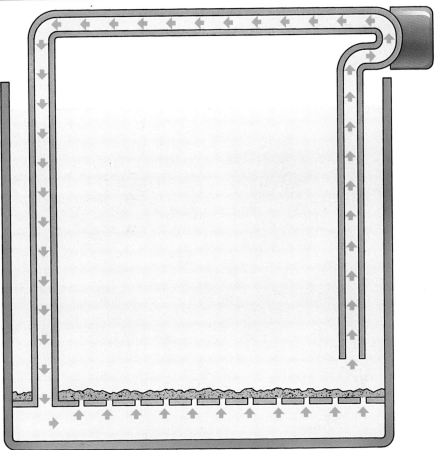

It may be desirable to put other materials into the filter chamber. Peat may be added when breeding certain acid-loving fish. Charcoal is sometimes used to remove damaging substances from very 'old' water. But these are exceptional circumstances: for normal use, filters of this type operate for years with a minimum of fuss or maintenance.

Probably the most important type of filter is the 'biological' filter, or subgravel type. This consists of a large plastic plate, as near the size of the tank bottom as possible, which contains many perforations or slits to allow water to pass through. It incorporates small 'feet' which hold it about 1cm (½in) above the tank bottom. Some older designs consist of a grid of interlinked perforated tubes.

At the rear corner of the filter plate is a bubble airlift. The whole plate is covered with a layer of gravel at least 7.5cm (3in) thick. As the airlift operates, water is drawn down into the gravel and through the slits in the filter plate, before ascending the airlift and being discharged. Mulm is drawn into the gravel, which thus acts as the filter medium. This system is attractive in its simplicity, and has some important advantages — as well as some disadvantages.

Mulm trapped in the gravel is broken down by bacteria and made harmless. Normally, in deep gravel, bacterial action occurs under conditions that are anaerobic; that is, lacking in oxygen.

CENTRE: *The tank must be completely set up, and fully planted out, before the fish are added. Filters, heaters, and aerators should be fitted at an early stage to avoid disturbing the layout later on.*

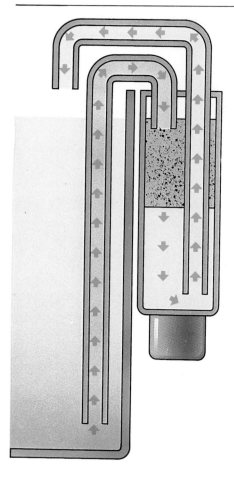

ABOVE: *In an external filter, an airlift and syphons are used to draw dirty water from the bottom of the tank, out into a plastic box containing filter medium. The cleaned water then passes back into the tank. This type of filter is very easy to clean out.*

The gravel turns black and becomes foul-smelling; it can poison the fish by releasing bacterial wastes. In the biological filter, however, the constant flow of water means that conditions remain aerobic. The bacteria which develop are of a different type, and are completely harmless. They not only break down mulm but also complete the cycle of wastes/ammonia/nitrites/nitrates; because the large amount of gravel can hold huge numbers of bacteria, they are very much more effective than if there were no subgravel circulation.

But there are drawbacks. Coarse mulm will not be drawn in, but will remain on the gravel surface. Fish which dig in the gravel will dislodge clouds of trapped sediment. And, if the air supply fails and the water-flow ceases, the bacteria die very quickly and conditions become anaerobic and foul.

Obviously a reliable air pump is a necessity. Use of a bottom or outside filter in conjunction with the biological filter is sensible, as the combination removes coarse mulm as well as small particles. It is wise to rake through the gravel occasionally, so that trapped sediment is released and can be carried away by the other filter mechanisms.

Filtration for the Marine Aquarium
The marine aquarium is a highly unstable environment and needs special care and equipment. The beginner will probably find more success by starting out with the cheaper and more durable freshwater fish. For those starting with marines, however, the special equipment needed for filtration is discussed in Part Three, on page 135.

MAINTENANCE AND HYGIENE

In addition to the continuous cleaning action of filters, a certain amount of other routine cleaning-up is required in both freshwater and marine aquaria. Some debris may be too large for the filters to cope with, so manual cleaning will be required. The simplest method of clearing debris too large for the filters is to use a syphon. Take a length of plastic hose long enough to touch the bottom of the tank on the inside and to hang down well below the level of the bottom on the outside. If you suck the dangling end of the tube so that water is drawn up the tube (and take your mouth away before the column of water reaches it!), a jet of water will be syphoned out, and continue to flow as long as the end of the tube is held below the level of the tank bottom. Use the part of the tube inside the tank like a vacuum cleaner to suck up all visible debris, and direct the jet of water leaving the syphon into a bucket for disposal. Don't hold the end of the tube too close to the gravel, plants or fish: the suction is quite powerful and could cause damage.

Also available are automatic syphons in which, by an ingenious system of small reservoirs, water starts to flow as soon as the end of the tube is submerged.

A further, more sophisticated type works from the aerator supply. This device is a bubble airlift in which the flow of water sucked up is directed into a nylon bag which catches the suspended debris. This type of cleaner operates completely submerged, and returns cleaned water straight into the tank. It is useful for marine aquaria, where one does not wish to discard the carefully made-up artificial 'seawater' — but be very careful that no metal is used in the apparatus.

Overfeeding is the primary cause for the build-up of mulm in the aquarium, and can be very dangerous. Bacteria proliferate at a tremendous rate on the uneaten food, depleting the oxygen in the water and frequently producing poisonous toxins as well as a foul-smelling and poisonous gas, hydrogen sulphide. Very few fish die from starvation; underfeeding normally only slows their growth. Overfeeding, by contrast, causes ill-health and bloating, while the decay of excess food can cause a sudden and catastrophic collapse of the aquarium ecology, killing all the fish in a few hours. Give only enough food that the fish can consume it all within five minutes. If necessary, feed twice a day, using small amounts each time. This rule obviously applies mainly to dried or artificial foods but, even if you are using live foods which can survive for a time in the aquarium, never give them to excess. All living foods use oxygen, and so could rob the fish of their oxygen supplies.

It will be necessary to clean the glass inside the tank occasionally, due to overgrowth of micro-organisms. If lighting levels are too high (see pages 55 and 134) algal overgrowth may also occur. In a freshwater tank, a razorblade fixed in a plastic holder can be used as a scraper, and the material removed can be syphoned out of the tank. Keep the blade well clear of the fillet of silicone rubber along the edge of the tank, or you could create leaks.

In the marine tank, razorblades must not be used, nor any other metal object. A nylon pot-scourer works well, but the metal staple holding it together must be removed. Coarse fibrous plastic scouring pads from hardware shops can be used, and if so should be reserved exclusively for the job of tank-cleaning.

The Complete Clean-Out

Once in a while you may need to clean out the tank completely. Catch the fish (see page 45) and transfer them to your prepared quarantine or hospital tank. Syphon out all the water, and make a space in the gravel so that the syphon tube can get to the bottom and remove the last drops. *Never* attempt to move the tank until all the water and gravel have been removed.

Shovel out the gravel and, if it is to be reused, place it in a bucket and run a hose in it, stirring constantly until the water runs clear. If the gravel is discoloured, add a small amount of hydrogen peroxide or bleach, and allow it to stand for 12 hours. Then rinse thoroughly, and allow the gravel to soak in fresh water for at least

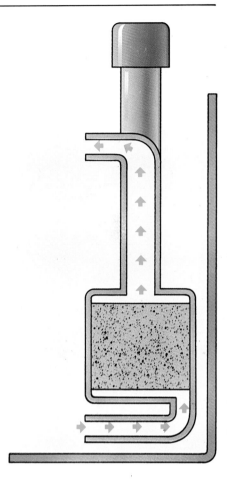

ABOVE: *An internal filter consists of a box containing filter medium, through which water is drawn by a bubble airlift. It is cheap and efficient, but rather obtrusive, and messy to clean out.*

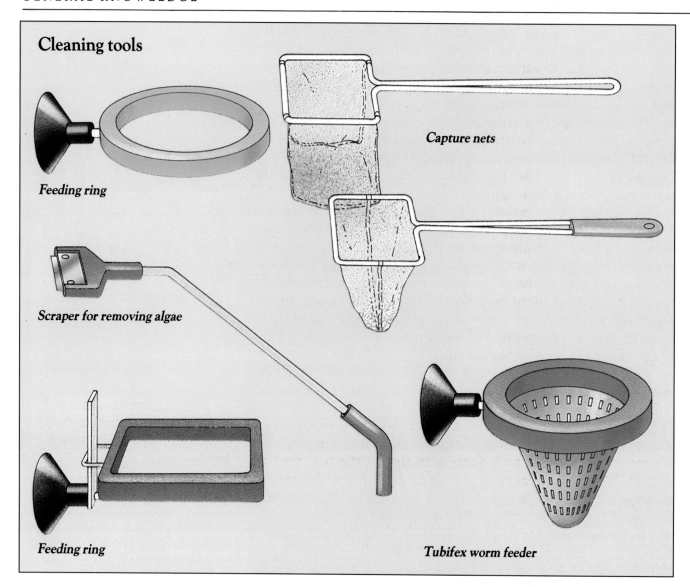

Cleaning tools

Feeding ring

Scraper for removing algae

Capture nets

Feeding ring

Tubifex worm feeder

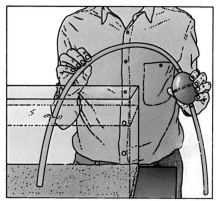

ABOVE: *The syphon, or syphon pump, is used to remove water from the tank with the minimum of disturbance. It can be used to replace some of the water, or to suck out loose mulm that has not been cleared away by the filter.*

a week, with frequent changes of water. It's much easier to discard and replace the gravel!

The tank can be washed and cleaned with a plastic or nylon scourer, and rinsed well; take great care not to scratch the glass while cleaning it. Although the scratches will be invisible when the tank is refilled with water, they provide weak spots from which a crack could begin.

INTRODUCING THE FISH

Part of the secret of successful fish-keeping is to buy healthy fish to start with. Just like any other animal, healthy fish actually *look* healthy. Examine the fish in the dealer's tank carefully. Look for those which are brightly coloured and bold with erect fins; avoid small or stunted fish. If possible, ask for them to be fed while you watch so that you can be sure they are feeding well. And make sure that the dealer catches the one you actually want.

Your fish will be put into water in a plastic bag, which is then inflated with oxygen and tied off with a rubber band. The temperature of the water will soon begin to drop, so you must protect the bag from cold. Wrap it up in a scarf or, if it is small enough, put it under your coat to keep it warm. Experienced aquarists carry fish in containers packed with insulating foam polystyrene, or even in large, wide-mouthed vacuum flasks. Get the fish home as quickly as you can to avoid chilling and shock.

When you get the fish home, do not rush to tip them into the tank. Turn out the tank lights to keep the fish calm, and float the sealed plastic bag, complete with fish, in the tank for at least 30 minutes while the temperatures gradually equalize. Now open the bag and use a gentle scooping movement to introduce small amounts of tank water to the water in which the fish were carried. Do this gradually, as the pH or hardness in the dealer's tank may have been quite different from that in your own, and the fish will need time to adjust.

When you finally tip the bag over and release the fish, they will normally dive to the bottom and hide behind plants or rocks. This is customary; it may even be several days before the fish regain their usual confidence and bright colours, and begin to feed normally.

If you are introducing new fish to an already well populated tank (after quarantining — see below), follow the same procedure but, as you slowly mix tank water with that in the bag, feed the other fish. Most aquarium fish are highly territorial, and even normally peaceful fish may attack a newcomer: feeding will distract them and give the new fish a chance to settle down. This is most important with marine fish, each of which will protect its own place in the tank. It may be helpful to shift all the coral in the marine tank at the same time as introducing new fish, as this disrupts all the territories and destroys any advantage held by the original inhabitants.

Quarantine Procedures

It is bad practice to introduce a fish straight from the dealer's tank into an established aquarium. However healthy it looks, a fish may carry a disease which takes several days to develop. Sometimes the stress of being moved will cause an underlying disease to become more severe. It is bad enough to lose a newly purchased fish through disease, but it can be a tragedy if a whole tankful is affected.

The sensible answer, before introducing a new fish to an established tank, is to quarantine it for a few days. For this you need a quarantine tank, a small tank (how small depends on the type of fish you use it for) fitted out like the larger tank. It will not need gravel, even for marine fish, as the fish will not be in there long enough to cause any serious nitrite build-up.

Adjust the temperature to about 25°C (77°F), as this increases the rate at which parasites (if any) will develop. Check the fish

Introducing the fish to the tank
1 Turn the lights down, and float the sealed plastic bag containing the fish in the tank for at least 30 minutes, to allow the temperatures to equalize.
2 Open the plastic bag, and, with gentle scooping movements, introduce the tank water to it. Give the fish plenty of time to adjust.
3 Tip over the bag to release the fish into the tank. It may take several days for the fish to adjust properly to its new environment.

43

daily for any signs of illness or skin parasites and, if these appear, treat as recommended on pages 70 and 147. For marine fish, remove 25 per cent of the water every three days and replace it with properly aged seawater, to prevent build-up of toxins. After a week, the temperature can be gradually lowered to the normal level, and the fish can be transferred to a plastic bag and introduced to the main tank in the normal way. It may all seem an unnecessary complication, but it will pay dividends: you will have a healthy tankful of fish.

Should you be unfortunate enough accidentally to introduce disease into your main tank, the quarantine tank makes a useful 'hospital' tank. It is easily cleaned and disinfected after use.

PROBLEMS AND SOLUTIONS

Holidays

What happens when I go on holiday? In most cases, the short answer is, provided that your fish are generally well cared-for, nothing! Fish do not suffer from starvation in the short term, especially in a well planted freshwater aquarium. In a long-established marine aquarium, which has a good growth of algae and other organisms on the rocks or coral, fish will be able to find enough food to keep them going for a few days. The lights can simply be left on for a week's holiday, and this minor disturbance should not upset the fish or plants too much.

If your fish are especially valuable or delicate, or if you will be away for an extended period, you can plan accordingly. Fit a timeswitch to the lights on the tank. Timeswitches can be purchased from any electrical shop, and are easily programmed to switch lights on and off at predetermined times.

Do *not* give a massive feed before you leave. Make up individual packages of food and label them 'Monday', 'Tuesday', etc, so that a friendly neighbour can drop them into the tank regularly. Cut down on the normal quantities of food just in case something begins to go wrong while you are not around to spot the first signs of trouble or to syphon out uneaten food.

Power Cuts

What about power cuts? If you think of how long it took your tank to heat up to the proper temperature after it was first switched on, you will realize that it will also take a long while for it to cool down. Most power cuts last only an hour or so, and the temperature in a large tank will not drop much in this time. Small tanks cool off more quickly, and can be insulated by covering them with blankets. If the temperature drops more than 4°C (7°F) you will need to take measures to warm things up. For a freshwater tank, small amounts of hot water can be added, very gradually, stirring the water well to avoid 'hot spots'. Reheating a marine tank is more difficult, as seawater cannot be heated as it reacts with cook-

ABOVE: *Discus fish are notoriously finicky creatures. They are difficult to feed, sensitive to water conditions, and susceptible to disease. But the delight of watching a devoted mated pair spawning and raising their fry can make keeping them well worthwhile.*

ing utensils. The only course is to fill a plastic container with hot fresh water and to float it in the tank, refilling it with more hot water as it cools off. In marine tanks more damage will be caused during a prolonged power cut by lack of aeration and filtration than by chilling.

Fumes and Smoke

An air pump draws any fumes in the room into the aquarium water (see pages 33-5). It's best, therefore, to keep the pump where there will not be too many fumes. If you are painting the room, extend the tubes on the pump so that it can be moved elsewhere, or switch off aeration until the worst smells have faded. Encourage room ventilation by opening the windows, and keep the tank well covered. Fish show distress at dissolved smoke or fumes by 'gasping' at the surface, and this should be a signal to change the water or, at least, part of it.

An oily film may develop on the surface, and this can reduce the amount of oxygen dissolving in the water. It is simply removed by floating a sheet of newspaper or other absorbent paper on the surface and quickly removing it. The oil film will come away too.

Moving Tanks

If at all possible, don't. The older types of tank with metal frames, especially the larger ones, will leak if moved, however carefully. Never attempt to move any tank until it has been emptied completely. All-glass tanks with bonded seams have a slight flexibility, and can usually be moved, while empty, without causing leaks.

Catching and Handling Fish

At some time, it will be necessary to catch a fish for treatment or for transfer to another tank. Your fish will have got to know their tank intimately, and will be skilful in avoiding your attempts to catch them. Chasing them around the tank is often disastrous: not only does it upset the other fish, but plants and other tank arrangements can be dislodged. It is best to stand a long-handled net in the tank for a few hours until the fish are accustomed to it, then to move it slowly so as to catch the fish against the front glass. Always transfer the fish to a bag containing water from the original tank, and be sure to equalize the temperatures before releasing it into the new tank.

A metal-framed nylon net is acceptable for freshwater fish, but all-plastic nets must be used for marine fish. For long-spined fish, and for some very spiky Catfish, it is best to fix a polythene bag over the net frame, so that fins are not caught in the mesh and damaged.

Handle fish as infrequently as possible. If the slimy mucous coating over their scales is damaged, micro-organisms can enter and cause disease. Fish should be handled only when it is necessary to treat them by swabbing their skin surface, and then only with wet hands, which are less likely to damage the mucous coating.

When Thing Go Wrong

If the proper balance in the aquarium is disturbed it soon becomes obvious. Fish gasp at the surface or lie on the bottom. Discoloured or cloudy water means that all is definitely not well.

Get into the habit of checking regularly that you can see all the fish. A sick fish may hide away and die, quickly fouling the water. Sudden blackening of the gravel is a sure sign that things are going wrong, and you must investigate swiftly. Usually this effect is a result of prolonged overfeeding, or it may be that gravel over a biological filter has become too tightly packed to allow water to flow through it. Stirring the gravel gently, together with vigorous aeration and syphoning-out of the sediment you dislodge, may improve matters.

If the plants begin to die off, check that they have enough light. It is quite normal for certain types of freshwater plant to shed their leaves when transplanted to a new tank, and they will usually recover quite rapidly.

Check the tank temperature daily, especially if your fish seem to be sluggish and go off their food. If obvious signs of disease are seen, treat as recommended on pages 70-1 and 147.

Foreign Bodies

Quite often, you will find unexpected organisms in your aquarium. Eggs and spores get carried in with plants and live food, and you may get Snails, Leeches, Worms and various other small creatures introduced in this way. Most are harmless, and their presence indicates that tank conditions are healthy; many will simply be eaten by the fish.

Snails are unsightly and, contrary to traditional advice, are an unnecessary nuisance in the tank: they eat plants and foul the tank with their droppings. They can be removed or crushed against the glass and left for the fish to eat. You can collect snails for disposal by floating a lettuce leaf in the tank overnight: by morning, the snails will have congregated on it, and the whole can be removed.

Malayan sand snails are the only type which might be worth introducing. They are small elongated freshwater snails which live buried in the gravel. They fulfil a useful scavenging job, and their constant burrowing prevents the gravel from becoming too tightly packed and anaerobic.

Leeches are brown or grey worm-like creatures which sometimes feed on the fish. They should be caught and killed whenever possible. Ideally, one would wish not to introduce them to the tank in the first place, and some writers recommend dipping any new plants, to which the Leeches might be clinging, in a dilute salt-water solution before putting them in the aquarium; unfortunately, this process often kills not only the Leeches but the plants as well. One way of dealing with the problem is to introduce to the tank a Pufferfish (*Tetraodon* spp. — see pages 128-9); with luck, this will eradicate the Leeches by the simple process of eating them; it will also eat snails — shells and all.

ABOVE: *A simple, daily inspection can tell you that all is well in your aquarium, because a healthy aquarium actually looks healthy: the fish are active and plump, and*

the plants are well coloured and growing rapidly. You should notice if anything is wrong in good time to take corrective action.

In the marine tank, many unusual organisms may appear, especially if live Shrimps are fed to the fish or if live corals or other invertebrates are introduced. Many marine organisms grow from young which float almost invisibly as plankton, and the adult forms may develop in your aquarium. Usually, as soon as these creatures are big enough, they are eaten by the fish, which constantly search through the gravel and in cracks in the coral for suitable food. Only very seldom will these 'foreign' organisms cause problems.

Leaks

If a tank springs a leak it is usually only a gradual seep along one edge. You will need to empty the tank to effect a cure. Dry it out very thoroughly, then run a fillet of silicone-rubber adhesive (obtainable from aquarium dealers) right down the affected edge on the *inside* of the tank. The fillet can be smoothed and shaped with a finger to make it unobtrusive. Do not just apply a patch over the point where the leak appears; water may be running along beneath the surface of the existing silicone or mastic and popping out somewhere else. Before refilling the tank, allow the silicone to dry or cure for at least 24 hours, as it gives off toxic fumes of acetic acid.

Equipment Failures

Because unusual problems can arise, it is wise to own a spare set of thermostat, heater and cheap plastic tank.

PART TWO
THE FRESHWATER AQUARIUM

Setting up a freshwater aquarium is relatively straight-forward, provided that you plan carefully before you start. There is no need to buy the most expensive equipment, plants and fish. On the other hand, buying the cheapest is always a false economy. Make sure you get things right first time, as mistakes may be difficult and expensive to rectify. If you buy a small tank, you will always wish you had a larger one. A small, cheap air pump will not only wear out rapidly but may be very noisy and will probably never supply as much air as you require. The worst item of all to try to economize on is the fish. The only reason for a fish to be cheap is because it cannot be sold easily — and this usually means that it is of obviously poor quality.

If you have read the first part of this book, you should have a good idea of what fish need for a healthy life in the aquarium, and this will influence the way in which you set up your tank. However you do this, your tank will still represent something of a compromise, as it is impossible to create a totally natural environment in a tank kept in the average home. Remember that, while the tank must be acceptable to the fish as a home, it must also be an asset to *your* home.

LEFT: *The magnificent Blue discus,*
Symphysodon aequifasciata haraldi, *has colours to rival the most exotic marine fish. A large and temperamental fish, it must be kept with its own kind, and it is advisable to keep a mated pair.*

HABITATS

NATURAL HABITATS

How closely should your aquarium resemble the fishes' natural habitats?

Most fish selected by importers and dealers for the home aquarium are highly adaptable to various conditions, and they need to be. In nature, freshwater environments are subject to sudden violent fluctuations in temperature and water conditions due to rain and seasonal changes, and the fish are adapted to cope. Thus it is relatively easy to keep freshwater fish from various contrasting habitats together in the aquarium, under 'average' conditions, although, for perfect health or for breeding, more insight into their real requirements may be necessary.

The most difficult habitat to recreate is the fast-flowing stream where the water has a high oxygen content. Fish from this habitat usually prefer lower temperatures. They either are powerful swimmers, enabling them to keep position against the current, or perhaps have sucker mouths to cling to stones. In contrast, fish from deeper, slower-moving rivers are very easy to keep, as their natural habitat, like that of lake-dwelling fish, is not too different from that in the aquarium. In all cases, the water may be hard or soft, acid or alkaline, depending on the rock and soil over which the water flows. But generally the stream-dwelling fish will be intolerant of the dirty-water conditions which are part of the natural habitat of river dwellers. Many of the hardiest and most successful aquarium fish live in drainage ditches and swamps in Southeast Asia or South America: they are naturally tolerant of filthy water with low oxygen levels, and consequently can easily survive a certain amount of aquarium mismanagement.

The nearer fish live to the sea, the more tolerant they become to salt water. Some, like the Archerfish, live entirely in brackish water. This is a difficult environment to reproduce. The normal aquarium plants do not live in brackish water, which quickly becomes turbid.

Probably the most extreme habitat of all is that occupied by 'seasonal' fish, represented in the aquarium by some of the Egg-laying toothcarp family. They live in puddles and pools in very dry territory. Their pools fill with rain only during the wet season, and then rapidly dry up, going through various stages of foul water and mud.

In order to reproduce in the aquarium the wide range of habitats experienced in the wild it would be necessary to keep most species separately. We set up a 'natural-looking' aquarium, but

ABOVE: *In a large, well-planted aquarium, there may be little need for additional decoration with rock-work. However, it can be difficult to balance slow- and fast-growing plants and keep the tank looking attractive without constant pruning and replanting. It is sensible to choose plants that grow at about the same rate.*

TOP: *Judicious use of rocks, plants, and waterworn wood creates a very attractive aquatic environment, and also provies a range of suitable hiding places for shy fish. In this arrangement, a few large specimen plants, rather than clumps of fast-growing ones have been used.*

this bears little real resemblance to the conditions under which the fish would naturally live. In the wild, clear water and bright light are the exceptions, not the rule. Aesthetic designs and plants are for *our* benefit — the fish would be just as happy swimming among flowerpots as among expensive and carefully arranged rock terraces in the aquarium. The breeding tanks of the expert aquarist are normally plain water-filled boxes, with no attempt to recreate a 'natural' appearance. Fish spawn happily on pieces of slate, nylon wool, flowerpots or beds of marbles.

SETTING UP YOUR FRESHWATER AQUARIUM

You should plan your new aquarium carefully before starting to set it up: it will be difficult to make changes later.

First, decide where the tank is going to go. It will need to stand on a very solid base, preferably a purpose-designed one. For the

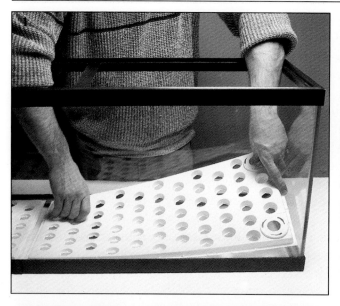

Setting up the tank
1   *The baseplate of a biological, or subgravel filter (see page 39) is placed in the bottom of the tank.*
2   *The bubble airlift is located in the rear corner of the filter plate.*
3   *The plate is covered with gravel, to a depth of at least 7.5cm (3in).*
4   *A submerged heater with a thermostat (see page 32) is placed in the tank. Before being switched on, the heater should be raised to about 5cm (2in) above the gravel. It can be attached to the side of the tank with rubber suckers.*
5   *Fitting the air pump to the bubble airlift. It is advisable to tidy and secure any trailing wires to avoid accidental disconnection.*
6   *Decorating the tank: waterworn wood, if well soaked in advance to remove any impurities, and aquatic plants make attractive additions.*
7   *A liquid crystal strip thermometer (see page 32) is a simple and inexpensive way of monitoring aquarium conditions. It can be attached easily to the outside of the tank.*

modern all-glass aquarium, you will need a baseboard of very thick blockboard or flooring-grade chipboard. This must be absolutely flat because otherwise the tank may crack as it fills. Small irregularities can be taken care of by covering the whole base with a single thin layer of foam polystyrene, of the grade used for ceiling tiles; this will squash down beneath the filled tank. Check carefully that there are no pieces of grit on the prepared surface, and then carefully position the tank.

You will probably be using a biological filter (see page 39); make sure it is as large as can be fitted into the tank.

Next comes the gravel. Some people like to use brightly coloured artificial material; this is a matter of personal taste — or lack of it. Fish are indifferent about this, as they are about other aquarium oddities such as sunken 'galleons' or 'divers'. Always use gravel purchased from a proper aquarium dealer, which will not contain limestone or other material which dissolves in the water. The size of the gravel particles should vary from 3mm to 6mm (⅛-¼in) across. Any smaller and there will be insufficient space between the particles of gravel for adequate water circulation through the filter. Larger pieces of gravel leave spaces in which uneaten food can lodge and decay.

Gravel needs thorough washing to remove dust. Place it in a plastic bucket and run a hose into it for at least half an hour, stirring frequently to allow debris to be floated away. Do not use detergents; these can be highly poisonous to fish.

Now place the gravel in the tank, first covering the filter plate with a level layer to hold it all in place, then banking the gravel towards the back of the tank. At its shallowest, the gravel depth must be at least 5cm (2in). Gravel banked up in this way will soon slump back to a level layer, thanks largely to the activity of fish digging in the bottom for food. If you want, you can prevent this by the use of rocks built into terraces, behind which the gravel is retained and built up in steps or small pockets. Use only stone sold specially for the purpose. This is usually York stone, sandstone, slate, granite or volcanic rock, none of which will dissolve in the aquarium water. Do *not* use limestone, unless you have a special need for very hard, alkaline water. The most decorative rock is waterworn, but this is quite expensive. Small pieces can be locked into place by a dab of silicone adhesive (remember to give it time to cure before adding water).

Waterworn wood is sometimes used for decoration. This must be very old to be safe, and should be soaked for a week or so to remove impurities. It usually needs anchoring with rocks to hold it in place.

Always remember to position rocks so that they are built up towards the rear and sides of the tank: this creates an illusion of greater depth. If you are going to keep shy or retiring fish, it is worth constructing some small caves or hiding places at this stage. Paradoxically, the more hiding places there are, the more confident and less inclined to hide the fish will be.

Next, the heater(s) and thermostat can be installed. The heater must be positioned against the back of the tank, either horizontally or at a slight angle. Plastic suckers fitted with a clip can be used to hold it in place. It can be concealed behind rocks, which should be placed so that they allow plenty of room for water circulation. Never allow the heater to touch the rocks or gravel, or it will quickly become covered with an impenetrable layer of gravel and a cement-like deposit. This can cause it to burst.

The heater in place, the thermostat can be positioned. Fully submersible types are installed exactly like the heater, as are combined submersible heater/thermostats. Some types of thermostat are suspended vertically in the water from the tank surface, and must not be fully submerged; special fixing clips will be provided for this type. If you have an external thermostat, it should be attached to the back or side of the tank with contact cement or double-sided adhesive tape.

Electrical connections must be made *exactly* according to the instructions. It may be necessary to purchase a small terminal

ABOVE: *This magnificent planted aquarium requires only the addition of the fish to bring it life.*

LEFT: *The Tiger or Sumatran barb,* Barbus tetrazona *is an aquarium favourite. It is bold, attractive, and hardy, and, like many of the genus, it is quite easy to breed. However, it must be treated with caution in the community tank, for the Tiger barb is a fin nipper, and often pesters slow-moving fish; it is also almost impossible to catch in a well-planted tank.*

block from an electrical supplier to make the connections. Ensure that any electrical connections are well protected from drips or splashes, and tucked away tidily behind the tank. Do not switch on to test the circuit until *after* you have filled the tank!

At this stage, the air pump can be installed, together with the filter. There are many varieties of corner and outside filters, and they should be assembled exactly as instructed. The air line is usually made of flexible clear PVC, and should not be too narrow, or the air-flow will be restricted. The air tube is simply pushed onto the nipple provided on the filter. If it is tight, heat the PVC tube in hot water to soften it. You can purchase three- or four-way connectors to allow you to connect two or more filters. An aerator stone can be installed at this stage. It is useful to incorporate small screw valves which allow the air-flow to the filters and the aerator to be varied to give maximum efficiency; otherwise, you may find nearly all the flow going to power just one airlift.

Don't forget to fit the thermometer. It may be easier to attach while the tank is empty.

The tank can now be filled. It is best to stand a glass or plastic bowl on the gravel and to pour water into this, thus breaking up the flow which would otherwise shift the gravel. Cold water can come from a bucket or hose. Do not be in too much of a hurry, and keep checking that there are no leaks. Fill the tank to within 5cm (2in) of the top, and switch on the thermostat and heater. You will soon see the water shimmering slightly above the heater. Turn on the air pump, so that the aerator circulates water and speeds up the heating process.

You *must* leave the tank for at least 24 hours before adding plants or fish. It will take several hours to heat up, but, more important, the aeration will drive off the chlorine which is always added to disinfect normal tap water, and which is toxic to most fish. Use the 'waiting' time to check that the tank has come up to the proper temperature.

The lights can be installed at this stage. A simple metal or plastic canopy, containing fluorescent tube(s) and all the necessary fittings, is placed on the glass tank cover. Do not use incandescent bulbs: these become very hot, and have a short life when operated on their sides under an aquarium canopy.

For a tank of 60×30×40cm (24×12×15in) a 30 Watt tube is sufficient; for 90×40×40cm (36×15×15in), you should have 60-80 Watts. It is worth paying the extra for special tubes which stimulate plant growth. It may also be a good idea to buy a special dimmer-switch to reduce the sudden glare for the fish when the lights are switched on in the morning (normal room dimmers will not work with fluorescent tubes).

Position the canopy towards the front of the tank. This causes the light to be thrown back towards the fish, illuminating their colours. If the canopy is too far back, the fish will be silhouetted against the light and appear very dark.

All that now remains is to add plants and fish.

PLANTS FOR THE FRESHWATER AQUARIUM

All green plants live by means of photosynthesis. Materials absorbed from the roots — or, in the aquarium, from the surrounding water — are used by the plant, together with sunlight or artificial light, to make the food the plant needs. Importantly, the plant takes in carbon dioxide and produces sugars, which it uses, and releases oxygen through tiny pores in the leaves. You can see this process taking place in the aquarium: tiny bubbles of oxygen are produced on the leaves of certain plants in bright light. This provides a valuable source of oxygen for the fish. A further benefit is that the carbon dioxide which the fish produce as a waste product is used by the plants. Moreover, the plants use the breakdown products of fish wastes and decayed material.

Photosynthesis takes place only in bright light. At night, a different process comes into play, by which the plant uses oxygen and releases some carbon dioxide. Supplementary aeration is therefore advisable.

Some aquarists use realistic plastic plants: these need no lights and last indefinitely, but of course have none of the valuable qualities of real plants. They are very useful, however, in giving temporary 'instant' plantings while the living plants are developing, and can also be used with fish which would destroy or eat normal plants.

Aquarium plants are foliage plants. Some grow completely submerged, in deep water, while others are bog plants which will thrive only in shallow water, or grow better part-submerged. Still others are floating forms which do not root into the gravel, or which produce long floating leaves. So, as with any plant arrangement, careful thought is necessary to make the best of the plants you use.

Generally speaking, the principles of plant arrangement are simple. Small, low-growing plants are used in the foreground, and taller types at the back and sides. A few larger, attractive specimen plants can be put in the foreground where they can be clearly seen. Always leave some clear gravel over which fish can feed without overlooking food particles. It is advisable to leave some channels between groups of plants which increase the illusion of depth by making the viewer want to 'look around the corner'.

Always remember that certain types of plant grow or spread very rapidly to form large clumps which can swamp less vigorous neighbours, so allow plenty of space between plantings, and be prepared to prune them heavily to maintain a tidy shape. It takes some experience to visualize the eventual appearance of a plant if it is rooted 'dry'; when supported by water it will spread out and change its shape.

ABOVE: *This well-planned planting arrangement demonstrates how similar plants can be grouped together to produce a natural effect, and also shows how plants can be graded by height, with the tallest at the back of the tank. This creates an illusion of greater depth in the tank.*

LEFT: *The Emperor tetra,* Nematobrycon palmeri, *is a relative newcomer to the aquarium world. Apart from the beautiful tail fin, its colours are pale. Consequently, it looks its best in a heavily planted tank, with subdued lighting.*

It is usually best to plant after filling the tank. Water plants can simply be pressed into the gravel and will take root very quickly. Special planting sticks are available, consisting of a long rod with a fork at the tip. This fork is used to grip the roots and push them into position. All the roots must be covered, or the plant will quickly become dislodged. Large plants should be weighted down with stones, at least until they have rooted well and are secure in the gravel. Some dealers sell lead wire to wrap around plant roots and hold them down, or to secure bunches of spindly-stemmed plants, but this is not a good idea: although lead itself is nearly inert, other impurities may leak out into the water.

Buy only the healthiest plants. Check the leaves carefully and remove snails or the jelly-like patches of snail eggs. Select plants from those growing in the dealer's tank; avoid plants sold

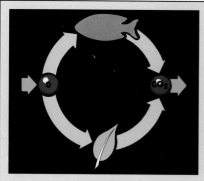

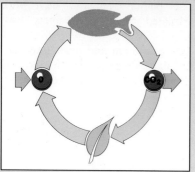

During daylight hours, plants release oxygen, which is needed by the fish. In darkness, plants release carbon dioxide and use oxygen themselves. Consequently, in a well-planted tank aeration is particularly important at night.

unrooted in shallow trays. Many plants are just as badly affected by chilling as are fish. You can carry them home wrapped up in damp paper. Plant them as soon as possible.

Plants grow only slowly in 'new' aquaria, which contain few nutrients: in established tanks there is a high concentration of nitrates and other materials, and so plant growth is rapid.

Some aquarists put a layer of well washed peat, or even of sterile peat compost, beneath the gravel when starting up a new tank. This assists plant growth, but can also stimulate the growth, or overgrowth, of algae if sufficient light is present. In addition, fish digging in the bottom soon dislodge the buoyant peat or compost, creating an unsightly effect. If you do adopt this practice, remember that plants must be rooted 'dry', as any disturbance of the gravel in a water-filled tank releases the compost beneath.

The problem can be avoided by potting individual specimen plants in miniature plant pots containing peat, which is 'sealed in' with a layer of gravel, and then pressing the pots into the aquarium gravel so that they are hidden. This has the additional advantage that plants can be moved with a minimum of disturbance to their roots or to other plants.

Some plants grow very rapidly and, instead of spreading out, become very long and float untidily, or grow straight up vertically out of the water. These should be pruned mercilessly, to encourage bushier growth. Remove all dead or straggly leaves or shoots to prevent decay.

Normally, the fastest-growing plants produce most oxygen and have the highest uptake of nitrates and other undesirable waste products. But, if there is insufficient light, oxygen production and other useful functions of these plants stop suddenly, while slower-growing plants will continue to grow and metabolize as usual.

Material pruned from fast-growing plants can be easily used for propagation. Simply gather the cut-off tips into bunches and press them into the gravel, securing them with a stone: the bunches will root within a week or so. This should be a regular job, with older and less healthy growth being discarded and replaced by newly rooted plants.

Some plants spread by means of runners, which either appear on the gravel surface or run along beneath the gravel; small new plants appear from time to time along the runners. These can be severed and replanted elsewhere, or left to spread into a dense clump.

It may be preferable to start out with a collection of mixed fast- and slow-growing plants. The fast-growing types, which often deteriorate after a while, can be progressively removed as the slow-growing and more desirable plants become established.

Do not neglect the potential of floating plants. Certain of these have trailing roots, used by egg-scattering fish while spawning. Others can be used to adjust lighting levels by providing shade. However, floating plants may quickly overgrow the water surface, and so need constant thinning-out.

DIRECTORY OF FRESHWATER AQUARIUM PLANTS

Acorus gramineus
(Dwarf rush; Japanese rush)

A bog plant from East Asia, often grown as a complete aquatic. It grows from a creeping rhizome which lies just beneath the gravel surface. Stiff reed-like leaves are produced in a fan-shaped spray, sometimes up to 30cm (12in) in height. The variegated form, which is striped with yellow, is the one most commonly grown. There is a dwarf form which grows only to about 7cm (2¾in) in height, and which is very useful in the foreground of the tank. All *Acorus* need plenty of light, and benefit from being planted in loam or peat. Propagate by separating side shoots from the rhizome.

Alternanthera sessilis

A red-leaved, semi-aquatic plant which grows well completely submerged. Stems are woody and heavily branched, with spear-shaped leaves up to 7.5cm (3in) long. The stems are red and the undersides of the leaves intensely red. *A. sessilis* usually deteriorates after a few months, first shedding its leaves. Propagates easily from cuttings. No special water requirements, but prefers coolish temperatures.

Anubias spp.

A group of bog plants from tropical Africa which grow very slowly but eventually form large specimen plants of great beauty. They have tough waxy leaves up to 12cm (4¾in) in length, carried on 15cm (6in) stems in a stiff spray. Dwarf forms are available. Because of their slow growth rate, these plants command high prices, variegated types with silvery leaves being especially expensive. Grow in a mixture of loam and peat, under subdued light. Propagate by division of the rhizome. They prefer neutral-to-acid pH and soft water.

Left: *Anubias* spp.
Right: *Aponogetom* spp.

Aponogetom spp.

A. crispus is a beautiful aquatic plant from Ceylon, producing large strap-shaped leaves which are bright green and crinkled along the edges. Grows to a height of 30cm (12in) or more, and can almost fill a small aquarium. The delicate leaves may be attacked by snails. Needs strong light for vigorous growth. The bulb must be planted in a rich compost. Very difficult to propagate. A flowering stem may be produced, carrying a hooked inflorescence above the water surface. In common with other *Aponogetom* spp., *A. crispus* has a winter resting period when part of the foliage may die back. Prefers neutral pH soft water.

A. fenestralis (Madagascar lace-leaf plant) is strictly for the specialist grower. Produces large leaves, up to

Acorus spp. and *Alternanthera* spp.

Aponogetom spp.

length, carrying rounded fleshy leaves, usually pale green but sometimes with a red tinge. The stems will grow above the water, and a small flower may be produced. Propagate by pinching off the tips and replanting them — this encourages the original plant to bush out. It is best to start cuttings off in a few centimetres of water, transferring them back into the tank when they are properly rooted. No special water requirements.

Barclaya longifolia
Large and robust relative of the Water lily, coming from Southeast Asia. The leaves are elongated, with wavy edges, and are bronze-green in colour with reddish stems. It is uncommon, and not too easy to grow.

Cabomba spp.
An old-established aquarium plant from North and South America, *Cabomba* is an excellent oxygenator. Grows very rapidly to a length of 90cm (3ft) if not pinched out. The leaves are finely divided, and arranged in pale green fans. Some varieties are reddish. Propagates very easily from cuttings, which are planted in bunches directly into the gravel. Old plants become stringy and should be discarded. Requires strong light and prefers soft water with a slightly acid pH. Very useful as a spawning medium for e scattering fish.

20cm (7¾in) long, which consist only of the leaf veins, producing a beautiful network. A similar species, *A. henkelianus*, has brownish foliage and more elongated leaves with fewer of the lacelike holes.

Aponogetom spp.

A. ulvaceus is a magnificent plant from Madagascar, with 25cm (9¾in) leaves, very broad, and twisted or waved. Its requirements are as for *A. crispus*, but this plant is even larger. Beware of buying dormant bulbs of this or other types: they usually turn out to be the related *A. natans* from Ceylon, which is useless for the aquarium.

Azolla caroliniana
(Fairy moss)
A tiny floating fern found in South, Central and North America. It forms a dainty clump, coloured pale green or, in strong light, reddish brown. In the right conditions it grows very rapidly, and may need to be scooped out of the tank regularly. *Azolla* is usually introduced accidentally, but has a useful purpose, in moderation, of shading the tank. Thrives in any water conditions, and propagates very rapidly.

Bacopa caroliniana
(Baby's tears)
From North America, a semi-aquatic plant, which grows well submerged. It has long stems, up to 60cm (2ft) in

Left: *Bacopa* spp. Right: *Aponogetom* spp.

Cabomba spp.

Cardamine lyrata

A semi-aquatic plant from Japan, Korea and China, this has long slender stems, carrying rounded pale-green leaves which resemble those of watercress. It grows under moderate light and has no special water requirements. Propagate from cuttings, which are best grown as bog plants before transfer to the aquarium. Usually deteriorates after a few months.

Ceratophyllum demersum
(Hornwort)

A brittle-leaved plant distributed through most temperate and tropical areas, C. *demersum* has long branching stems covered with dense whorls of dull green, spiky leaves. Easily propagated from cuttings, but will grow as a floating plant, without rooting into the gravel. Prefers cooler temperatures than those usually found in the tropical aquarium. A very good oxygenator.

Ceratopteris thalictroides
(Floating fern; Indian fern)

This beautiful fern comes from the tropics of Asia and Africa. It has soft, pale green fronds deeply subdivided into smaller leaflets. Daughter plants are produced along the edges of the fronds, and drop off to produce new plants. C. *thalictroides* grows either as a floating plant, with fronds extending above the surface, or can be rooted into the gravel and grown completely submerged. It grows very rapidly in slightly acid, soft water, and prefers strong light. The shape of the fronds is variable, and there are at least two other very similar species available. The trailing roots of the floating form are very useful shelter for fish fry. Sometimes the floating and submerged forms are sold as different species.

Cryptocoryne spp.

A very large and diverse group (at least 50 species, perhaps many more) of bog or submerged plants from Southeast Asia. They are very variable in colour and form, even within a particular species, and are therefore difficult to identify with any certainty.

In general, *Cryptocoryne* have elongated, tough leaves, coloured mid-green to deep olive. Many are red- or purple-tinged, especially on the undersides of the leaves. They grow, depending on species, from 7cm to 60cm (2¾-24in), and some grow best when part-submerged. *Cryptocoryne* grow best in moderate light or in shade, and usually thrive in soft acid water. They grow only slowly, so are expensive to buy, and do best if rooted in a mixture of peat and gravel. They reproduce in the aquarium by means of small plants produced on shoots running beneath the gravel, and will form dense clumps if left to their own devices. Their capacity for producing oxygen and removing nitrates is comparatively low, due to their slow growth rate. Most, and particularly the expensive large-leafed types, have the habit of dropping their leaves on being transplanted or even when the water is changed. Usually, these leaves are regrown quite quickly, once a good root system has been established.

The following species are most often available:

C. affinis (C. *haerteliana*). One of the faster-growing of the genus; reaches a height of 15-20cm (6-8in). It has elongated leaves which are dull bluish-green on the upper surface and purple underneath, and have prominent leaf veins. Responds well to some loam mixed with the gravel.

Cryptocoryne spp.

Cryptocoryne spp.

C. becketti. Often called *C. cordata*, this plant occurs in two forms, each growing to about 18cm (7in) in height. One form has oval leaves, the other type elongated. Leaf colour is olive-green, with a reddish-purple underside. Grows most rapidly under bog conditions, with foliage above water level.

C. blassii. Beautiful specimen plant reaching a height of 40cm (15¾in) under good conditions. Has broad, pointed leaves up to 15cm (6in) long, carried on long stems. Upper surface of the leaf is dark green or reddish, underside crimson. Leaf surface is usually heavily dimpled. Grows best completely submerged and, once established, spreads rapidly. Grows well in hard or soft water, but does not tolerate very alkaline conditions.

C. ciliata. Large species, growing to about 40cm (15¾in). Leaves are of an elongated heart-shape, and are pale green, unusually for a *Cryptocoryne*. The plant will tolerate hard, alkaline water, and even slightly brackish conditions. For propagation, it is best grown as a bog plant in rich compost.

C. griffithii. Broad, bluntly pointed leaves are up to 7cm (2¾in) long, and carried on long stems to a height of 25cm (10in). It is a very variable plant, and leaf colouring may be from pale green to dark-brownish green on the upper surface, with reddish-purple beneath. In some forms the leaves are attractively flecked with brown. Moving the plant causes leaf rot. Do not overcrowd.

C. lingua. Small species growing to 10cm (4in) high. Leaves are blunt-tipped, tapering into a flattened stem. Grows more rapidly as a bog plant. Do not expose to strong light, which stunts the growth. Prefers soft acid water.

C. nevillii. Occurs in several forms, notably the dwarf type, which grows to only 5cm (2in) in height. It is very useful as a 'carpet' plant for the foreground of the tank. Leaves are mid-green, pointed and elongated. It

grows best under bog conditions but, once established as a submerged plant, will spread steadily.

C. thwaitesii. Very attractive plant, up to 15cm (6in) high, whose leathery leaves have deeply serrated edges and are coloured olive or brown, mottled with dark brown on the upper surface. Grows very slowly, and may take two years to reach full size. Requires rich peaty compost.

C. wendtii. Very popular plant found in various forms. Usually grows to about 20cm (8in), with leaves that are reddish-olive on the top, purple underneath, and have undulating edges. Smaller forms are also available. Relatively easy to propagate, and tolerates most water conditions.

C. willisii. Sometimes misnamed *C. undulata*, this plant has narrow undulating leaves, reddish below and with an olive or brownish upper surface. Grows easily and quickly to about 25cm (10in). Spreads quickly to produce dense clumps.

Echinodorus spp.
(Sword plants)

A genus of plants, mostly from North and South America, which roughly correspond to the *Cryptocoryne* plants of Asia in both habitat and appear-

Left: *Hypoestes* spp. Right: *Echinodorus* spp.

ance. Most are large and robust, and may need to be grown in pots of compost if they are to thrive. They are less sensitive than *Cryptocoryne* to water conditions, and can tolerate hard alkaline water. In the aquarium, they spread by means of long runners on which small plantlets are produced. If the runner is weighted down, the plantlets root into the gravel and can soon be separated.

E. berteroi (Cellophane plant). Large plant, naturally growing semi-submerged. Juvenile leaves are slender and delicate; as the plant grows these become larger and coarser until they float on the surface, and are eventually carried upright as coarse, heart-shaped leaves above the water. These leaves can be. cut back to restart the whole process.

E. brevipedicellatus. Small, fast-growing plant, up to 17cm (6¾in) in height. Sword-shaped leaves are about 3cm (1¼in) broad. Quickly produces long strings of young plants on runners.

E. grisenbachii (Chain sword plant). Small form, growing to about 10cm (4in) in height, with slender leaves. Spreads very rapidly to produce strings of smaller plants; forms a dense growth on the bottom of the tank.

E. paniculatus (Amazon sword plant). Probably the best known tropical aquarium plant, with large tough leaves up to 45cm (17¾in) in length, produced in a very large spray which soon fills the tank. Leaves vary in width from 3cm to 8cm (1¼-3¼in), depending on growing conditions. This plant grows strongly under moderate light.

E. tenellus (Pygmy chain sword plant). Tiny plant, seldom growing to more than 5cm (2in). Spreads steadily to form a grass-like carpet. Larger forms are also available, but are much less attractive.

Eleocharis acicularis
(Hairgrass)
Beautiful North American bog plant best described by its popular name, Hairgrass, growing to about 15cm (6in) when submerged. Grown out of water, the thin stems sometimes produce tiny plantlets at the tips, but submerged it usually spreads by means of its creeping root. The fine stems are often grazed

Left: *Echinodorus* spp. Right: *Elodea* spp.

Hygrophila spp.

63

Hygrophila spp.

down to stumps by herbivorous fish. Prefers slightly acid conditions, and moderate light.

E. *vivipara* (Umbrella hairgrass) is similar to E. *acicularis*, but grows to 20cm (8in) in height. Produces plant-lets at the tips of the stem, which in turn produce further plantlets, causing the whole plant to spread out grace-fully.

Elodea spp.

Several species of the American genus *Elodea* are commonly grown in the tropical aquarium. All are fast-growing aerators, with long floating stems and whorls of small, bright-green leaves. They are propagated by pinching out the tips, which root very rapidly. They require strong illumination, but usually deteriorate slowly and need frequent replacement. They do not tolerate acid water. Usually available as E. *canadensis* or the much larger E. *densa*.

Hygrophila guianensis

Popular plant from tropical America, with long (10cm; 4in) pale green pointed leaves and tough stems. May grow very large, and tends to grow out of the water unless pinched out. Becomes very 'twiggy' as leaves drop. Prefers neutral pH and moderate water hardness. Propagates easily with cuttings, which root more readily under bog conditions.

H. *polysperma*, from Southeast Asia, is similar but has smaller, blunt-tipped leaves. A 'bunch' plant, with thin stems, which bushes out well if the growing tips are pinched out. Needs strong light and normal water con-ditions. Grows very rapidly when con-ditions are right.

Lagenandra spp.

L. *lancifolia* is a bog plant related to, and resembling, *Cryptocoryne* spp., and found in Sri Lanka. Grows to a height of about 18cm (7in), with tough, fleshy olive-green leaves which have a mildly serrated edge. Grows fairly quickly in soft, slightly acid water, and spreads by means of side-shoots which produce a dense clump.

L. *ovata* is a very large species from Sri Lanka, up to 45cm (17¾in) in height, with very leathery, pale green leaves; these are tough enough to with-stand most herbivorous fish. Grows slowly in most water conditions, and can thrive in alkaline or brackish water. Can be induced to spread by snipping out the crown of the plant, which can itself be used as a cutting.

L. *thwaitesii*, a Sri Lankan bog plant, has beautifully marked deep green leaves, edged with silver, and carried on red stems. Grows to about 20cm (8in) in height. The silver varie-gation may temporarily vanish after transplanting, or in poor light.

Limnophila sessiliflora
(Ambulia)

A plant from Africa and Asia which is very similar to *Cabomba* in both appearance and the techniques required for its care. It really prefers cooler temperatures, and may become leggy after a time in the tropical tank.

Lobelia cardinalis

A garden plant which is often offered for sale but is not at all suitable for permanent aquarium use.

Ludwigia arcuata

A popular bog plant from North America which resembles *Hygrophila* spp. A 'bunch' plant with slender stems, and narrow 2cm (¾in) leaves, coloured pale green or, in strong light, reddish. Will develop aerial leaves unless pinched out regularly. Appreciates a rich compost.

Left: *Lobelia* spp.   Right: *Myriophyllum* spp.

Nomaphila spp.

L. natans is a much larger and more vigorous species from the southern USA. It has broad leaves with a bronze tinge, coloured bright red beneath (the colour may not develop at high temperatures). Does not usually survive permanently in the tropical tank, and must be replaced by fresh cuttings.

Myriophyllum spp.

Marsilea hirsuta
(Four-leaved clover)
Curious little Australian bog plant, looking exactly as its popular name suggests. It survives quite well submerged, and requires strong light. It spreads slowly by means of sideshoots.

Microcanthemum micranthemoides
A dainty little plant from the USA, with tiny oval leaves on slender stems. It creeps along the tank bottom, making dense thickets, not more than 8cm (3¼in) high. Easily propagated from cuttings. Tends to accumulate sediment in an untidy tank. Needs strong light.

Myriophyllum spp.
(Water milfoil)
Very popular plants, found in most temperate and tropical regions, which are, however, not ideal for decorative use. They produce whorls of very fine leaves on long slender stems, growing very rapidly. They are excellent oxygenators but, due to their rapid growth rate and need of very strong light, quickly become leggy and unattractive. They are, nevertheless, very useful in the breeding of egg-scatterers, or for temporary use while slower-growing plants are becoming established. Generally tolerant of normal water conditions, and easily propagated from cuttings.

Nomaphila stricta
(Giant hygrophila)
A close relative of *Hygrophila*, *Nomaphila* comes from Southeast Asia. It has bright green pointed leaves about 10cm (4in) in length, carried in pairs on stiff woody stems. It grows rapidly, straight out of the water unless pinched out regularly; this practice causes it to branch attractively. It is very susceptible to attack by snails. Cuttings root very easily. Grows well in peat or loam, and thrives in hard water of neutral pH. Discard old, woody plants, and replace with fresh cuttings.

Ludwigia spp.

Nymphoides spp.

Nuphar spp.
(Spatterdock)

N. japonicum (Arrowhead spatterdock) is a large-leaved Japanese relative of the Waterlily. The leaves are bright green and arrowhead-shaped, although a reddish-leaved variety is sometimes available. Like all its relatives it is a greedy feeder, and must be planted in a mixture of loam and peat. When purchasing, be very careful — as with other Spatterdocks — that the large rhizome is healthy; damaged rhizomes can rot very rapidly. Grows well under most water conditions.

N. pumilum is a small European Spatterdock with rounded, lettuce-like leaves which are rather fragile and may be nipped by herbivorous fish. Care as for *N. japonicum*.

N. sagittifolium (Cape Fear spatterdock) is a large and choice specimen plant from the southern USA. It has very large elongated heart-shaped leaves, which have undulating edges. Can grow very large, in the strong light it needs, but size can be restricted by pruning. Care as for *N. japonicum*.

Nymphoides aquatica
(Banana plant)

Odd relative of the Waterlily from the southern USA. It has rounded leaves, 7.5cm (3in) in diameter, pale green or reddish in colour, often speckled in red, and with red leaf veins. Its popular name derives from the swollen roots. Grows easily in bright light and normal water conditions. Propagate by division of sideshoots.

Pistia statoites
(Water lettuce)

An interesting floating plant found in most tropical areas, *P. statoites* has a floating rosette of velvety leaves like a miniature lettuce, about 10cm (4in) across, and trailing roots some 20cm (8in) long. Very useful as cover for your live-bearers. Propagates by runners bearing small plants. Lives in most water conditions, but can be scorched by very strong light.

Riccia fluitans
(Crystalwort)

Pretty floating moss from most tropical areas. It forms a loose floating mass just beneath the surface, but, because of its delicate branching structure, cuts out little light. It provides cover for young fish, and is eaten by herbivorous fish. In addition, *Riccia* is an excellent oxygenator. Prefers soft water with neutral pH.

Sagittaria latifolia
(Giant sagittaria)

A very useful American plant, producing long strap-like leaves up to 45cm (17¾in) long and 2cm (¾in) broad. It forms dense thickets, spreading quickly once well established. An excellent oxygenator. It may produce arrowhead-shaped aerial leaves on long stems. Prefers hard water and neutral pH, with moderate light.

Sagittaria subulata

The most common type of *Sagittaria*; like *S. latifolia* from America. Produces bright green leaves, 30cm (12in) or more in length, and up to 1cm (½in) broad. A very useful plant, both decoratively and as an oxygenator. Grows very rapidly and may become reddish in strong light. Care as for *S. latifolia*.

Syngonium spp.
(Goose foot)

A pretty plant with deeply lobed

Sagittaria spp.

leaves, widely sold for but totally unsuited to growth in the aquarium.

Synnema triflorum
(Water wisteria)

This pretty but rather untidy plant from India and Malaysia looks very like *Ceratopteris*, with finely divided leaves

of variable shape, pale green in colour and very brittle. Aerial leaves may be produced, and these are darker. Grows easily under bright light. Propagate from cuttings. Discard old plants as they deteriorate.

Vallisnaria spiralis

Normally grown as the variety *V. spiralis tortifolia*, this plant is found in most tropical areas. It closely resembles *Sagittaria*, having leaves up to 40cm (15¾in) in length and 1cm (½in) broad. The *tortifolia* form is tightly spiralled (it is known as Corkscrew vallisnaria) and very attractive. This plant is highly decorative and a good oxygenator. It spreads rapidly into dense clumps, but may take some time to become fully established. Prefers water of medium hardness and neutral pH, and requires very strong light.

An extremely large species, *V. gigantea*, can be used in very deep tanks.

Vesicularia dubyana
(Java moss)

Pretty creeping moss from the East Indies and Malaysia. It has very fine stems with tiny pointed leaves, and grows to form a dark-green mat on the tank bottom, or can be trained over rocks. Requires shade to prevent algal overgrowth. Prone to becoming coated with sediment in untidy tanks.

Left: *Syngonium* spp. Right: *Vallisnaria* spp.

FEEDING FISH

LIVE FOOD

In their natural state, most fish eat live foods — small animals of various types which the fish catch among water plants or in mud on the bottom. Fortunately most aquarium fish are omnivorous; that is, they can be educated to eat almost anything. Some important exceptions will eat only live food, and some herbivorous fish enjoy an occasional treat of live *Daphnia* or an earthworm.

In this country, live foods can be difficult to obtain on a regular basis. Most are seasonal, because of fluctuating water temperatures, and it is necessary to breed some foods to ensure a regular supply. Fortunately this problem has been overcome to a large extent by the development of freeze-dried foods (see page oo).

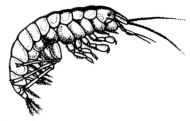

Brine shrimp

Brine shrimps, or *Artemia*, are used in the freshwater aquarium mainly to feed fry, but are a staple food for the marine aquarist's fish. Brine shrimps are small crustaceans, up to 6mm (¼in) long, which develop in saltwater from tiny eggs which resist drying-out for years. They live naturally in lagoons where salinity may be very high, and are quite easy to hatch under artificial conditions. Mix 20g of sea-salt with 1 litre of ordinary tap water (½oz/pint) in a shallow glass dish, and sprinkle on the surface a pinch of Brine-shrimp eggs. Specially treated eggs, in which the tough shells have been removed to improve the hatching rate, are also available. Leave the dish in a warm sunny place, and the Brine shrimps will

hatch within 12 to 24 hours. Newly hatched shrimps can be used to feed fish fry: pour them through fine mesh, rinse to remove the salt, and wash them into the rearing tank.

You may be able to grow the shrimps to a more useful size, although this can be difficult. They feed on algae and microorganisms which develop in strong sunlight, or can be fed with commercially available Brine-shrimp food dripped into the tank. If you want to set up a 'production line' for Brine shrimp, use a series of jam jars for culture, starting one up each week, and providing constant aeration.

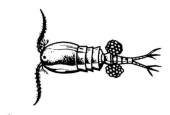

Cyclops

Cyclops are similar to *Daphnia* but much smaller — usually some *Cyclops* will be found in among a supply of *Daphnia*. They can be distinguished as they swim in a straight line, rather than with the jigging action of *Daphnia*. *Cyclops* are relished by most fish, but should not be fed to very young fry, which they may attack. They are seldom available from dealers.

Daphnia

Daphnia, or Water fleas, are relished by most fish. They are tiny swimming crustaceans, often coloured pinkish-red, and can be found swarming in puddles and pools in warm weather. They are only about 2mm (¹⁄₁₀in) in length, so can be eaten by all but the

smallest fish; they can be bought from most dealers. *Daphnia* should be fed in small quantities, as they can cause intestinal disturbance in greedy eaters. If you buy a large quantity at one time, remember that they will need aeration: *Daphnia*'s oxygen requirements are quite high. Examine *Daphnia* carefully in a glass container before you tip them into the tank: sometimes dangerous intruders like Damselfly or Dragonfly larvae may be found mixed in with them; these should be removed

Earthworms are excellent for larger fish such as Cichlids. They must be washed well and cut into small pieces to avoid them escaping into the gravel and polluting the water. Scald them with boiling water (which kills the worms immediately and removes slime and mucus) and then chop them up with a razor blade. Earthworms are probably the most complete and nutritious fish food of all.

Earthworm

Infusoria cultures can easily be produced for feeding the smallest fry. Infusoria are single-celled animals which can be grown in a broth of boiled hay or of dried lettuce leaf crumbled into boiling water. Add a tiny pinch of mud from a water butt or long-standing puddle to 'seed' the cooled broth and place the jar containing the culture on a warm windowsill. Within a week millions of infusoria will develop, and these can be fed to the fry with a dropper.

Mealworms can readily be purchased from pet dealers. They are wiry brown caterpillar-like creatures, about 2cm

(¾in) long, and are eaten by strong-jawed fish like Cichlids, *Pantodon*, *Toxotes*, and of course Piranha. Mealworms float if placed carefully on the water surface, so are useful food for surface-feeding fish like *Pantodon*. They survive well in the bran in which they are sold.

Mealworm

Mosquito larvae are easily raised in the summer, as mosquitos and gnats lay their eggs in any exposed water, such as a bucket or a bowl left in the garden. The larvae are comma-shaped or, depending on their stage of development, more elongated, and can be collected from the surface with a net. They are eaten greedily by most fish, and are an excellent food source.

Mosquito larvae

Tubifex or Sludge worms are an old aquarium standby. They live in heavily polluted water, partly buried in the mud. The worms are bright pink, 2-3cm (¾-1¼in) in length, and weave constantly to and fro. *Tubifex* is now not so easy to find in the dealers'

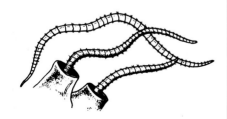

Tubifex

shops, since the cleaning up of rivers has eliminated much of their natural habitat. Most fish enjoy eating them but, due to their unpleasant living habits, *Tubifex* can introduce disease, and need careful cleaning. *Never* feed them to your fish unless they are bright pink and very active.

They are purchased in a tangled mass, which can be left in a container under running water, to flush out debris and impurities. Feed in small quantities, dropping a lump of *Tubifex* into a floating feeder or a container with perforations through which the worms creep, to be picked out by the fish. Worms escaping to the tank bottom will mostly be found by the fish; if they become established in the gravel, Catfish, Loaches or other bottom-feeders will root them out.

Whiteworms

Whiteworms, or *Enchytrae*, and the related Grindal worms, are small terrestrial worms which can be purchased from specialist dealers. They are cultivated in trays of damp earth and leaf mould, on which are placed pieces of dampened bread. The worms are about 1cm (½in) long, and will be found clustered around the bread. They are relished by fish, but are very fatty and rich, and cause ill-health if used too heavily. They are given in an ordinary *Tubifex* feeder.

OTHER FOODS

Freeze-dried Foods have been introduced relatively recently, and provide a means of giving Brine shrimp and *Tubifex* in a clean and hygienic manner. Freeze-dried foods are usually

accepted by fish which normally eat only live foods, although they may need some coaxing at first. These foods are supplied as pellets which can be simply pressed against the inside of the glass or crumbled into the water. Especially with *Tubifex*, this reduces the risk of introducing disease, as the freeze-drying process kills most of the dangerous organisms. *Do not* supply the foods until they have thawed out!

Dried Foods are probably the most widely used of all. Some live foods, such as *Daphnia*, are available dried, but these are not as nutritious as the freeze-dried forms.

Other dried foods are mixtures of various substances ground into crumbs, flakes or pellets of sizes suitable for various types of fish. These provide an excellent balanced diet, and should be given only in small pinches. To stop the floating dried food spreading out over the surface, it can be dropped into a small floating feeding ring, beneath which the fish will congregate. Different grades of dried food are available for fish of all sizes, and also for herbivorous species.

Vegetable Foods include chopped lettuce and specially prepared foods, which are essential to the health of such fish as *Molliensa* spp. that normally feed on algae. Lettuce must be chopped finely and fed in only very small amounts, as it quickly fouls the water.

Miscellaneous Foods, such as chopped egg yolk, liver and many other items, can be given occasionally in very small amounts. A shelled prawn, suspended in the tank by a thread, makes an excellent treat for the fish, and will soon be completely eaten. A swatted housefly will also be eaten by larger fish, but be sure it has not first been sprayed with insecticide. A greenfly-covered shoot from a garden plant will soon be picked clean, but must be removed quickly after feeding to avoid contamination.

RECOGNIZING AND TREATING DISEASES

Fish are susceptible to numerous diseases, some of which are highly contagious, and prompt treatment is needed to prevent losses. It must be remembered that imported fish can be swimming in your tank within a few days of being caught in an Asian swamp or an Amazon pool, due to speedy air-freighting, and you may unwittingly introduce diseases developing in an apparently healthy fish. Conscientious dealers quarantine their fish, but there are some dubious sources from which diseased fish are common. Luckily, most of the common diseases are easy to treat.

The topic of fish diseases is so complex that it would need a whole book to discuss it thoroughly. Fortunately, most of the proprietary medicines available are broad-spectrum, killing most disease organisms. It therefore does not usually matter if you are unable to identify the precise disease affecting your fish, as the treatment will usually help.

White Spot or ichthyophthiriasis, is the most widespread and dangerous disease affecting freshwater fish. It is caused by a microscopic protozoan, *Ichthyophthirius*, and is highly contagious. Small white specks up to 1mm (¹/₃₂in) in diameter appear on the body of the fish, usually first on the fins. They disappear in a day or so as the parasites drop off and proliferate on the tank bottom, then reappear in progressively greater numbers, covering the fish and weakening them so that they die within a few days. The damage to the fish's protective skin also allows the entry of other types of disease organisms. This disease is always introduced from new fish which have not yet developed signs of white spot. Quarantine prevents white spot spreading in your main tank.

White spot is treated by various proprietary medicines which are added to the water. Some are toxic to plants, and this means that the fish must be transferred to your quarantine/hospital

tank for treatment. Detailed instructions will be provided for safe use. Always raise the tank temperature a few degrees during treatment (even if the fish have been transferred to another tank): this speeds up the development of the parasites, which in their free-swimming form will be susceptible to the drugs, or will simply die if the fish have been removed from the tank. With this, as with other diseases, sterilize the net used for handling fish by dipping it in boiling water to kill off the parasites.

Oodinium, or velvet, is another common disease, and usually follows chilling; a related disease affects marine fish. Oodinium resembles white spot,

but the spots are very small, and affected fish look as though they have been dusted with white powder. The microscopic parasites are present in most tanks, but do not cause obvious disease unless the fish are weakened by chilling or other problems. Even then, only a few fish are usually affected, the most susceptible types being Cyprinids, Labyrinth fish, and Egg-laying tooth-carps. Once again, proprietary drugs are available for treatment, which is not usually difficult.

Tuberculosis is common among imported fish, or fish which have received a poor diet. Affected fish are lethargic and become hollow-bellied, with inflamed gills. It is not particularly

Fungal infection

infectious, and *never* affects humans. Infected fish are best disposed of humanely.

Dropsy is not a disease, but a symptom of other illnesses. The fish become bloated with fluid, so that the scales stand out like a pine cone. It is incurable, and affected fish should be humanely killed.

Dropsy

Flukes are parasitic flatworms, sometimes affecting imported fish. They have an extremely complex life-cycle, involving birds, crustacea or snails as alternate hosts, so cannot normally spread in the aquarium. They sometimes cause an infected fish's eyes to bulge, and lead to blindness. The condition is untreatable.

Fungal infection

Fungal Infections are quite common after some damage to the skin or fins. They appear as a cotton-wool-like growth, usually on the fins, and gradually spread over the body. Fungus is easy to treat, by removing the infected fish to the hospital tank and immersing it in water to which sea-salt has been added at a rate of half a teaspoonful to one litre of fresh water (¼teasp/pint). Alternatively, various proprietary treatments are available. Brackish-

White spot

water fish kept in freshwater are particularly susceptible to fungus (notably *Tetraodon fluviatilis* and *Scatophagus argus*), and for this reason seldom thrive in the freshwater tank.

Crustacean Parasites are uncommon in the aquarium, but are sometimes introducd with live *Daphnia*. The Fish louse, *Argulus*, is a 5mm (³⁄₁₆in) shrimp-like organism which clings to the fish and feeds on blood. These parasites are easily seen; if the fish is caught in a net, the Fish lice can be rubbed off or picked off with tweezers. Anchor worms look like worms, but are actually crustaceans. They are up to 2cm (¾in) long, and threadlike, burrowing into the skin of the fish and feeding on its tissue. Anchor worms can easily be seen, and are killed by catching the fish and painting the worms with 1 per cent potassium per-manganate solution (don't let this get into the gills of the fish). Do not try to pull the worms off, as they are firmly anchored in the skin.

Disposing of Sick Fish

A seriously ill fish is a menace to its tank-mates, and should be disposed of. Do not flush fish down the toilet; this is inhumane. A fish can be killed instantly by throwing it hard against a solid floor.

Human Health

Fish diseases are *not* transferable to humans. There have, however, been rare reports of a skin condition caused by organisms living in very unhygienic and badly kept aquaria, which enter the skin through cuts and abrasions. So, if you have an open wound on your hands, it makes sense to wear household rubber gloves when working on your tank.

DIRECTORY OF FRESHWATER FISH GROUPS

Many of the photographs of the fish described in this section depict them in aquaria. It must be appreciated that most fish change colour depending on mood and condition, and so the photographs may not always show them in typical colouring or posture.

The entries on individual species give indications as to compatibility, food requirements, water requirements, preferred habitat and water-temperature range. The key to the abbreviations used is:

CYPRINIDS

This group, the Carp family, includes many of our common fish of rivers and streams: Carp, Roach, Bream, Tench, Dace and Bleak are all typical Cyprinids. The group is the largest of all freshwater families, comprising more than 1,500 species, and is found in all continents of the world except South America, Australasia and Antarctica. More than 300 species have been kept in the aquarium, although far fewer are kept regularly. They vary in size from 2cm (¾in) to over 2m (6½ft; the Indian Mahseer, a sporting fish).

Most Cyprinids are elongated, with large scales, and either have no teeth or have only blunt teeth in the throat: mostly herbivorous or omnivorous, they gulp their food rather than bite it.

Typical Cyprinid, showing barbels.

Many have at the sides of the mouth small barbels or whiskers which they use to help find food while grubbing about in the bottom. Their fins have no supporting spines, and, except when they are ripe with roe and in breeding coloration, it is often difficult to distinguish the sexes. Most are shoaling fish, and of these the Barbs, Rasboras and Danios will not thrive if kept singly. They breed in groups, scattering their eggs on the bottom or, more frequently, among fine-leaved plants. Some types attach the adhesive eggs to the plants, but most scatter them at random — and will eat the eggs greedily if they can. Spawning generally takes place after a wild chase, with the males scattering their milt as the females deposit their eggs.

Many of these fish come from rivers rather than still waters, and are powerful and restless swimmers. They generally prefer soft, acid water, but most of those currently popular are well adapted to most tap waters.

Barbs

This group of fish is common throughout Africa and Asia. Barbs are active fish, requiring good oxygen levels. The genus may be described variously as

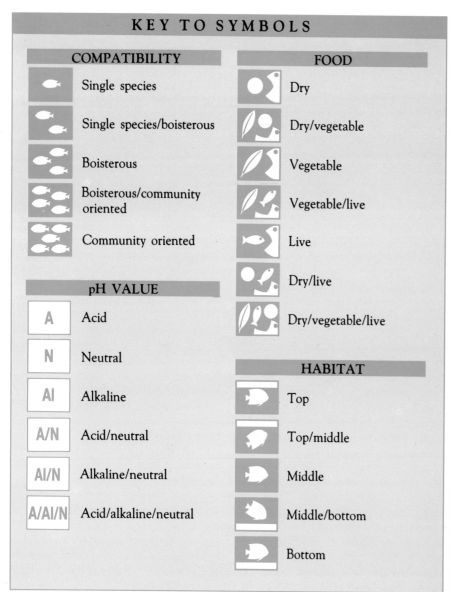

KEY TO SYMBOLS

COMPATIBILITY

- Single species
- Single species/boisterous
- Boisterous
- Boisterous/community oriented
- Community oriented

pH VALUE

A	Acid
N	Neutral
Al	Alkaline
A/N	Acid/neutral
Al/N	Alkaline/neutral
A/Al/N	Acid/alkaline/neutral

FOOD

- Dry
- Dry/vegetable
- Vegetable
- Vegetable/live
- Live
- Dry/live
- Dry/vegetable/live

HABITAT

- Top
- Top/middle
- Middle
- Middle/bottom
- Bottom

Balantiocheilus melanopterus

Barbus, *Puntius* or *Capoetes*; *Barbus* is the universally recognized name.

Most Barbs breed easily in the aquarium, after suitable conditioning with good feeding. The breeding tank should be reasonably large, and filled to a depth of about 18cm (7in) with clean rainwater which has been filtered through peat. Place a few bunches of *Cabomba* or *Myriophyllum* in the tank for use as a spawning medium. The eggs are not very adhesive, so it is a good idea to include a layer of glass marbles to trap eggs which fail to be caught in the plants. Heat the water to 2°C (3.6°F) above that in the tank in which the fish are normally kept, and introduce the fish to the breeding tank in the evening. Spawning should take place within 48 hours, after which the fish should be removed. Hatching takes place within another 48 hours. Start feeding with the finest proprietary food for fish fry, and keep well aerated.

Rasboras

This is a group of about 30 species native to Malaysia and Indonesia. All are small, elongated, fast-swimming fish, and live in shoals in swiftly flowing streams. They lack the mouth barbels of the Barbs. Colouring is generally subtle, and, as they are difficult to sex, it is best to spawn them as a group.

Spawning is not easy. They require a shallow tank with soft, strongly acid water which has been filtered through peat. They are best spawned on finely divided spawning mops made of unravelled nylon wool, as they feed greedily on their eggs and can easily seize the adhesive spawn from plants. Eggs usually hatch within 48 hours, and the growing fry need good aeration. There are many other *Rasbora* species available from time to time than those listed on pages 80-1. They are generally similar in their requirements: all require neutral or acid pH and soft water, and all are peaceful shoaling fish.

Danios

This group includes fish of the genera *Danio* and *Brachydanio*. They are familiar surface-feeding fish from India, Burma and Sri Lanka, and are very active and hardy. They breed very easily, scattering their eggs on a bed of marbles in about 10cm (4in) of water: deeper water gives them time to eat the eggs as they sink to the bottom. The eggs hatch quickly and the young are easy to raise, provided they are started off on suitable small-sized foods.

Balantiocheilus melanopterus
(Silver shark)

23-26°C (73-79°F)

This large and beautiful shoaling fish comes from Thailand. It grows up to 30cm (12in) in length in the wild, but is smaller in the aquarium. It is a fast swimmer and a powerful leaper, and needs plenty of room; a predator, it is not to be trusted with small fish. It is coloured silver and has large, erect orange-yellow fins with jet-black edges. It is long-lived and hardy, and is best suited to the community tank with other large fish. It has not yet been bred, and is difficult to sex.

Barbus arulius
(Arulius barb)

24-25°C (75-77°F)

A fairly large fish from Malaysia, growing to 12cm (4¾in) long. The young are blotched with irregular black patches which become more intense as the fish matures. Most unusually for a Barb, the male develops long trailing

Barbus conchonius

Barbus cumingii

Barbus fasciatus

fin-rays from the dorsal fin. This is a hardy and long-lived Barb, which is fast-swimming but quite peaceful. It needs plenty of swimming space, and should be given vegetable food in its diet. It breeds in typical Barb fashion, but is not prolific. The water should preferably be well aged.

Barbus arulius, *showing dorsal filaments.*

Barbus conchonius
(Rosy barb)

18-25°C (64-77°F)

This fish comes from Southeast Asia and has been an aquarium favourite for many years. It is active, bold, and peaceable, reaching a length of about 10cm (4in). Both sexes are normally glossy green and silver, with a black spot near the tail and, in the male, black-tipped fins. In breeding conditions, the male blushes a brilliant rosy pink while the fins become red, with dense black tips. These fish spawn extremely easily and, if well fed, keep in breeding coloration for much of the year. Very hardy, and may dig actively in the gravel.

Barbus cumingii
(Cuming's barb)

22-27°C (72-81°F)

A small Barb from Sri Lanka, seldom growing to more than 5cm (2in) and so suitable for most community tanks. It has large conspicuous scales, coloured silver with a golden tinge. There are two smudgy black vertical bars on the sides, and the males have orange-red fins. It spawns in typical Barb fashion, although reluctantly, and seems to need matured rainwater to induce spawning.

Barbus everetti
(Clown barb)

25-27°C (77-81°F)

A large Barb from Southeast Asia, in which the male grows to 14cm (5½in) and the female to 11cm (4⅓in). They are colourful while young, with a brownish-pink body coloration and wedge-shaped blackish bars; the fins are red. This Barb is very hardy and peaceful, and does best in a shoal in a large tank. It is a plant-eater, and should be kept with leathery-leafed plants like *Anubias*, *Lagenandra* and the larger *Cryptocoryne* species. It breeds very easily, and is extremely prolific. Small fish are the most attractive, as in the adult the colours are less marked and the appearance becomes rather coarse.

Barbus fasciatus
(Zebra barb; Striped barb)

22-26°C (72-79°F)

A medium-sized Barb from Sumatra and Borneo, growing to about 11cm (4⅓in). It is unusual in that the thin black stripes run lengthwise (in almost all other Barbs stripes or bars are vertical). The body is silver. It is slimmer than most Barbs, and less inclined to

Barbus filamentosus

root in the bottom. It breeds fairly easily, but is not as hardy or prolific as others of this genus.

Barbus filamentosus
(Filament barb; Black-spot barb)

20-25°C (68-77°F)

This Barb from Southeast Asia reaches 15cm (6in) in length. Its coloration is confusing: while young, it is barred in black, with four vertical stripes, but as it matures these fade, and the adults are silvery gold with a single large black spot near the base of the tail, level with the anal fin. The outer edges of the tail are red, with black tips, and the dorsal fin is rosy pink. In the male, the dorsal fin rays are extended and often ragged-looking. A very active and curious fish, it is extremely prolific and breeds easily in a large breeding tank. Males in breeding condition develop tubercles on the face, which look superficially like a disease symptom. Needs adequate vegetable supplementation to its diet.

Barbus lateristriga
(Spanner barb)

20-25°C (68-77°F)

A large Barb from Southeast Asia, which grows up to 18cm (7in) long, and is rather prone to digging about in the gravel. It is greyish-silver, with two vertical black bars and a thin line extending back towards the tail, making a 'spanner' shape. The colour is intense in young fish, but becomes more diffuse in adults, which can look coarse and uninteresting. This fish is very active, and may bully smaller Barbs, keeping them away from food. It breeds in typical Barb manner, but it may be difficult to induce spawning. Once bred, it is enormously prolific.

Barbus nigrofasciatus

Barbus nigrofasciatus
(Black ruby)

20-26°C (68-79°F)

A beautiful and well behaved Barb from Sri Lanka, this fish is very deep-bodied, and grows up to 6cm (2⅓in) in length. Colouring is normally subdued, with a pinkish-grey body crossed with faint black bars. In females, the bases of the fins are predominantly black, and in males the whole dorsal fin is black. In breeding condition, males glow with an intense purplish-red colouring, and the blackish areas become deep velvety black. A group of males kept together seem to compete for the females' attention by remaining in breeding coloration for most of the time. This is a very active, inquisitive but peaceable fish, ideally suited to the community aquarium. Does not do well in very hard water.

Barbus oligolepis
(Chequer barb; Island barb)

20-25°C (68-77°F)

A small Barb from Sumatra, growing to 5cm (2in) and thriving in a small shoal. The body is of iridescent silver tinged with pink, and two rows of scales along the side are alternately coloured black and silver, giving a chequerboard appearance. The fins are red, edged with black, except for the tail fin, which is plain red. The colours intensify when breeding is imminent. These fish are very active and peaceable towards other species, although the males fight among themselves — without causing any real damage. Sometimes difficult to persuade to spawn, but once started is quite prolific.

Barbus schwanenfeldi
(Tinfoil barb; Tinsel barb)

20-25°C (68-77°F)

An aquarium giant, which grows to 45cm (17¾in), from Southeast Asia. Most aquarists come across this fish by accident, having purchased it as an attractive juvenile. Unfortunately it

Barbus semifasciolatus

Barbus stoliczkanus

grows swiftly and keeps on growing, not being significantly stunted by a small tank. It has large, bright silver scales and reddish fins, edged with black, and the body is very deep and broad. It swims very quickly and is a prodigious leaper, so the tank must be tightly covered at all times. Surprisingly for such a large and robust fish, it is largely vegetarian, and will speedily graze most plants down to stubble; it will also gulp any small fish it can catch. This fish is tough and long-lived, and breeds readily provided it is given proper conditions and a large enough breeding tank.

Barbus semifasciolatus 'schuberti'
(Schubert's barb)

20-25°C (68-77°F)

This fish came originally from China, and is usually sold as a 'sport' called B. schuberti, which is pale gold with faint traces of the black bars found on the original, undistinguished wild fish. Fins are deep orange. It grows to about 8cm (3¼in), and is a very peaceful, shoaling fish. One of the easiest Barbs to breed, it can be kept in breeding condition throughout most of the year. Less liable than most Barbs to eat small tank-mates. Tolerant of most water conditions.

Barbus stoliczkanus
(Stoliczk's barb)

20-25°C (68-77°F)

A small Barb from Southeast Asia, growing to about 6cm (2⅓in). This is one of the most attractive members of the group, but is coloured subtly, rather than with the bold coloration of the most popular species. The large conspicuous scales are black-edged There is a distinct black spot near the base of the tail, and another by the gills. The fins are red-tinged and, in the male, the dorsal is brilliantly coloured, bright red with black edging and irregular black patches. When breeding, males become suffused with a rosy pink colour. A peaceful shoaling fish, this breeds readily in typical Barb fashion.

Barbus schwanenfeldi

Barbus tetrazona
(Tiger barb; Sumatra barb)

20-25°C (68-77°F)

This small fish from Southeast Asia is the most widely kept of all Barbs, and is very boldly coloured. It grows up to 7cm (2¾in) in length, and is very deep-bodied. It is a brassy yellow overall, with four sharply edged broad black bars. Males have bright red fins and a reddish-brown head, while females are less colourful. They are aggressive shoaling fish, squabbling among each other, and irritate fish such as Angel-fish and Siamese fighting fish by nipping at their long trailing fins. They are not particularly aggressive to other species, however. Their oxygen requirement is high, and they do not tolerate overcrowding well. Albino varieties are available.

Barbus tetrazona

Barbus titteya

Barbus titteya
(Cherry barb)

22-26°C (72-79°F)

This pretty Barb from Sri Lanka grows to only 4.5cm (1¾in). It is an extremely active shoaling fish, living naturally in small streams, and so does not tolerate overcrowding in the aquarium. Both sexes have a black longitudinal stripe. Females are brown overall, with reddish fins. In males, most of the body is a brilliant cherry-red, the colours being exceptionally marked during spawning. These fish are especially active when spawning, and care must be taken that the females are not driven too violently. The young are proportionately tiny, and difficult to rear to a large enough size to eat normal foods. Very peaceful with other fish in the community aquarium.

Brachydanio albolineatus

Brachydanio spp.

   A/N/Al

20-25°C (68-77°F)

B. albolineatus (Pearl danio) is a slim, fast-swimming fish from Southeast Asia, growing up to 6cm (2⅓in) in length. It has long trailing barbels, which are unobtrusive unless specifically looked for. It is a subtle pearly pink, with metallic green tints — this colour is developed properly only in strong light and with proper feeding, especially of live foods. These fish are constantly on the move, and may jump. They will not thrive unless kept in a small shoal. They breed very easily, and are prolific; as the eggs are non-adhesive, plants are unnecessary in the spawning tank. The fish are very agile and quick to eat their spawn, so use shallow water of depth no greater than 10cm (4in) to shorten the time taken for the eggs to drop into the bed of marbles or glass rods on the tank bottom; some aquarists use a plastic spawning trap. Spawn in pairs, or as a shoal. The eggs of these and other Danios hatch quickly, and the fry are fed at first on infusoria or extremely fine prepared food. They reach maturity in about 18 weeks.

B. frankei (Leopard danio), a comparative newcomer to the aquarium, comes from Southeast Asia. It is shaped very like B. albolineatus, but has a yellowish-silver body heavily dotted with deep blue speckles. B. frankei grows to about 6cm (2⅓in); the females are perhaps a little longer and much plumper than the males. As with other Danios, it is a fast-swimming, surface-living shoaling fish which tends to jump, so the aquarium must be well covered. Breeds as B. albolineatus, but is not very prolific, probably due to reduced fertility in the males. Keeping two males per female improves the fertility, but it is still not an easy fish to breed. This is probably a reflection of its 'newness'.

B. nigrofasciatus (Spotted danio) is a small Danio from Burma, and grows to only 5cm (2in). It resembles a hybrid between B. frankei and B. rerio, although it is a species in its own right. It is brown on its back, and has silver undersides; it has a long blue stripe along its side, and is speckled with blue on its belly. Not an easy fish to spawn, as it is difficult to get into proper condition.

B. rerio (Zebra fish) is the 'standard' Danio; it comes from eastern India and grows to about 6cm (2⅓in) in length. It has an olive-green back and silvery-gold sides and belly. Sides and fins are marked with broad blue longitudinal stripes, and the dorsal fin is outlined in white. A very active and completely peaceful shoaling fish, it is bold and always swims at the front of the tank. Allow plenty of clear swimming space between the plants. Highly recommended for the beginner, as it is hardy and easily bred — but do not keep singly as it thrives in groups of six or more. As with other small Danios, B. rerio lives for only 2-3 years.

Danio malabaricus
(Giant danio)

   A/N

20-25°C (68-77°F)

The true giant of the Danio family comes from India and Sri Lanka. It grows to nearly 15cm (6in), but is just as peaceful as its smaller cousins. It is deep-bodied, coloured a metallic sky-blue with yellow lengthways streaks; the belly is pale pink, and the lower fins are reddish. It needs to be kept in a shoal, and precautions must be taken to prevent it jumping out of the tank. Breeds easily in Barb fashion and is prolific, but large amounts of live food are necessary to get the fish into spawning condition.

Brachydanio frankei

Brachydanio rerio

Danio malabaricus

Gyrinocheilus aymonieri

Epalzeorynchus spp.

22-25°C (72-77°F)

E. kallopterus (Flying fox or Pal fish) is a popular scavenging fish from Thailand, growing up to 12cm (4¾in) in length. It has a long cylindrical body, slightly flattened underneath, and this suits its bottom-living habit. It has an undershot mouth, with horny lips, and grazes continually on algae as it grubs about among the plants. The upper surface is brown, the underneath silvery-yellow. Along the sides are a bright gold stripe and a bold brown stripe. Fins are held stiffly erect and tipped with white. This fish is aggressive and territorial, being something of a bully and prone to rush at other fish, although not doing any physical damage. It is also irritatingly restless, and sometimes dashes madly about, disturbing the whole tank. Not known to have bred in captivity.

E. siamensis (Siamang) is very similar, but thicker-bodied and with a more general gold colour overall. Some have green speckles towards the rear of the body.

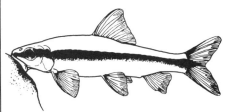

Epalzeorhyncus, showing sucker mouth.

Esomus spp.

22-24°C (72-75°F)

E. danricus, the so-called Flying barb, is actually more closely related to the Danios, which it resembles in appearance and habit. It is a small shoaling fish from India, Sri Lanka and Malaysia, growing to 10cm (4in) in length. The colouring is silver with a dark green lengthways stripe, and the fish has long pectoral fins — the sign of a powerful jumper. E. danricus has very long trailing barbels. The fish swim rapidly, and must be kept in a shoal;

they leap wildly when disturbed, so the tank must be well covered. A peaceful fish, but one which will eat small tank-mates such as baby live-bearers. Needs plenty of live food to get into spawning condition, and can then be spawned like the Barbs, in clumps of fine-leaved plants.

E. malayensis (Malayan flying barb) is very similar in all respects, but has a faint lengthways stripe and a conspicuous black spot on the base of the tail.

Gyrinocheilus aymonieri (Sucker loach)

22-30°C (72-86°F)

From Thailand, this fish, despite its popular name, is not a Loach at all (technically, it is not truly a Cyprinid either). It is a large fish, growing up to 15cm (6in) in the aquarium, and looks very much like the common Gudgeon of British rivers. It is light brown with darker bars and speckles. Its most notable feature is its large undershot sucker mouth, with which it industriously scrapes algae and other debris from the glass or plant leaves — in fact, it is further modified so that water can be taken in through a special aperture and passed out of the gills without the fish having to stop feeding. It is certainly the most efficient tank scavenger available, but has a few drawbacks. It is nervous, almost impossible to catch in a tank with plants, and prone to rush about when scared. It becomes aggressive when large, and irritates large passive fish like *Pterophyllum* and *Symphysodon* by attempting to treat them as a leaf on which to graze; however, it does not bother small fish. Not known to have bred in the aquarium, probably due to some missing

Labeo bicolor

element in the vegetable diet. Feed with chopped lettuce if no algae are present. Needs well aerated conditions and clean water.

Labeo bicolor (Red-tailed shark)

23-27°C (73-81°F)

A handsome fish from Southeast Asia which can grow up to 15cm (6in) but is usually smaller. It is velvety black overall, including the fins (which are tipped with white), except for the tail, which is a rich orange-red. The undershot mouth is surrounded by short barbels, with which the fish finds food buried in the bottom. It grazes on algae, and will also eat live foods. This is a somewhat schizophrenic fish, usually shy and nocturnal but on occasion becoming very aggressive: it is most aggressive towards members of its own species, and keeping them together causes continuous running fights which disturb the community tank. Has been bred in typical Barb fashion, but needs very careful conditioning and soft, acid water. Suitable for the community tank with other robust fish such as Cichlids.

Labeo erythrurus (Red-finned shark)

22-25°C (72-77°F)

From Thailand, a similar fish to *L. bicolor* but more elongated, with a blackish-green body and reddish fins and tail. There is a dense black patch at the base of the tail. Grows to about 12cm (4¾in), and is less shy than *L. bicolor*, often feeding in mid-water. Adults are territorial and may be aggressive. Breeds occasionally, in the same way as *L. bicolor*.

Morulius chrysophekadion (Black shark)

22-25°C (72-77°F)

A close relative of *Labeo*, this fish comes from Southeast Asia. It is similar to *Labeo* in most respects but is much less aggressive. It grows to 45cm

(17¾in) or more and is very active, so it needs a very large tank. It is an algae-grazer, and very effective as such, although it is so large that it frequently damages tank plants as it grazes. It has an elongated body with an undershot sucker mouth, and very large fins which are always held erect. When young, it is a dense velvety black all over, but in mature fish each scale has a golden spot, making the fish appear a warm bronze-black colour. Very hardy and long-lived. Needs plenty of algae or, if this is not available, must be fed fresh vegetable matter.

Rasbora heteromorpha

Rasbora borapetensis

22-25°C (72-77°F)

From Thailand, this grows to about 5cm (2in). It is a typical Rasbora, slim-bodied and fast-swimming near the surface. It thrives in small shoals. The body is silvery, with a greenish back and a vivid dark lengthways stripe along the sides, edged with gold. The fins are tinged with red, and there is a red patch at the base of the tail. A pretty, inoffensive fish which breeds in typical Rasbora fashion, although less readily than do other species. Requires soft, acid water in a shallow breeding tank, with fine-leaved plants or nylon spawning mops to catch the adhesive eggs. Like other Rasboras, this fish appreciates peat, either in the compost or in an outside filter.

Rasbora heteromorpha (Harlequin fish)

23-26°C (73-79°F)

A very popular fish from Southeast Asia, this is much more deep-bodied than other Rasboras. It grows to about 4.5cm (1¾in), and is a peaceful shoaling fish, although males often squabble. Colouring is a delicate orange-pink, with a bold blue-black wedge-shaped patch extending back from the midsection almost to the tail. The eyes are bright red. Males are generally brighter-coloured, especially during breeding, when they have a crimson or purplish flush. For years this fish was impossible to breed, but breeding has now become commonplace, although special conditions are required. The spawning tank has to be deeper than that usually used and well planted with broad-leaved plants like *Cryptocoryne* or *Lagenandra*. The water must be soft and acid, and the tank well shaded. The fish deposit their eggs on the undersides of the leaves, and must then be removed. It spawns best in groups of six to ten fish. *R. heteromorpha* is still a rather delicate fish, which may not thrive if water conditions are not to its liking. Do not keep with fish likely to bully.

Rasbora pauciperforata

Rasbora maculata
(Spotted rasbora; Pygmy rasbora)

23-26°C (73-79°F)
A tiny fish from Southeast Asia, growing to only 2.5cm (1in), this is bright red, with a few large and conspicuous blue-black spots. The fins are red edged with black. A brilliantly coloured fish when in good condition, but very sensitive to water conditions, it is probably best kept in a single-species tank, with a peat substrate instead of gravel: this provides the water conditions the fish need and shows off their colours to best advantage. Once well established these fish are quite hardy. For breeding, rainwater and peat are a necessity, and even then spawning is difficult. Not very prolific.

Rasbora pauciperforata
(Red-striped rasbora; Glowlight rasbora)

21-25°C (70-77°F)
A small, fast-swimming Rasbora from Sumatra which grows to about 7cm (2¾in), this fish is silvery-coloured with an olive back and a bright red lengthways stripe which is edged below with a fine black line. The eyes are bright red. This is a nervous fast-swimming fish, difficult to breed and not very prolific. Breeding and care as for *R. heteromorpha*.

Rasbora trilineata
(Scissortail)

20-25°C (68-77°F)
A popular fish from Southeast Asia which may grow to 15cm (6in) but is usually smaller. The body is translucent, with silvery sides and a dark-brown line running along the sides into the tail. Each lobe of the tail fin has a conspicuous black patch, edged with white. The tail is continuously flicked open and shut, to give the fish its popular name of Scissortail. It is very peaceful and is an excellent community fish, spawning relatively easily, but requiring a larger than normal tank, due to its relatively large size.

Rasbora vaterifloris
(Fire rasbora; Pearly rasbora)

23-26°C (73-79°F)
A small fish from Sri Lanka, growing to only 4cm (1½in), this has a similar shape to *R. heteromorpha*, but much larger fins. Coloration is an overall pink or pearl sheen, with red fins. There is some doubt as to whether all the fish available are actual *R. vaterifloris*, and a less colourful species may sometimes be imported. Rather delicate and difficult to breed. Best treated like *R. heteromorpha*, and given very soft, acid water and a peat substrate.

Rasbora vaterifloris

Tanichthys albonubes
(White cloud mountain minnow)

18-22°C (64-72°F)

An aquarium favourite for many years, originally from China, and requiring lower temperatures than most aquarium fish: these fish can survive in unheated tanks in a warm room. Being used to sudden temperature changes in the mountain streams they inhabit, they are very hardy. They grow to about 6cm (2⅓in), and are slim-bodied. The body is olive-green above and white below. A dark green stripe, edged above with gold, runs along the length of the body, ending on the tail with a black spot. The fins are yellow, edged with red, and the tail is bright red. The colours are very pronounced in the young fish, fading with age. Among the easiest of all egg-layers to breed, these spawn in pairs on bunches of fine-leaved plants after a prolonged courtship. Unusually, there is no need to remove the parent fish after spawning: they generally ignore both eggs and young.

CHARACINS

One of the largest fish groups of all is the Characin family, in which are found many of the most familiar aquarium fishes. Characins are immensely diverse, and have filled almost all the possible habitats (or ecological niches) available to them, apart from the sea. They are typically from Central and South America, especially the Amazon area. A few have made their way up into North America, and others are found in Africa.

They have certain specific characteristics which are important in classification. Characins have teeth, unlike the Cyprinids; these may be small and rudimentary, or very large and obvious, as in the Piranha. They have also an adipose fin, a small fleshy fin on the back between the dorsal fin and the tail (this is found also in some other groups, like the Catfish). Inevitably, the rules never hold true all the time, and a few Characins have lost their teeth or adipose fin, making identification difficult. Body-shape is

Abramites microcephalus

no guide to the relationships of fish, and the Characins include flattened disc-like fish as well as typically slender, round-bodied fish adapted for fast swimming.

One notable Characin characteristic is the 'Characin hook', which is sometimes useful in sexing fish. This is a very small hook at the tips of the rays of the anal fin (and sometimes other fins), and is found only in the males. When the smaller species are caught in a fine-mesh net, males often cling by their hooks to the net for a few seconds. This is not an infallible test, and works only with quite small fish.

Characin, showing characteristic teeth and adipose fin.

Many of the most popular species are known as Tetras, a widely used name which technically encompasses only fish of the genera *Hyphessobrycon* and *Hemigrammus*. In practice, however, the term is used more widely to describe any small Characin.

Some species described here as Characins have recently been shifted by the taxonomists to other groups.

Aquarists are highly resistant to such changes, however, so these fish are listed under their familiar classification, which they will probably retain for years to come.

As would be expected from their teeth, Characins are usually carnivorous, benefiting from occasional feeding with live or freeze-dried *Daphnia* or *Tubifex*, although for much of the time they are quite content with proprietary dried foods. Live foods are important, however, when conditioning Characins for breeding. This group is notoriously difficult to breed, especially the newly imported species. Also, they exemplify the classic problem of the commercial fish breeder, in that wild fish are usually larger, more vigorous and much better coloured than their tank-bred cousins (see page 19). Ease has replaced bright colouring as the key object in breeding, interfering with the normal process of natural selection whereby the most spectacularly coloured males usually win mates and thus achieve breeding success. Some Characins now available are no more than pale reflections of the wild fish — but they are, of course, much cheaper, as the cost of catching and importing the wild fish has been eliminated.

To breed Characins, the following broad guidelines are helpful. (Bear in mind that individual species may have particular needs; these are discussed in more detail under the headings for those species.) Characins are normally bred in pairs rather than shoals, and there is some difficulty in sexing the breeding fish. There are seldom differences in colouring or finnage between males and females, although females are typically deeper-bodied and plumper. The plumpness of a ripe female can be more easily spotted if the fish are examined from immediately above, when females with bulging flanks can be identified. Males are usually smaller than females and, when they are in breeding condition, their colours may become more intense. Easiest of all is simply to watch a group of potential breeders and isolate those which seem to pair off. Characin eggs are semi-adhesive: some will cling to plants and others will fall to the bottom. They are best spawned in a tank containing a bed of marbles or glass rods, together with a selection of nylon spawning mops, which the fish treat like natural plants. It is best to fill the spawning tank to a depth of (for small fish) 20cm (7¾in) with rainwater, in which peat has been thoroughly stirred and then filtered off. Heat the tank to 26-27°C (79-81°F), and make sure that it is only dimly lit, shading it with paper if necessary. If you prefer, the spawning tank can be planted with fine-leaved plants — but note that there is a risk of introducing infection, as natural plants cannot be sterilized.

The fish will probably spawn at night after a great deal of chasing. The eggs are tiny and difficult to see, so it is important to check the breeding tank carefully each day. Remove the fish as soon as they have completed spawning. The fry hatch very quickly, and special attention to the proper food on which to start smaller species is needed, as the fry have very small mouths. Once over the first week or two, they grow very swiftly and are generally hardy.

Abramites microcephalus
(Marbled headstander)

23-27°C (73-81°F)
This fish from the 'headstander' group comes from the Amazon basin and Guyana. It is relatively large, growing to about 12cm (4¾in), and has a rather fat body with a dispro-

Alestes longipinnis

portionately small head (hence the name *microcephalus*). The colouring is subdued: irregular greyish-brown bars on a lighter background, with a bright yellow adipose fin. Its claim to interest is its headstanding attitude, tilting downwards at an angle of 45°. It is partly vegetarian, and nips pieces out of the plants as well as out of the fins of slow-moving tankmates. It is shy and retiring, hanging stationary among the plants for long periods, but tending to dash out at other fish occasionally. It is aggressive with its own kind, and is not known to breed in captivity. It is a powerful jumper, so the tank must be well covered.

Alestes longipinnis
(Long-finned characin)

23-25°C (73-77°F)
This West African Characin is a peaceful shoaling fish growing to about 15cm (6in), but normally smaller. It is silvery overall, and has very large red eyes. There is a short black stripe running into the tail, and in the males the dorsal fin is extremely elongated and broken into separate rays. This fish is not commonly seen in the aquarium, as its colouring is not exceptional and it is difficult to breed.

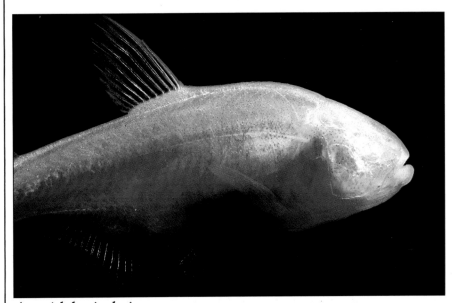

Anoptichthys jordani

Anostomus anostomus

Anoptichthys jordani
(Blind cave-fish)

20-26°C (68-79°F)

This very odd cave-dwelling fish from Mexico has lost its eyes completely, together with its skin coloration, due to its natural habitat: underground streams. It is a descendant of a normal-eyed fish common in Mexico but seldom kept in the aquarium. *A. jordani* is a plump, pearly pink 7cm (2¾in) fish, and is constantly on the move, seeking food. Surprisingly, it does not suffer in competition with tankmates which have normal eyes; this probably indicates that most fish hunt food by smell. It is able to avoid bumping into obstructions, and can be scrappy, nipping at the fins of other fish. For breeding it is best kept in a dimly lit single-species tank. Breeds quite easily in typical Characin fashion in hard, alkaline water.

Anostomus anostomus
(Striped anostomus)

25-27°C (77-81°F)

A large 'headstander' from South America, growing to 15cm (6in), this fish has a long cylindrical body and a small pointed head. The body is coloured gaily with broad blue-black lengthways stripes interspersed with yellow ones. The fins are blood-red. As with the other 'headstanders', *A. anostomus* normally swims with its body inclined at an angle of 45° or even more. For such a large fish, it has a comically small mouth, set on top of the snout: this means that, to feed from the bottom, the fish must stand absolutely erect on its head or even roll onto its back. It is very likely that, in nature, it feeds on organisms growing on plant stems — its mouth would be in the right position for this. Probably because of some dietary deficiency, it does not breed regularly in captivity. Can be aggressive with its own kind, but peaceable if kept singly with other species or in a large group in a single-species tank. A powerful jumper and an occasional fin-nipper.

Aphyocharax rubripinnis
(Bloodfin)

18-26°C (64-79°F)

This fish from Argentina grows to about 5cm (2in) long. It is a shoaling fish, coloured silvery green with blood-red fins — although, due to intensive and careless breeding, those currently available lack the brilliant fin colouring of the wild fish. The males have the characteristic 'Characin hook' on the anal fin, which can be used to sex them (see page 82). Breeds very easily, and two males should be used per female. After a courtship chase, the fish leap clear of the water, depositing eggs as they fall back. The eggs should be collected on spawning mops or fine-leaved plants. Breeds at the upper end of the water-temperature range.

Arnoldichthys spilopterus
(Red-eyed characin)

24-28°C (75-82°F)

This extremely attractive fish from Nigeria grows to 6cm (2⅓in). It has very large, pearly scales, a silvery lengthways stripe, and a black spot on the dorsal fin. The eyes are large and bright red. The males have red-speckled anal fins. This fish is much more peaceable than would seem from its exposed teeth, and is a suitable inhabitant of the community tank, doing best in a shoal, in soft, acid water, with plenty of swimming space. It has not been bred in captivity.

Carnegiella marthae

Carnegiella spp.

22-30°C (72-86°F)

C. marthae (Black-winged hatchetfish) is a small fish widely distributed in South America, and is typical of its group. It has a grossly enlarged 'chest' consisting of muscles which beat the elongated pectoral fins very rapidly to allow the fish to 'fly' for 2m (6½ft) or more, probably mainly to escape predators. It is a delicate shoaling fish, growing to no more than 3.5cm (1⅓in), and seldom surviving for long in the aquarium. It is silvery with an indistinct pale stripe along the sides. It breeds occasionally, in soft, acid water filtered through peat. Keep the tank well covered.

C. strigata (Marbled hatchetfish) is very similar, and comes from the Amazon basin and Guyana. It grows to 4.5cm (1¾in), and is attractively marbled with brown markings on a silvery body. It is hardier than *C. marthae* and more suited to the community tank, with non-aggressive tank-mates. It is slightly easier to breed than *C. marthae*, but just as prone to jumping out of the tank. Provide plenty of floating plants to act as cover.

Cheirodon axelrodi

Cheirodon axelrodi
(Cardinal tetra)

23-27°C (73-81°F)

Sometimes incorrectly called *Hyphessobrycon cardinalis*, this little fish comes from the Rio Negro in Brazil and grows to about 4cm (1½in). It is one of the most brilliantly coloured freshwater fish, with a fluorescent blue-green stripe extending from the snout

Carnegiella strigata

through the eye to the tail root. The underside, from snout to tail, is a brilliant red. It is a typical fish of jungle pools, preferring the 'black water' achieved in the aquarium only by filtering soft, acid water through peat. When originally imported, it was extremely difficult to spawn but, due to selective breeding, it is now easier, reproducing in typical Characin fashion in well planted tanks containing soft, acid water. *C. axelrodi* needs a great deal of conditioning with live food if it is to be bred successfully.

Chilodus punctatus
(Spotted headstander)

20-28°C (68-82°F)

This attractive 'headstander' from South America grows to about 8cm (3¼in). It has subdued colours, predominantly silvery-gold, with each of the large scales carrying a dark patch so that the fish has a mottled appearance. There is a dark lengthways stripe, and the dorsal fin has a few dark spots. This

Chilodus punctatus

Copeina arnoldi

fish has a very small mouth, and grazes on algae or small organisms. In the community tank it may go hungry if kept with greedy tankmates; it usually needs supplementary vegetable food, such as lettuce or oatmeal. Has been bred occasionally in captivity. Keep in soft, acid water.

Copeina arnoldi
(Spraying characin)

22-28°C (72-82°F)

A small Amazon shoaling fish which grows to 8cm (3¼in). It is very slim and has a large mouth. The upper lobe of the tail is elongated, especially in the male. The body is greenish-silver, with a red-tinged belly, and there is a conspicuous black spot in the dorsal fin and on the gill cover. Males have reddish fins. It is interesting mainly for its incredible spawning behaviour.

It must be spawned in a few centimetres of soft, acid water, with plenty of overhanging plants — a potted houseplant placed in the tank serves very well. The mating pair selects a suitable site by examining the leaves overhanging the tank; then they leap out together, sticking to the leaf surface for a few moments while the eggs and sperm are deposited. The eggs are adhesive, and stick in a cluster. The fish repeat the process until several hundred eggs have been deposited, after which the female takes no further part in looking after them. The male, however, stations himself beneath the

eggs, and every few minutes flicks water over them using his elongated tail lobe. After 36-48 hours, the fry hatch, and are washed into the water by the spray thrown by the male fish. The parent fish must now be removed to prevent them from eating the fry. The young are very tiny, and quite difficult to raise. This and *C. guttata* are the only commonly kept Characins to show any interest in their eggs, except in the eating of them.

Copeina guttata
(Red-spotted copeina)

22-28°C (72-82°F)

A fairly large shoaling fish from the Amazon region which grows to 15cm

(6in), this is less attractive than *C. arnoldi* and less commonly available. It has an elongated shape, is bluish-grey, and has large scales. The fins are reddish, tipped with orange; in the male the upper lobe of the tail is enlarged. In breeding males, the colours are intensified and there is a row of red spots along the flanks. In both sexes there is a black spot in the dorsal fin.

There are two odd points about this fish. Almost uniquely, tank-raised fish are larger than wild stock; and, like *C. arnoldi*, these fish reproduce in a remarkable way, this time guarding their eggs like Cichlids. The male digs out a depression in the gravel by beating with his tail and picking up stones in his mouth. The female lays her eggs in this nest and, after fertilizing the eggs, the male drives her away. He guards the eggs until they hatch, 48 hours later, and must then be removed so that he does not eat the fry.

C. guttata is very prolific, producing up to 1,000 eggs in a single spawning. It is a powerful jumper, and so the tank must be well covered. Spawn in neutral or slightly acid water.

Corynopoma riisei
(Swordtail characin)

22-26°C (72-79°F)

This peaceful shoaling fish comes from Trinidad and Venezuela and grows to a length of 7cm (2¾in). It is silvery-coloured and not very distinctive,

Distichodus spp.

Gasteropelecus sternicla

apart from the extended lower lobe of the tail and the long flowing dorsal and anal fins of the male. The male also has a curious appendage trailing from his gill covers: this is a long antenna, with a thickened tip, and is usually carried close to the body. During breeding, which takes place in typical Characin conditions, the gill appendage is held out stiffly at right angles to the male's body. Somehow, the male manages to transfer a packet of sperm *into* the female, although he lacks any apparent sexual equipment to carry this out: it is thought that the gill appendage plays a part in depositing the sperm. Once inside the female, the sperms fertilize the eggs, which are laid some time later and attached to plant leaves. The sperm is stored and may continue to fertilize eggs for the rest of the female's life, or at least for several spawnings.

Distichodus sexfasciatus

24-28°C (75-82°F)

A handsome, active shoaling fish from Africa, this grows to 25cm (10in), and is gold-coloured with six distinct velvety-black vertical stripes on its deep body. The fins and eyes are red. Despite its size, this fish is very peaceful, and needs plenty of vegetable material in its diet. It has not been bred in the aquarium. Provide plenty of swimming space and no plants — they will be quickly eaten.

Exodon paradoxus

24-28°C (75-82°F)

A beautiful shoaling fish with a thoroughly nasty temperament, *E. paradoxus* comes from South America. It grows to about 15cm (6in). Brilliant silver with purplish highlights and two large black patches on the sides, it has bright red fins It is a very active swimmer, and a vicious predator, harassing and killing fish much too large for it to eat. It has been bred occasionally, after prolonged conditioning with a wide variety of live foods, and needs soft, acid water filtered through peat.

Gymnocorymbus ternetzi

Gasteropelecus sternicla
(Common hatchetfish)

24-30°C (75-86°F)

From South America, a typical Hatchetfish which is hardier than *Carnegiella* spp. It grows to about 7cm (2¾in), and has a very flattened and deep-chested silver body with a black stripe from gills to tail. It needs to be kept in a shoal, and is longer-lived than most Hatchetfish, although it is not known to breed in the aquarium. Will not withstand chilling. A very powerful leaper.

Gasteropelecus sternicla, showing enlarged, muscular chest and pectoral fins for 'flying'.

Gymnocorymbus ternetzi
(Black widow)

23-25°C (73-77°F)

From Paraguay and Brazil, this grows to about 5cm (2in). It is slim and deep-bodied, with a very large anal fin. It is silver, with three narrow vertical black

Hemigrammus erythrozonus

bars; the rear half of the body, includ-ing the anal fin, is velvety black. Unfortunately, the black fades to a dull grey as the fish ages, and also if it is frightened or the water conditions are not satisfactory. Males are smaller and noticeably slimmer than females. Adult specimens may be bullies, and should not be kept with small or slow-moving fish. Breeds fairly easily, in typical Characin fashion. All specimens now in captivity are believed to be descended from an original trio first imported to Germany; the inbreeding means that many deformed young are produced.

Hemigrammus armstrongi
(Golden tetra)

23-25°C (73-77°F)

There are many similar species of *Hemigrammus* available from time to time. Almost all are hardy, peaceful and difficult to breed.

H. armstrongi is a typical small shoaling Tetra, growing to 4.5cm (1¾in), from Guyana. It is slim and elongated with a shiny gold body and a black base to the tail. *H. armstrongi* are timid shoaling fish and not easily spawned; moreover, when spawned in the aquarium they do not have the gleaming metallic colours of wild fish, but are an uninteresting green (this is almost certainly the result of a dietary deficiency). They require some vegetable supplement to the diet.

Hemigrammus caudovittatus
(Buenos Aires tetra)

18-28°C (64-82°F)

A large and rather boisterous Tetra from South America, growing to 10cm (4in) or more. It has a silvery-green body, a red anal fin and red lobes to the tail; a black line runs along the rear of the body and into the tail. It is very active: too much of a bully for the average community tank containing small fish, and an irritating fin nipper; it is particularly scrappy when in breed-ing condition. Best kept with larger Cichlids, which can return as good as they get. Tends to eat plants. Breeds quite easily in a large spawning tank. Has a wide temperature range.

Hemigrammus erythrozonus
(Glowlight tetra)

22-27°C (72-81°F)

One of the most popular Tetras, this pretty little fish from Guyana grows to 4cm (1½in). It has a bright silver body with a brilliant red line running through the eye from nose to tail, and a red patch on the dorsal fin. The tips of the fins are white when in good con-dition. An active shoaling fish, it hugs the bottom more than most Tetras. Breeds quite easily, in typical Characin fashion, provided it is in soft, slightly acid water.

Hemigrammus ocellifer

Hemigrammus ocellifer
(Beacon fish; Head-and-tail light tetra)

23-27°C (73-81°F)

A medium-sized Tetra from Guyana and the Amazon region, this grows to 4.5cm (1¾in). It is slim, with a silvery-yellow body and a dark spot on the

Hemigrammus caudovittatus

Hyphessobrycon bifasciatus

shoulder: its brilliant spot of yellow-orange at the tail root and its glowing red eye with a yellow spot are the so-called head-and-tail lights. These Tetras have the 'Characin hook', which can be used for sexing the fish (see page 82). Tolerates fairly hard, alkaline water, and breeds quite easily.

Hemigrammus pulcher

Hemigrammus pulcher
(Pretty tetra)

26-28°C (79-82°F)

This medium-sized Tetra from the Amazon Basin grows to 6cm (2⅓in) and is very similar to *H. ocellifer*, but deeper-bodied. It has a short black bar on the rear of the body, extending nearly to the tail, and above this a deep red patch. This fish is rarely seen, as it is less colourful than many other Tetras and is reluctant to breed, except in well aged rainwater containing peat.

Hemigrammus rhodostomus
(Red-nose tetra; Rummy-nose tetra)

23-25°C (73-77°F)

A slim-bodied Tetra from the Amazon region which grows to 6cm (2⅓in). In healthy fish, the whole head is bright crimson and the tail is marked in black and white, like that of the Scissortail (see page 81). A dark stripe runs along the rear of the body into the tail. It is a hardy and bold shoaling fish but, largely because it is very difficult to breed, is not available as often as it should be. Even when persuaded to breed it is not very prolific, and the spawn is very likely to become fungussed.

Hemiodus semitaeniatus

23-25°C (73-77°F)

This large hardy fish from Guyana and the Amazon region grows up to 20cm (7¾in). It is slim and highly streamlined with a very large, stiffly erect tail, and swims in a head-down attitude. It is bluish-silver, and the sides are marked with a bold black spot and a black line extending along the flanks and down into the lower lobe of the tail. It can leap well over 1m (3ft 3in) out of the water, so the tank must be carefully covered. A very active but peaceful fish, it eats anything — especially the plants. Not known to have bred in captivity. *H. gracilis*, a similar but slightly smaller species with a slimmer body, is occasionally available.

Hyphessobrycon bifasciatus
(Yellow tetra)

23-25°C (73-77°F)

Apart from those listed here, there are many other species of *Hyphessobrycon* available from time to time. These are often difficult to identify, and are uniformly difficult to breed.

H. bifasciatus is a small Tetra from Brazil, growing to 4.5cm (1¾in), coloured golden-yellow with a silver lengthwise stripe and two vertical grey stripes; there is a large spot on the tail base. It breeds in typical Characin fashion, but rather reluctantly. The

Hyphessobrycon callistus callistus

'Characin hook' (see page 82) can be used for sexing.

Hyphessobrycon callistus callistus
(Jewel tetra)

23-25°C (73-77°F)

An aggressive, fast-swimming Tetra from Paraguay, this grows to 4cm (1½in). It is deep-bodied, with a rosy pink overall colouring. The dorsal fin is black, and there is an elongated black spot just behind the gill. The anal fin is fringed with black. Does not breed easily, needing prolonged conditioning with live foods and soft acid or neutral rainwater.

H. callistus serpae (Blood tetra) is probably a variety of H. callistus callistus. It is found in South America and grows to 5.5cm (2¼in) long. It is extremely similar in habit and temperament, but the fins have less of the black marking and the shoulder spot is less intense. The body colour is more of an orange-red.

Hyphessobrycon erythrostigma

Hyphessobrycon erythrostigma
(Bleeding-heart tetra)

23-25°C (73-77°F)

This large Tetra from South America grows to 8cm (3⅛in) and is extremely deep-bodied. It is known also as H. rubrostigmata, both specific names referring to the blood-red patch in the middle of the flank. The general body colour is salmon pink with a bluish lustre. The dorsal fin is striped in pink, white and black; in males it is very elongated. There is a thin black line running vertically through the eye.

Hyphessobrycon flammeus

Hyphessobrycon herbertaxelrodi

Very beautiful fish, these are expensive because they are not easy to keep in good condition and are particularly difficult to breed: best results are achieved if the sexes are conditioned separately before being put together for breeding. If they can be persuaded to spawn, very large numbers of eggs are produced. Needs very soft water with a neutral to slightly acid pH.

Hyphessobrycon flammeus
(Flame tetra)

22-25°C (72-77°F)

A small fish from Rio de Janeiro, growing to 4.5cm (1¾in), this is a typical Tetra, thriving in small shoals, and with attractive but often subdued colouring. The front part of the body is silvery-gold with two thin vertical black bars. The rear is, or should be, bright red, as are the anal fins. Unfortunately, this fish has deteriorated badly since domestication, and is seldom seen with the brilliant colouring of the wild fish. Breeds very readily in typical Characin manner. It can be sexed easily, the anal fin being black-edged in the male. Prefers neutral pH and soft water.

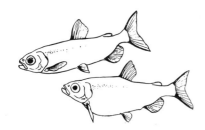

Male (top) and swollen, ripe female.

Hyphessobrycon herbertaxelrodi
(Black neon)

23-26°C (73-79°F)

This small slim Tetra from Brazil, named after a well known US aquarist, grows to 4cm (1½in), and is a relatively new introduction. It has a silvery body with a bold lengthways black stripe, above which is a brilliant metallic green stripe. This peaceful shoaling fish has become very popular, and breeds readily if spawned in small groups in soft water with a slightly acid pH. The young develop relatively slowly.

Hyphessobrycon ornatus
(Flag tetra)

23-25°C (73-77°F)

A fairly large Tetra from Guyana; very similar to *H. erythrostigma*. Grows to 6cm (2⅓in), and is often sold as *H. rosaceus*, a related and very similar fish. The body is pearly red, and the fins flushed with red. The dorsal fin has a black blotch and a white edge, and in the male is very long (in *H. rosaceus*, the male does not have this elongated dorsal fin). Difficult to breed, and the wild fish always have more intense

Hyphessobrycon ornatus

colours. They are sometimes difficult to establish, being sensitive to water changes. The males often fight, but without causing damage.

Hyphessobrycon pulchripinnis
(Lemon tetra)

23-25°C (73-77°F)

A pretty but subtly coloured Tetra from the Amazon region, this grows to 5cm (2in) and is slim-bodied. The body is silver overall with bright yellow markings on the dorsal and anal fins. The anal fin is edged with black, and the eye is bright red. This peaceable

shoaling fish is seen to best advantage in subdued light, with dark-leaved plants, to emphasize the subtle colouring. Breeds fairly easily, in typical Characin fashion.

Leporinus affinis
(Black-banded leporinus)

25-27°C (77-81°F)

Also known as *L. fasciatus*, this South American fish grows to 30cm (11¾in). It is elongated, with a muscular cylindrical body, and is a fast swimmer and powerful jumper. It is generally yellow; in mature adults it is bright orange

Hyphessobrycon pulchripinnis

Leporinus striatus

Micralestes interruptus

Moenkhausia pittieri

crossed with wide black bands which run right around the body. Mainly herbivorous, and peaceful with fish of its own size, preferring to be kept in a shoal, it will chew most plants down to stumps. Not known to have bred in captivity.

L. striatus (Striped leporinus) is very similar, but has lengthways black stripes on a gold-coloured body and grows to 25cm (9¾in).

Metynnis roosevelti
(Silver dollar)

24-27°C (75-81°F)

A large Characin from Guyana and the Amazon, growing to 15cm (6in), with a flattened, immensely deep body (the depth is at least two-thirds of the length). The body is brilliant silver, often with some glittering silver speckles in the darker upper surface. There are brown blotches on the rear, and the tail is tinged with orange. An active shoaling fish and very peaceable, it is an unsurpassed plant-eater which will chew up even the toughest plants. Needs large amounts of vegetable food. Can be bred in very large tanks, in typical Characin fashion, but requires deep water. Prefers soft, slightly acid water.

Metynnis schreitmuelleri

M. schreitmuelleri (Silver dollar) is very similar, but grows to 18cm (7in). The body is plain silver, with a grey-green back.

Micralestes interruptus
(Congo tetra)

23-27°C (73-81°F)

Also known as *Phenacogrammus inter-ruptus*, this lovely fish comes from

Zaire. It has very large opaline scales, which reflect constantly changing colours. It grows to 12cm (4¾in). The black middle rays of the tail are greatly extended into a ragged fringe; in the male, the dorsal and sometimes the anal fin rays are similarly extended. The finnage is seldom as spectacular in tank-raised fish as in wild ones. This fish breeds reluctantly and needs soft, acid water strained through peat. It is extremely prolific once spawning has been established. It does best in a shoal and is very peaceful except with small fish.

Moenkhausia pittieri
(Diamond tetra)

23-26°C (73-79°F)

This peaceful shoaling fish from Venezuela grows to 5.5cm (2¼in). It is deep-bodied and pearly-coloured, with glittering scales. Males have elongated dorsal and anal fins. The eye is red. It breeds relatively easily, in typical Characin fashion.

Moenkhausia sanctae-filomenae
(Glass tetra)

20-25°C (68-77°F)

This peaceful fish is from the La Plata region of South America, and grows to

Moenkhausia sanctae-filomenae

about 7cm (2¾in); it is often confused with the larger and quite aggressive M. oliglepis. It has a stocky silvery-green body, with a large black blotch at the base of the tail, and a conspicuous red eye. Females are noticeably deeper-bellied than males. It is an active shoaling fish, and picks at fine-leaved plants. The dorsal and anal fins are white-tipped. Breeds quite easily if conditioned well on a mixed diet and kept in slightly hard water.

Nannaethiops unitaeniatus
(One-striped African characin)

23-28°C (73-82°F)

A small Characin from West, Central and East Africa, growing to 6.5cm (2½in), this is a shy peaceful fish, with a brown back and yellowish belly. It has an iridescent coppery lengthways stripe and, below this, a bold bluish stripe running through the eye. It breeds very easily and is prolific, but will not thrive in a community aquarium with boisterous tankmates. Needs soft, acid water.

Nannostomus spp.

25-27°C (77-81°F)

N. beckfordi 'anomalus' (Golden pencilfish) comes from South America, and grows to 4.5cm (1¾in). Related to 'headstanders' like Anostomus and Leporinus, they swim in a more or less level manner. They are active shoaling fish with slim elongated bodies (hence the popular name) which have a dark-brown lengthways line, bordered above with gold. The fins are tipped with bluish white; in the male the tail, dor-

Nannaethiops unitaeniatus

Nannostomus beckfordi 'anomalus'

sal and anal fins have a blood-red patch. They have very small mouths, and can eat only tiny food particles: in a crowded community tank with greedy tankmates they may go short of food. Breed in normal Characin fashion, depositing eggs in spawning mops or clumps of fine-leaved plants. It is usual to allow two males to each female, the rivalry between males encouraging spawning. They will spawn more successfully in small groups. The fry are very difficult to rear initially, as their mouths are extremely small: only the finest foods can be given. Infusoria is the only practicable diet for young fry.

N. marginatus (Dwarf pencilfish) grows to only 4cm (1½in), and comes from Guyana, Surinam and the Amazon. It closely resembles *N. beckfordi 'anomalus'* (in fact, it may be simply a subspecies of it; many similar *Nannostomus* species frequently hybridize). It has a dark-brown back, and three dark horizontal stripes along the sides, separated by gold bands. Dorsal and anal fins are red.

N. trifasciatus (Three-striped pencilfish) grows to 6cm (2⅓in), and comes from the Amazon and Guyana. It is rather delicate and difficult to breed. It has three lengthways golden stripes.

Nematobrycon palmeri
(Emperor tetra)

22-26°C (72-79°F)

A relatively 'new' Tetra from Colombia, growing to 7cm (2¾in), this very active fish thrives only in a shoal. The body is elongated. Males are yellowish-brown with metallic green highlights, and have a broad black lengthways stripe; the tail is distinctive.

the central rays being extended into a long spike, and the dorsal fin is also elongated. Females are less colourful, and have less spectacular finnage. Breeds fairly easily, in typical Characin fashion, but is not very prolific. Males often squabble, though without causing damage. Not too sensitive to pH or water hardness.

Paracheirodon innesi

Paracheirodon innesi
(Neon tetra)

20-25°C (68-77°F)

Formerly known as *Hyphessobrycon innesi*, the Neon tetra is a long-time aquarium favourite. It came originally from the Amazon region, but for many years all the available fish have been tank-bred. It grows to 4cm (1½in). Although it was, when originally imported, a delicate fish, thriving only in soft acid water, and very difficult to breed, the modern tank-raised fish are very hardy, and are raised in huge numbers — although they are still

Nannostomus trifasciatus

Nematobrycon palmeri

quite difficult to spawn. The back is greenish-olive, and a metallic-blue stripe runs along the side from nose to tail. The flanks are silvery, and the lower rear part of the body is crimson. The fish breed in slightly acid water, which should be as soft as possible; matured rainwater filtered through peat is the ideal. They spawn best at a temperature of 24°C (75°F). They are susceptible to a specific Neon disease (Plistophora), which is difficult to treat.

Poecilobrycon eques
(Tube-mouthed pencilfish; Knightly pencilfish)

22-27°C (72-81°F)

A small fish, very closely related to *Nannostomus*, and originating from the Amazon region. It grows to 5cm (2in), and unlike other 'headstanders' swims head-up, at an angle of 45° or even more. It is torpedo-shaped, like *Nannostomus*, and has a bold black stripe along the side, continued down into the lower lobe of the tail. The anal fin is red and black, and is tipped with white. Breeding and care are as for *Nannostomus* (see page 93).

P. unifasciatus (One-lined pencil-fish) is very similar, differing sig-nificantly only in having part of the black tail-marking replaced by red.

Pristella riddlei
(X-ray fish)

20-26°C (68-79°F)

A well-known, hardy shoaling fish from the Amazon, Guyana and Venezuela, this grows up to 5.5cm (2¼in), and is noteworthy for being semitransparent. It has a silvery body with a greenish back. The dorsal, anal and pelvic fins are white with a black spot, and the tail is glowing pink when

the fish is in good health. It is a bold but peaceful community fish, thriving even in hard water, although it needs soft or neutral water for breeding. Does not tolerate temperatures at the lower end of the scale well.

Pristella riddlei

Prochilodus insignis

22-25°C (72-77°F)

A very hardy fish from Amazonia, growing to 30cm (11¾in) or more, this has a cylindrical body and large fins, and is a powerful swimmer and jumper. It is silvery overall, the tail and anal fins being marked with conspicuous horizontal black stripes. Despite its size, it is a completely peaceable vege-tarian, rasping away at algae with its enormous lips. It will destroy most plants in the aquarium, and must be given plenty of vegetable food. Not known to have been bred.

Poecilobrycon eques

95

Prochilodus insignis

Pyrrhulina rachoviana
(Fanning characin)

20-26°C (68-79°F)

This little South American fish is closely related to *Copeina*, and resembles that group in reproducing in a very un-Characin-like manner. It is elongated, with very large scales and erect fins; the upper lobe of the tail is somewhat enlarged. The colour is silvery, greenish on the back; in males there are some orange dots along the sides. There is a conspicuous black spot on the dorsal fin. In the male the anal and pelvic fins are red-edged.

It spawns like some Cichlids. The pair select a spawning site on a broad leaf and clean it well. After spawning, the male chases the female away and guards the eggs, fanning them with his fins until they hatch. He must then be removed, or he will eat the fry. Prefers soft, acid water for spawning.

Serrasalmus nattereri
(Red-bellied piranha)

24-27°C (75-81°F)

The notorious Piranha is found in much of South America; several species are available, but *S. nattereri* is both the easiest to keep and the most attractive. It is a large shoaling fish, growing to 30cm (11¾in), and is very hardy and long-lived; single fish are very nervous and rather shy. It has an oval body, very flattened but highly muscular. The lower jaw is bulldog-like and protruding, and the large interlocking triangular teeth can be clearly seen. The body is silver overall, darker on the back, with small glittering speckles. The underside is flushed with orange from the jaw to the tail, and the anal fin is orange. There are black streaks on the tail, and sometimes black mottling on the body. The fish is very pugnacious, though not as dangerous as its reputation suggests. It cannot be kept with any other species, and is occasionally cannibalistic. Piranhas can be fed on chunks of fish or meat, but need to be trained to take this dead food: a strip of fish or meat tied to a thread and jiggled in front of them will usually give them the idea,

Serrasalmus nattereri, with exposed cutting teeth.

and subsequently they will take this food immediately. They can give a very nasty bite, so keep your hands well out of the tank.

Piranhas have bred on occasion, in very large tanks. They pair off and execute an upwards roll into the floating plants where the eggs are laid. Sometimes the male guards the eggs until hatching. Though not particularly sensitive to water conditions, these fish prefer soft, acid water for spawning.

Thayeria boehlkei
(Penguin fish)

22-27°C (72-81°F)

One of three very similar species, all from the Amazon region, and all usually offered as *T. obliqua*, this grows to 8cm (3¼in) and has a plain silvery body with a dense black line running from the gills back along the body and down into the lower lobe of the tail fin. A peaceful shoaling fish, it positions itself in a tail-down position in the water. It is extremely agile and a good jumper, and is almost impossible to catch in a well planted aquarium. Easy to spawn and comparatively prolific.

T. obliqua is exactly as *T. boehlkei*, but with the stripe starting near the base of the tail.

Thayeria boehlkei

T. sancta-mariae is as *T. boehlkei*, but with the stripe starting at the base of the dorsal fin and with the lower lobe of the tail enlarged.

EGG-LAYING TOOTHCARPS

This group of fish belongs to the Cyprinodont family, popularly called Killifishes. They are very widely distributed throughout most of the tropics (except in Australia and most of the

East Indies). They are generally small, with elongated bodies, and are adapted for surface-feeding. They are predatory, eating insects and small fish, and have a generally pike-like appearance. It may be difficult to get them to take dried food. The body is cylindrical and muscular, with the dorsal and anal fins set well back. The tail fin is frequently very enlarged, and often lyre-shaped, with extended rays at top and bottom. The mouth is large, in keeping with their predatory habits; nevertheless, many species are peaceful in the community tank, provided they are not kept with much smaller fish.

In the wild, nearly all live in small pools which are heavily overgrown and subject to scouring-out by tropical rain. In these conditions, the water is very soft and acid, due to the large amounts of decaying material on the muddy bottom. This specialized habitat must be borne in mind when keeping these fish, which often do best in single-species tanks.

Some live in extreme conditions, with only a brief rainy season. They must grow and breed very rapidly, before the water evaporates in the dry season; their eggs survive in the muddy bottom until the next year's rain. These annual fish are often described as egg-buriers or substrate-spawners. They are obviously short-lived, but are very tolerant of changing water conditions, and are usually very beautifully coloured. Other types lay eggs on the surface of the mud, or hang them on plants.

Serrasalmus nattereri

Eggs can be purchased, ready to hatch, by mail order from specialists. However, fish of this group are among the easiest of all to spawn, provided their special requirements are understood. Nearly all require soft acid water, best obtained by soaking peat in rainwater and filtering well. They are relatively inactive, and will live and spawn in small tanks of about 40 × 20 × 20cm (16 × 8 × 8in). The bottom can be covered with well soaked moss peat, to a depth of 3cm (1¼in) or more; do *not* use sedge peat, which can be poisonous. Give some cover with floating plants, used by some species for spawning. A floating nylon spawning mop can be used instead.

Egg-laying toothcarps must be conditioned well with plenty of live food.

Keep them in threes or fours, with two or three females to each male. Spawning is prolonged and may be continuous. The plants or spawning mop must be removed every few days to another tank or a glass jar for incubation, while spawning continues. Annual species will bury their eggs in the peat, a pair of fish diving repeatedly into the peat to deposit a single egg each time. After spawning, remove the peat and allow it to dry until it is only slightly moist; then seal it in a polythene bag and keep it at about 22°C (72°F) for two to three months. When it is put back into the water, fry emerge within a few hours, and can immediately feed on newly hatched Brine shrimps.

A few species lay their eggs on the surface of the peat, and these are not resistant to drying. They hatch normally, though after a month or more.

All Egg-laying toothcarps grow at a tremendous rate after hatching. Because of their incredible colouring, they are well worth the extra trouble involved in their care.

Aphyosemion australe
(Lyretail)

20-24°C (68-75°F)
A short-lived fish from Gabon and Cameroon, growing to 6.5cm (2½in), this is typically bright-coloured. Males are predominantly brownish-red, with scarlet speckles. The tail is lyre-shaped, blue with red spots, with the upper and

Thayeria obliqua

Aphyosemion australe

lower spikes coloured orange with white tips. Females are brownish, with rounded tails. Usually an egg-hanger, although some individuals seem to spawn on the surface of the substrate.

Aphyosemion bivittatum bivittatum
(Red lyretail)

20-24°C (68-75°F)

A West African species, growing to 6cm (2⅓in), found in a seemingly limitless number of subspecies, all of which can be interbred. Most are brownish, with two dark horizontal bands. Males have extremely elongated dorsal and anal fins, and a lyre-shaped tail. The fins of the male fish are boldly marked in orange and blue, and are held stiffly erect. Breeds readily, and is an egg-hanger, but the fry grow more slowly than in most of the group.

A. bivittatum multicolor is a subspecies; it is slightly larger and heavier-bodied, and the males have less elongated fins.

Aphyosemion gardneri
(Steel-blue lyretail)

20-25°C (68-77°F)

An aggressive species from Nigeria, growing to 7cm (2¾in). It occurs in two colour varieties, males being either blue, spotted with crimson, or pre-dominantly yellow. As usual, females have more subdued colouring.

Aphyosemion gulare
(Gularis)

20-25°C (68-77°F)

A beautifully coloured fish from West Africa, growing to 8cm (3⅛in). Males are predominantly blue, with crimson speckles on the sides; the dorsal and anal fins and tail are marked brightly with blue and red. The tail is lyre-shaped. A very quarrelsome fish, it spawns on the surface of the substrate.

Aphyosemion sjoestedti
(Blue gularis)

20-25°C (68-77°F)

The most magnificent fish of the group, growing to 12cm (4¾in), although usually smaller. It is very aggressive with other fish, but quickly becomes tame and will take food from the fingers. In males the body is blue-green, marked with crimson bands and speckles. The tail has three distinct lobes, the central one rich yellow and the others blue and green. Unusually, the female of the species is well coloured, being green speckled with red. It is a substrate spawner, and hatching may take four months or more, although it usually starts after about six weeks.

Aplocheilus spp.

22-28°C (72-82°F)

A. blockii (Green panchax) is a typically pike-shaped panchax from Madras and Sri Lanka, and grows to 5cm (2in). It is relatively peaceable. Males are green with a line of red speckles along the sides, and have yellow fins fringed with orange. Females have plain yellow fins. There is a bright green spot on the gill cover of both sexes. Spawns near the surface, depositing eggs on the

Aphyosemion bivittatum

roots of floating plants or on spawning mops. Very hardy, and takes easily to dried foods.

A. dayi (Ceylon panchax) is a 9cm (3½in) fish from Sri Lanka which is rather shy and easily bullied. The colour is predominantly metallic green and gold, and metallic blue beneath. There are black blotches on the sides of the male which fade as the fish ages. The rounded tail and dorsal and anal fins are orange, with black speckles in the elongated anal fin. Breeds like *A. blockii*, but is generally much hardier.

Egg-laying toothcarp, burying eggs.

A. lineatus (Deccan killifish) is the largest *Aplocheilus*. It comes from India and Sri Lanka, and grows to 12cm (4¾in). Despite its size, it is peaceful, but because of its large mouth should not be trusted with very small fish. The body is yellow-green, marked with rows of glittering green spots. There are several dark vertical bars across the rear. The anal fin and the tail are blue edged with red. Produces extremely large eggs, and spawns on floating plants. The fry are correspondingly large, and feed immediately on newly hatched Brine shrimps.

A. panchax (Blue panchax) gives its specific name to the whole subgroup. It comes from India and Southeast Asia, grows to 7cm (2¾in), and is very variable in colouring (according to its source). Most are yellowish, with rows of metallic blue speckles, with a blue dorsal fin, yellow tail, and orange anal fin. The dorsal fin and tail are edged with black. Females have more subdued colouring. Breeds very easily, as for *A. blockii*.

Austrofundulus dolichopterus

20-25°C (68-77°F)
A recent import from Venezuela, growing to 4cm (1½in). An inactive fish, it

Aphyosemion gardneri

Aphyosemion sjoestedti

Aplocheilus lineatus

is best kept in a single-species tank, as more active tankmates will nip its long fins. The colouring is not exceptional: bluish grey, speckled with deep red, and an orange flush over the belly. The tail is lyre-shaped, but the most distinctive features are the enormous dorsal and anal fins, which are held stiffly erect; in the female, they are much shorter. Breeds readily in very soft acid water, depositing eggs on spawning mops or floating plants. Eggs are slow to hatch.

Cynolebias belotti
(Argentine pearlfish)

18-30°C (64-86°F)

A hardy species from the La Plata region of South America, this is deeper-bodied than other Egg-laying toothcarps, and has rounded fins.

Egg-laying toothcarps in spawning mops.

Males are dark blue-grey, covered with pearly-white spots over body and fins; females are grey, with darker spots and a pale belly. Typical annual fish, these are very short-lived. Spawn at about 26°C (79°F). They deposit eggs below the surface of a peat substrate, and these must be conditioned in nearly dry conditions for several months before being placed in water for hatching. Adults require heavy feeding during breeding, which, once started, will be continuous for several weeks.

Aggressive, and probably best kept in a single-species tank.

C. nigripinnis (Dwarf Argentine pearlfish) is another annual species from South America. It grows to 6cm (2⅓in), and is very aggressive. Males are midnight blue with green speckles over body and fins. Females are mid-brown, blotched with darker brown.

Cynolebias nigripinnis

Epiplatys spp.

24-28°C (75-82°F)

E. annulatus (Rocket panchax or *Clown killie*) is a small peaceful fish from Sierra Leone, Liberia and Guinea, growing to 4cm (1½in). It resembles *Aplocheilus* in appearance, care and breeding. This is the most gaily coloured of the genus, with a yellow body crossed by three broad brown bands. The centre of the tail is elongated, and the tail, dorsal and anal fins are marked with red and blue. This colouring is lacking in females, although they have the bold body-stripes. This fish is not usually inclined to take dried foods. It breeds in soft acid water, but may tolerate a few degrees of hardness, spawning best at 26°C (79°F). Eggs are deposited on spawning mops or plants, and hatch after a 1-3 week resting period. The proportion that hatches is low, due to bacterial attack.

E. chaperi (Finemouth panchax), also known as *E. dageti*, comes from West Africa and grows to 6.5cm (2½in). It is green, crossed by several dark stripes. In the male, the lower part of the rounded tail is prolonged into a short spike, and the throat and front of the belly are bright orange-red. Females have more subdued colours

Aplocheilus panchax

Austrofundulus dolichopterus

and yellow throats. It spawns as for *E. annulatus*, and is hardy and peaceful.

Jordanella floridae
(American flagfish)

18-24°C (64-75°F)

A tough, scrappy fish from Florida, growing to 6cm (2⅓in). It has a yellowish-brown body, and each scale has a metallic patch reflecting various colours, so it looks best in good lighting. It lives at somewhat lower temperatures than most of its relatives, and requires plenty of algae or other vegetable material in its diet. Spawning is unusual, and varies: sometimes eggs are scattered in the plants, but usually the male digs out a nest on the tank bottom, in which the eggs are laid. The male guards both eggs and fry and, most unusually, neither parent will eat the eggs or young fish.

Nothobranchius spp.

20-26°C (68-79°F)

N. guentheri are annual fish *par excellence*, from East Africa. They are very short-lived, but exquisitely coloured; they grow to 8.5cm (3⅓in). All have stocky cylindrical bodies and rounded fins and tail. They have specialized water requirements, needing a mixture of about 80 per cent hard neutral water and 20 per cent seawater. Colours are metallic blue, with each scale edged in red; fins are streaked with red, and the tail is red throughout. The tail and dorsal fins are black-edged. These fish are very aggressive, the males constantly squabbling.

Eggs are buried in the peat substrate, and must be conditioned by part-drying for three months. If they do not hatch, repeated drying-out and submersion may be necessary, because hatching in the wild does not necessarily occur at the first sign of rain after the dry season.

N. palmqvistii is probably a subspecies. This 8.5cm (3⅓in) fish comes from Tanzania and is very similar in colouring, but lacks the black edging to the fins, which are generally more yellow. Very short-lived.

Jordanella floridae

Nothobranchius guentheri

Nothobranchius palmqvistii

Nothobranchius rachovii

Pachypanchax playfairi

Pterolebias longipinnis

N. rachovii is a more peaceful species. From Mozambique, it grows to 5cm (2in). It is quite delicate and more temperamental than the other species. The colouring in the males is exceptional: brilliant fire-red, with vertical bands of metallic blue speckles. The fins are turquoise-blue, and the tail is edged with orange and black. The female is a very plain grey-brown. Spawning takes place on the surface of the peat substrate, and eggs must be conditioned by drying for four to six months before hatching is attempted.

Pachypanchax playfairi

21-25°C (70-77°F)

A hardy and aggressive panchax from Zanzibar and the Seychelles, this grows to 10cm (4in), although usually less. The overall colour of the male is yellowish-green, sprinkled with small red speckles; fins are yellow, speckled with red and edged with black. Females are brown, with a black blotch near the base of the dorsal fin. The species' chief peculiarity is that the scales stand out at an angle to the body, as if the fish were suffering from dropsy; this is most marked during breeding. They spawn in floating plants or nylon mops, like the other panchaxes, and eggs hatch without having to be dried out. They prefer a small amount of salt to be added to the water.

Pterolebias longipinnis
(Longfin)

20-25°C (68-77°F)

A quarrelsome but beautiful fish from Brazil and the lower reaches of the Amazon, growing to 10cm (4in), this has a greenish-grey body which, in the male, is crossed by many blue bars. The belly is pinkish-brown. Old males develop enormous flowing tails and enlarged dorsal and anal fins; these are barred heavily with blue-grey. Females are drab brown fish. *P. longipinnis* are short-lived, but breed easily. The breeding pair dive deep into the peat substrate to deposit their eggs, so at least 7.5cm (3in) of peat should be provided. The eggs need a dry resting

Rivulus urophthalmus

period of three to four months before hatching is attempted.

P. peruensis (Peruvian longfin) is a very aggressive, active but short-lived fish from Peru and the Upper Amazon. Like *P. longipinnis*, the male of this species has a long flag-like tail, although less exaggerated. Males grow to 7.5cm (3in) and are yellow-brown with a metallic blue patch on the gills and another on the tail, which has also a broad orange stripe. The body and fins are marked with dark bars and metallic blue speckles. Care and breeding are as for *P. longipinnis*, but the water must be very soft and acid.

Rivulus urophthalmus
(Green rivulus)

23-25°C (73-77°F)

One of numerous *Rivulus* spp. kept in the aquarium, this is a modestly coloured but popular fish from South America, and grows to 8cm (3¼in). It has a powerful cylindrical body, and hangs motionlessly near the surface on the lookout for floating or flying prey. It will leap without warning to catch flies near the water surface. Very oddly, these fish leave the water periodically to lie on the surface of floating leaves; the reason for this is not known.

This species and its relatives are very peaceful. The male is green, with rows of small red speckles along the flanks, while the female is brown with a black patch on the tail-base. Both sexes have rounded tails. They breed very easily, depositing their spawn in small clumps on plants or spawning mops.

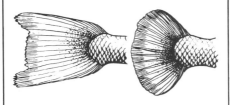

Rounded and lyre-shaped tail fins.

LIVE-BEARING
TOOTHCARPS

These fish comprise the other part of the Cyprinodont group (see page 96), technically called the Poeciliidae family but universally referred to as Live-bearers. They give birth to well developed young, although technically they are not viviparous but ovoviviparous, producing normal spawn, but retaining it in the female's body until after hatching. They are New World fish, found from the USA down through Central America and as far south as Argentina, many thriving in brackish water or even entering the sea. Some are algae eaters, and most need some vegetable supplements in their diets. All are small fish by aquarium standards. Toothcarps, whether egg-laying or live-bearing, are popularly called Killifishes.

Their breeding is particularly interesting. Unusually, the females are larger than the males — sometimes very much larger. The males possess a special rod-like sex organ called the gonopodium, which is formed from an adaptation of part of the anal fin. The gonopodium can be extended sideways, and is used to deposit a packet of sperm into the vent of the female to effect fertilization. This takes place after prolonged and often frantic courting of the large and usually indifferent female by the tiny male.

A pregnant female becomes extremely fat, and a large dark spot can usually be seen on her flanks, just above the vent. Pregnant females are delicate, and will abort their young if disturbed. Broods are small, especially with young females, and the newborn fish are about 0.5cm (¼in) long and able to swim and feed immediately. Breeding is carried out in heavily planted tanks, so that the young can escape their predatory parents. Except for *Molliensia* spp., which are particularly delicate while pregnant, most aquarists confine pregnant females in a simply made breeding trap; in a heavily planted tank, however, no trap should be needed: some of the young should escape for long enough to grow too big to be eaten.

Breeding is continual, even in the community tank, and, once fertilized, females can produce several batches of young from the same packet of sperm. This makes selective breeding from colour varieties rather difficult unless fish are kept rigorously apart except when breeding. Very many colour varieties have been produced, as these fish hybridize easily, even between different genera, and Live-bearers seen in the aquarium almost always bear little resemblance to their wild ancestors.

In general, the Live-bearers are peaceable and very hardy fish, ideal for the community aquarium, and breed freely.

Molliensia latipinna
(Sailfin molly)

23-27°C (73-81°F)

Molliensia are sometimes now classified as *Poecilia*.

M. *latipinna* is found from the USA to Yucatan, and is a largish fish of up to 12cm (4¾in), although usually smaller in the aquarium. It has been found in the sea as well as in freshwater, and will not thrive unless 1 teaspoonful of salt is added for each 5 litres (1.1gal) of water. They are mainly herbivorous, and require large amounts of chopped lettuce or specially prepared dried food. Stocky, with very pointed snouts, they are very thick through the base of the tail. Males, and especially wild males, develop enormous sail-like dorsal fins, usually carried stiffly erect. The body is green, with several rows of dots forming fine horizontal stripes, and the tail is streaked with metallic blue. A velvety black form is also available. They breed very easily, and the female does not usually eat the young; she is very delicate while pregnant, however, and should not be disturbed. This fish will thrive singly, in pairs, or as a shoal.

M. *velifera* (Sailfin molly), from Yucatan, is the largest of the Mollies, growing to 17.5cm (7in). A peaceful shoaling fish, it closely resembles M. *latipinna* but has an even larger dorsal fin and is metallic blue-green with sparkling dots arranged in horizontal lines.

Molliensia sphenops
(Molly)

23-27°C (73-81°F)

Scarcely ever seen in its 'wild' form now, this fish was found originally from Mexico to Colombia, and grows up to 10cm (4in). It closely resembles M. *latipinna* in body-shape, but lacks the enlarged dorsal fin. It has been selectively bred into many brightly coloured hybrids as well as the well known Black molly form, which is velvety black all over. There is also a hybrid with a lyre-shaped tail, as well as types with trailing fins. Unfortunately, these hybrids

Molliensia latipinna

have often been inbred to such an extent that deformed or dead offspring are common. Care and breeding are as for M. *latipinna*, and salt should be added to the breeding tank as above. Needs large amounts of vegetable food for good health.

Poecilia reticulata
(Guppy)

18-30°C (64-86°F)

The Guppy, known variously as *Platypoecilia* and *Lebistes*, originates in South America, and has been an aquarium standard since its introduction in 1908. It is an ideal aquarium fish — hardy, prolific, peaceable and, in centrally heated homes, thriving even in unheated aquaria. Females grow up to 6cm (2⅓in) and males to 3cm (1¼in). The differences between the sexes are very marked. The females are uninteresting greenish fish, and extremely fat when pregnant. The tiny

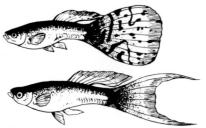

Male guppies, showing tail variations due to selective breeding.

males are brilliantly coloured, and have vastly extended dorsal fins and tails, almost unrecognizably different from those of their wild ancestors. They are obtainable in literally any colour, and are always visible at the front of the aquarium, being very bold and active. The domesticated forms are by no means as tough as the 'wild' fish, being highly inbred. These fish do best at a temperature of about 24°C (75°F).

Poecilia reticulata (wild type)

Xiphophorus helleri
(Swordtail)

18-25°C (64-77°F)

A well-known fish originating from Guatemala and Mexico, the Swordtail grows to 10cm (4in) or more. In the wild it is a green fish resembling the Mollies, but with a long sword-like extension to the tail of the male. Swordtails are very active, greedy

Xiphophorus helleri

shoaling fish which sometimes annoy other fish in the community tank. The wild type is seldom seen, and the brightly coloured fish commercially available are hybrids with X. *maculatus*. They are usually marked in red, blue and black, and some are available with sail-like dorsal fins. They are very hardy, and easy to breed. X. *helleri* sometimes change sex for no apparent reason.

Xiphophorus maculatus
(Platy)

18-25°C (64-77°F)

Also known as X. *variatus*, this fish has been extensively hybridized. Apart from the absence of the male tail spike, it is almost indistinguishable from X. *helleri*, although a little smaller. These fish are available in a huge range of colour types, and are hardy and easy to breed. They require a good deal of vegetables in the diet.

CICHLIDS

The Cichlids are a major group of freshwater fish with a very wide distribution: they are found in the southern USA, Central and South America, Africa, parts of the Middle East, India and Sri Lanka. The aquarist is concerned only with the American and African species, as well as the *Etroplus* spp discussed on page 109. Cichlids are related to the common Perch, and share many of the Perch's characteristics. Spiky-rayed fish, they vary in shape from elongated pike-like forms to rounded and flattened types. Their dorsal and anal fins carry the characteristic spines, and the lateral line is broken into two distinct parts. They are generally predatory, possessing powerful teeth. Most are fish for the enthusiast, as they are often large and aggressive; few are really suited to be community fish, except with other Cichlids or large powerful fish. As most dig in the gravel and uproot plants, it is difficult to keep the tank as attractive as with other types of fish. Most inhabit still or slow-moving waters, and in the aquarium are not particularly active. Some are shoaling fish, but when breeding all species pair off and drive away other fish from their particular territory.

Their unusual breeding behaviour and the colour changes they go through are the primary reasons for

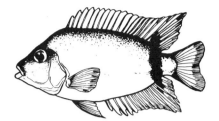

Typical Cichlid, showing spiny fins.

keeping these fish, a few of which have become peaceful and domesticated aquarium standards. They are best considered in major groupings according to their original habitats.

As with most aquarium fish, the classification of Cichlids is extremely confused.

African Cichlids

These are relative newcomers to the aquarium, and some require special treatment. Most of the popular African Cichlids are relatively small. Their natural habitats are quite varied.

West African species generally require soft acid water, like the majority of aquarium fish. Most spawn in a small cave or, in the aquarium, an upturned flowerpot.

East African species usually come from Lake Malawi. The conditions in this enormous body of water have resulted in the evolution of a huge variety of small territorial Cichlids (known locally as 'mbuna'), which are frequently coloured as brightly as marine coral fish. In the aquarium, these fish must be kept in hard, alkaline water to which some salt has been added. Other similar selections come from Lake Tanganyika and Lake Victoria, all having roughly similar requirements. Most are best kept in large mixed groups, when obvious pairs can be identified and removed for breeding.

American Cichlids

These fall into two convenient groups. The big boisterous species formerly popular have been largely replaced by the smaller and more easily handled African Cichlids. The other group, colloquially known as Dwarf cichlids, are a much easier proposition, often doing well in the community aquarium and not usually being aggressive except when breeding.

Xiphophorus maculatus

Cichlid Breeding in General

Cichlids are usually bought as adolescents, and pair off as they mature. With the more aggressive species it can be dangerous to introduce a pair of adults, as they will often fight; they may, however, be kept together separated by a sheet of glass until they get used to each other. Specific comments on breeding are given in the section on each particular species, but in general a large unplanted tank containing a selection of possible spawning sites, such as rocks, waterworn wood, caves, etc, is required.

Cichlids spawning in an upturned flowerpot.

Most Cichlids are good parents but, should they eat the spawn or fry, you may need to make arrangements to rear the young by artificial means. Avoid disturbing the breeding fish: this is the usual cause of the parents starting to eat the eggs and fry. Adult fish usually need conditioning with plenty of live food before any attempt at breeding, and will make it obvious when they are in proper condition by marking out a suitable spawning site. This will be meticulously cleaned by both parents, and will be guarded fiercely until the fry have hatched and become independent. Most young Cichlids eat newly hatched Brine shrimps and *Cyclops* as soon as they become free-swimming. Mashed earthworms and whiteworms are eaten eagerly. Adult fish are not particular about their diet, eating any live or dead food they can fit into their mouths. Some also pick at algae, and a few species, though not those kept in the aquarium, are largely herbivorous.

Aequidens spp.

22-26°C (72-79°F)

A. curviceps (Flag cichlid or Sheep's-head acara) is a relatively peaceful Cichlid, growing to 10cm (4in), from the Amazon region. It has a short, deep body, and is green with dark-edged scales and a golden belly. There is a blue tinge to the flanks, and the dorsal and anal fins and the tail are marked with turquoise-blue. This is a good community fish provided it is not kept with very small tankmates. It does not dig up plants, and eats almost anything. Breeds readily, but young pairs often eat their eggs, which are deposited on a carefully cleaned stone.

A. latifrons (Blue acara) is a popular, relatively peaceful species. Known also as *A. pulcher*, it comes from Panama, Colombia, Venezuela and Trinidad, and grows to about 12cm (4¾in). It is grey, with conspicuous vertical bands covered with turquoise-blue speckles. The head and fins are especially brightly marked. Very prolific and easy to breed.

Aequidens latifrons

A. maroni (Keyhole cichlid) is very peaceful. From Venezuela and Guyana, it grows to about 12cm (4¾in). Its colour is very variable, but is usually predominantly creamy-grey.

Aequidens maroni

An irregular black blotch on the side resembles a keyhole in young fish, but becomes blurred in adults. There is a broad dark stripe along the sides, with some irregular marbling.

A. portalegrensis (Brown acara or Porthole acara) is a large — 25cm (9¾in) — and rather clumsy fish of the Acara group, from Brazil and Bolivia. Young fish are greenish-brown, but adults become dusty brown, with a broad lengthways stripe and blue speckles on the dorsal and anal fins and the tail. There is a conspicuous black spot at the base of the tail. This fish is more aggressive than other *Aequidens*, and prone to digging up plants.

Aequidens curviceps

Apistogramma agassizi

20-25°C (68-77°F)

A small shy Cichlid from the Amazon region, growing only to 8cm (3¼in) and very peaceful. It is one of the so-called Dwarf cichlids. All the related species have much the same requirements. This one is yellow-brown with a broad dark lengthways band running to the tip of the tail, which in the male is extended to a spearhead shape. The tail is orange, with a blue edge, and the dorsal fin is orange. The back is violet-tinged, and there are blue speckles on the head and body. Females are smaller and drab. These fish spawn on a rock or on a large plant leaf; the female guards the spawn, but quite often eats the eggs. This and the other *Apistogramma* spp. are very sensitive to water conditions: soft, acid water is essential for breeding.

Apistogramma ornatipinnis

22-27°C (72-81°F)

A small Cichlid from Guyana and the Amazon region, growing to 8cm (3¼in). Males are yellowish-brown, with a dark spot in the middle of the body and another at the root of the tail. A dark line runs through the eye. Males have a large, reddish lyre-shaped tail and a black-edged orange dorsal fin. These fish are more aggressive than *A. agassizi*, and also tend to dig up plants.

Apistogramma ramirezi
(Ram cichlid; Butterfly cichlid)

22-26°C (72-79°F)

This little fish from Venezuela is probably misnamed, belonging to a different genus, *Microgeophagus*. It grows to about 5cm (2in) and is brilliantly coloured, with a violet sheen on most of the body overlying a pink coloration. There is a large black spot on the side, and a black line running through the bright red eye. The fins are tinged with red, and in the male the first few rays of the dorsal fin are extended and

Apistogramma ramirezi

black. Unusually, females are almost as brightly coloured as males. Wild fish are usually better coloured and larger than tank-raised specimens, and in fact this species is quite difficult to breed. Unlike other *Apistogramma*, these fish usually deposit their eggs on a leaf rather than hiding them away. They tend to eat their spawn. They require frequent changes of a proportion of the tank water.

Astronotus ocellatus
(Oscar; Marbled cichlid; Velvet cichlid)

20-25°C (68-77°F)

A *very* large and tough Cichlid from South America, this fish grows to 30cm (11¾in). It is very reminiscent of the tropical marine Groupers, having a powerful body, massive head and large

mouth, and thick leathery fins. It is deep blackish-brown with irregular creamy markings and orange speckles. There is a large, distinct black 'eye spot' near the tail, ringed in orange. This is a very active fish which wriggles through the water and appears to bustle up and down the tank. It becomes very tame, and will take chunks of meat or fish from the hand, and allow itself to be stroked. It is peaceful with fish too large to eat, but has an extremely large mouth and an appetite to match. *A. ocellatus* needs a very big tank with plenty of swimming room and without plants, which it would soon tear out. A red variety, where the red speckles cover most of the body, is often available. This fish can spawn when as small as 10cm (4in), digging a pit in the gravel in which the eggs are laid, or depositing them on a rock. The brood is enormous, and it is well to ensure a ready market for the young fish before starting to breed.

Cichlasoma biocellatum
(Jack Dempsey)

20-25°C (68-77°F)

This large Cichlid from the Amazon region is aptly named, being one of the most pugnacious of all. It grows to

Astronotus ocellatus

20cm (7¾in), and is extraordinarily beautiful. It is a good aquarium fish if kept in a single-species tank; otherwise, it will attack any other fish in the tank. Also, it will destroy all plants, as well as spending most of its time digging in the gravel. Its body is dark green or black, and each scale is marked with a brilliant turquoise-blue spot; these spots also cover the fins and tail. The dorsal fin is edged with red or orange. Males have long pointed extensions to the rear of the dorsal and anal fins. These fish breed easily and prolifically, after an energetic courtship in which the two fish grip each other's jaws and wrestle violently. Eggs are deposited on a cleaned rock or, occasionally, in a pit in the gravel. These fish eat almost anything.

Cichlasoma meeki

Cichlasoma festivum
(Festivum)

20-25°C (68-77°F)

This Cichlid is very timid and peaceful. In the wild, it is found with other timid species such as *Pterophyllum* (see page 112) and *Symphysodon* (see page 113), lurking among plant stems. It has a relatively small mouth, and can be trusted with other fish which are not too small and tempting. *C. festivum* has a deep, flattened body, a bright red eye, and long trailing spikes on its dorsal and anal fins; there is a black 'eye spot' on the tail-root. The most distinctive feature is a dark brown stripe running diagonally from the snout to the end of the dorsal fin. The body is green-gold. In adults the pelvic fins are prolonged into long threads. They are quite difficult to breed, but may be persuaded to deposit their spawn on a vertical rock or a large plant leaf.

Cichlasoma meeki
(Firemouth cichlid)

20-25°C (68-77°F)

A Cichlid from Yucatan and Guatemala, this grows to 15cm (6in) or sometimes more. It is aggressively territorial, but does not bother large fish of other species. The upper part of the body is strongly arched. The body is grey-green with darker vertical bars and a narrow horizontal bar. On the gill cover there is a conspicuous black 'eye spot' surrounded by a metallic blue border. Dorsal and anal fins are prolonged into points and, in mature males, the tail may be lyre-shaped. The whole of the underside is brilliant red, and during breeding the colouring seems to glow. The fish breed very easily, depositing their eggs on a rock and shifting the fry to a pit dug in the gravel. Tough plants may survive with this fish.

Crenicara filamentosa
(Chequerboard cichlid)

22-25°C (72-77°F)

This interesting Dwarf cichlid from South America is known also as *C. maculata*. It grows to 10cm (4in) and

Crenicara filamentosa

has a slim, elongated body. Males have an elongated lyre-shaped tail and long pointed pelvic fins. The body is yellow with two rows of square black patches along the sides. The fins are striped in blue and orange, and the dorsal is fringed with red. This is a shy, very peaceful fish which needs plenty of hiding places. It is an egg-hider, breeding like *Apistogramma agassizi*. It appears to need some vegetable matter in its diet, and may pick at algae growing in the tank.

Etroplus maculatus
(Orange chromide)

20-25°C (68-77°F)

A peaceful Cichlid from Sri Lanka and India, growing to 10cm (4in), this has a deep, flattened body, coloured orange-yellow and covered with rows of small red dots, with a large round blue spot on the flank. These fish do best in alkaline water with 1 teaspoonful of sea-salt per 5 litres (1.1gal) of water. Spawning is unusual. The eggs may be deposited on a rock or leaf, from which they hang on threads. The newly hatched fry are transferred to a pit in the tank bottom. They school closely for the first three weeks. *E. maculatus* is not too hard on tough plants.

Etroplus maculatus

E. suratensis (Green chromide) is a large shoaling Cichlid from Sri Lanka which grows to 40cm (15¾in), but is much smaller in the aquarium. It is very similar to *E. maculatus*, but has a light green body colour. Scales on the upper body are marked with pearly-white patches, and there are black spots on the belly. Care and breeding are exactly as for *E. maculatus*.

Etroplus suratensis

Hemihaplochromis multicolor
(Egyptian mouth-breeder)

20-25°C (68-77°F)

Known also as *Haplochromis multicolor*, this 8cm (3¼in) fish comes from East Africa, and is one of the more popular Cichlids despite its subdued colouring. It is very hardy and fairly peaceful. The colouring is modest, the body being yellow or brown with metallic highlights on the sides and fins. The colours vary quickly depending on the fish's mood, and sometimes it will be barred or striped. Females are smaller and drab, with noticeably larger mouths than the males. They are kept mainly for their interesting breeding behaviour. After elaborate courtship rituals, the male digs a pit in the gravel and coaxes the female into spawning. She picks up the eggs in her mouth, and at the same time pecks at an egg-like orange spot on his anal fin. He liberates sperm, fertilizing the eggs in her mouth. The male can now be removed, as he may be driven away by the female. The eggs are retained for 10-14 days in her mouth, during which time she will not eat. When the fry hatch they swarm around the female, diving back into her mouth whenever they are scared. She soon loses interest in them, and should then be removed.

This fish is very easy to breed and does best in hard alkaline or neutral water.

Herichthys cyanoguttatus
(Freshwater sheep's head; Texas cichlid; Rio Grande perch)

14-25°C (57-77°F)

The only Cichlid found in the USA, this fish's range extends south into Mexico. It is large and very aggressive, and destroys plants and tank-mates, resembling *Cichlasoma biocellatum* in many respects. It reaches a length of 30cm (11¾in) in large tanks, and is very beautiful. Adult fish are pearly grey, with faint dark vertical bars, and have a dark spot on the flanks and on the base of the tail. In both males and females the body and fins are covered with brilliant metallic-blue dots. They

Julidochromis ornatus

are very difficult to sex when young, but males over three years old develop a pronounced hump just behind the head. These fish breed easily, in typical Cichlid fashion, excavating huge spawning pits in the gravel. The young can immediately eat Brine shrimps. *H. cyanoguttatus* is very hardy, but does not tolerate old water; frequent partial changes of the tank water are essential.

Julidochromis ornatus
(Julie)

22-25°C (72-77°F)

One of the 'new' popular African Lake Cichlids, this comes from Lake Tanganyika. It is small, growing to 10cm (4in), and has a very slim body with a long dorsal fin extending along most of the back. The colouring is bright yellow, with three broad, black lengthways stripes, a large black spot on the base of the tail, and a black-fringed anal fin. It is shy, needing plenty of hiding places, and is territorial. It will live peaceably with other African Cichlids, each establishing its own territory. Unlike many Cichlids, it needs algae or other vegetable material in its diet. It breeds easily, depositing its eggs on stones. The eggs and fry are guarded by the male, or sometimes by both parents. It thrives only in hard alkaline water.

Labeotropheus fuelleborni

22-25°C (72-77°F)

A peaceful and beautiful Cichlid from Lake Malawi, one of the 'mbuna' group, this grows to 15cm (6in), and is bold and active, feeding on algae and other water plants as well as on live foods. The males and females look so different that they were originally thought to be different species. The males are a bright powder-blue, with darker vertical bars, while most females are blue. *L. fuelleborni* should be kept in hard alkaline water to which salt has been added at a rate of ½ teaspoonful per 5 litres (1.1gal). They breed easily, and are mouth-breeders, the females incubating the eggs. They need plenty of rocks and roots as hiding places.

Labeotropheus fuelleborni

Labeotropheus trewavasae

Nannacara anomala

L. trewavasae is a more aggressive species of Malawi Cichlid. This hardy fish grows to 15cm (6in), and is best kept with others of about its own size. The males are blue with numerous darker vertical bars and a bright red dorsal fin. Some of the females are similarly coloured, but others are mottled brown and orange, like *L. fuelleborni*. These fish breed easily, with the female incubating the eggs.

Nannacara anomala
(Golden-eyed dwarf cichlid)

22-27°C (72-81°F)

This small Cichlid from Guyana grows only to 8cm (3¼in) and has large, attractive fins. The males are dark brown, with a metallic tint to the sides. The eye is bright orange, and there is an orange edge to the dorsal fin. Females are mottled brown, with smaller dorsal fin and tail. They breed quite easily, hiding their eggs in a cave or an upturned flowerpot. Both sexes guard the eggs, but after hatching the female usually chases the male away. They do best in soft acid or neutral water. You should provide plenty of cover for these shy fish; they will not destroy the plants. Though very peaceful, they will attack other fish if they spawn in the community tank.

Pelmatochromis kribensis

23-30°C (73-86°F)

Now renamed *Pelvichromis pulcher*, but better known under its earlier name, this 9cm (3½in) Cichlid comes from Cameroon. It is very peaceful,

Pelmatochromis kribensis

Pseudotropheus auratus

although territorial, and is extraordinarily beautiful. The basic body colour is golden-brown, with a dark lengthwise stripe. In males, the central part of the tail-fin is elongated, and several black 'eye spots' develop on the tail as the fish ages. Both sexes have a brilliant magenta patch covering the belly and flanks; the colour of this is most intense in breeding pairs. They are industrious diggers, but do not damage robust plants. They pick at filamentous algae, and need some vegetable food. Breeding is of typical Dwarf-cichlid type, in an upturned flowerpot. The female drives the male away after spawning, and guards the eggs and young. These fish must be kept in soft water if they are to develop their full colouring, and do best in acid water filtered through peat.

Pseudotropheus spp.

22-25°C (72-77°F)

P. auratus (Malawi golden cichlid), an aggressive Cichlid from Lake Malawi, of the 'mbuna' group, grows to 12cm (4¾in). It is elongated and very fast-swimming, but likes to lurk in caves. The colouring is highly variable, dominant males in the tank usually being dark blue-grey, with two lengthways pale blue stripes. Other males and the females are pinkish-gold, with two bold lengthways stripes edged with gold and white. There are black-and-white markings in the upper lobe of the tail

in both sexes. Although aggressively territorial, this hardy Cichlid, once it has established a territory, will live in a tank containing similar or related fish. It breeds easily, the eggs being deposited in a nest dug in the gravel. The female incubates the eggs in her mouth, and broods the young for about three months. This fish must have hard alkaline water.

Pseudotropheus elongatus

P. elongatus (Elongated mbuna) is, as would be expected from its name, a long — 12cm (4¾in) — thin Cichlid of the 'mbuna' type. It is deep blue, with bright blue vertical stripes. The anal fin of adult males has yellowish 'eye spots'. Females are paler in colour. Care and breeding are as for *P. auratus*.

P. tropheops, from Malawi, grows to 15cm (6in). It is very varied in colour. Breeding males are deep blue, with a metallic turquoise spot on each scale. Females are golden-brown, with darker brown bands. Breeding and care are exactly as for *P. auratus*. This fish is very boisterous, and will destroy plants.

Pseudotropheus zebra

P. zebra (Zebra Malawi cichlid) grows to 15cm (6in). It comes in several colour forms, but most are blue, with several bold crossways dark blue bands and blue fins. There are numerous yellow spots on the anal fin of the male. Some colour forms are very pale blue, and others are almost black. This fish exemplifies the difficulty in classifying Cichlids; many of the Lake Malawi 'species' are probably just colour varieties, and seem to interbreed happily if none of their own type are available. Care and breeding are as for *P. auratus*.

Pseudotropheus tropheops

Pterophyllum scalare
(Angelfish)

24-28°C (75-82°F)

The Angelfish comes from the Amazon region. Some specialists classify *P. altum*, *P. dumerillii* and *P. eimekei* as separate species, but it is probable that they are merely local varieties. All aquarium Angelfish . are *P. scalare*, possibly interbred with these other 'species'. In any case, the domesticated Angelfish has been so interbred and selected to produce albino, golden, all-black and veil-tailed forms that it almost constitutes a new species. The 'normal' Angelfish grows to about 15cm (6in) in a large tank, and is exclusively a fish of the middle waters. The body is almost circular, and is flattened and disc-like, marked with four dark vertical bars. Two of these extend into the immense dorsal and anal fins. The body is silvery-gold, the eye red, and the tail mottled and barred with brown; the tail develops two spikes in mature fish. The pelvic fins are prolonged into long 'whiskers', which are often nipped by more active tankmates. These stately, slow-moving fish are very peaceful, although, like any Cichlid, they will eat small fish.

Breeding is not easy. Pairs must be selected from a shoal of adolescent fish, females being noticeably fatter. They must be kept in a large tank, at least 40cm (15¾in) deep, and provided with, for use as spawning sites, large-leaved plants or pieces of slate leaning against the tank side. The water should be soft, and of neutral to slightly acid pH; add 1 tsp of salt per 5 litres

Pterophyllum scalare

(1.1gal). Eggs are deposited on the selected spawning site, and guarded by both sexes. The parents herd the shoal of fry for two weeks, often shifting them to a pit dug in the gravel. Often the first few broods are eaten.

Symphysodon spp.
(Discus)

24-30°C (75-86°F)

Symphysodon are coveted and very expensive Cichlids from the Amazon region. All grow to about 18cm (7in) and vary only in their colouring; they are referred to colloquially as Discus fish. They are stately, shy, slow-moving fish with very flattened disc-like bodies. They have very small mouths and feed in mid-water on small live foods. Discus fish are best kept in a single-species tank, as they will not tolerate bullying. The only suitable tankmates are *Pterophyllum* (which may still bully them), *Cichlasoma festivum* and small *Corydoras*, which are very peaceful (see page 00).

For breeding, the tank is prepared as for *Pterophyllum*, and eggs are laid on a stone or leaf. When the eggs hatch, after about 50 hours, the fry cluster around the adults, feeding for the first two weeks on special nutrient slime produced on the body of the fish only during breeding. Since the fry have very tiny mouths, they are difficult to wean onto other foods. They attain their disc-like shape at about three months. These fish must be kept in soft, slightly acid water.

S. aequifasciatum (Green discus) is dark green with darker vertical bands. There are numerous wavy, horizontal iridescent green-blue bands. The eye is red, and a dark stripe runs vertically through it.

S. aequifasciata axelrodi (Brown discus) is similar, but has a dark-brown body crossed with only a few of the wavy blue horizontal bands.

S. aequifasciata haraldi (Blue discus) has a light brown body, completely netted with iridescent blue lines, which extend into the dorsal and anal fins and the tail.

S. discus (Discus) has a much lighter body colour than the other Discus fish. It is usually yellow-brown or even

Symphysodon discus

gold, with conspicuous vertical brown bars and a fine network of green-blue horizontal lines over the body and fins. The dorsal and anal fins are usually fringed with red.

Symphysodon aequifasciata haraldi

Tropheus duboisi
(White-spotted cichlid)

22-26°C (72-79°F)

This Dwarf cichlid from Lake Tanganyika grows to 7cm (2¾in). It is a peaceable but territorial fish, with a deep body. Juvenile fish are a beautiful velvety black with a broad saddle-like band of yellow-white. Females retain the white spots of the juveniles. These fish breed easily, spawning on a stone,

after which the female mouth-broods the eggs and young. Hard alkaline water is essential.

T. moorei is sometimes available. In this species the males have a maroon saddle, instead of the yellow of *T. duboisi*.

LABYRINTH FISH

The Labyrinth fishes are a large group of Asian and African fish, technically known as the Anabantidae, although sometimes classified into several different families. Their popular name comes from a special organ called the labyrinth, by means of which the fish can breathe air at the surface, and thereby live in habitats too low in oxygen for most other fish. The labyrinth consists of cavities on either side of the head which contain several bony plates covered with wrinkled tissue. This gives a large surface area through which oxygen can be absorbed. Some of these fish have become so dependent on this organ that they will die if prevented from reaching the surface to breathe atmospheric air. Every 20 seconds or so, the fish must swim to the surface, spit out a bubble of used air, and take in a further supply. The labyrinth develops a few weeks after hatching: prior to this the young breathe in the normal way. The gills are still used in the adult fish, but are not adequate to supply all the oxygen requirements.

The efficacy of the labyrinth can be seen in such fish as the Climbing perch, *Anabas testudineus*, which can survive out of water for several hours. It can travel overland by 'walking' on its fins and extended gill covers.

Labyrinth fish have another peculiarity, in that all the internal organs are compressed into the front part of the body, so that the rear of the body contains only the spine and muscles. The fish's body is thus remarkably flexible, as can be seen during courtship and spawning.

Cut-away diagram of the membranous labyrinth.

Labyrinth fish are nearly all predatory, and many are unsuitable for the community tank. As with other fish, their aggressiveness is particularly marked during breeding. They mostly breed very easily, and in a very characteristic fashion, being bubble-nest builders. The nest is constructed by the male, and consists of a raft of bubbles bound together by mucus from the male's mouth; its size may be up to 10cm (4in) in diameter and 5cm (2in) thick, although usually it is much smaller. It may include pieces of floating plant which help hold the nest together. The male then courts a female, sometimes very aggressively if she is unresponsive. A thickly planted tank is essential, so that the female can take shelter from the male if she is not yet ready to spawn. The male's courtship display is usually spectacular, with spread fins and brilliant breeding coloration.

When the female is receptive, she positions herself below the nest, and the male wraps himself around her, turning her over onto her back. Eggs are released in a spray and are imme-

Betta splendens

diately fertilized. The male then breaks the spawning embrace and catches the eggs in his mouth, blowing them into the nest; sometimes the female assists in this. The spawning embrace is repeated until all the eggs are expelled, after which the male drives the female away. She is best removed from the tank, unless it is very large. The eggs hatch in three or four days, and the young remain in the nest for another few days. Any which fall out and sink are caught by the male and spat back into the nest.

The young are very small and difficult to feed, taking only the smallest infusoria and dried foods. They are very susceptible to the effects of cold air when they begin to use their labyrinth, and so the tank must be well covered to protect them from draughts.

Once mature, most Labyrinth fish are very hardy and long-lived.

Betta splendens
(Siamese fighting fish)

26-32°C (79-90°F)

The famous Siamese fighting fish is a highly domesticated form of an uninteresting-looking fish common in Southeast Asia. The males are highly

aggressive, even when not breeding. The domestic *B. splendens* bears little resemblance to its ancestors. It grows to 7cm (2¾in), and thrives even in small aquaria. It has a slim body, and in the males the dorsal, anal and tail fins are enormously enlarged and veil-like. The fins are frequently kept folded, but when the male displays, which he does frequently, they are stiffly extended, and the fish also flares out its gill covers, presumably to make it look larger and more ferocious. Females are smaller and less brilliantly coloured. *B. splendens* have been bred into many superb colour varieties, usually in pink, red, maroon or blue. They are fairly peaceful in the community tank, except when getting ready to breed, at which time they should be isolated. They breed very easily, in typical labyrinth fasion, and should be kept in relatively shallow (20cm — 7¾in) acid water. Oddly enough, some closely related *Betta* spp. are mouth-breeders.

Colisa chuna
(Honey gourami)

24-27°C (75-81°F)

A small, recently imported fish from India, growing to 4.5cm (1¾in), this shares its physical characteristics with several other *Colisa* spp., having a deep, flattened body with long dorsal and anal fins. The pelvic fins are elongated and threadlike, and can be rotated in all directions to be used as sensory organs, like the whiskers of a Catfish. Both males and females are yellow-brown, but in breeding condition the colours of the male change, so that his body becomes orange-gold all over, with the head and belly deep blue. The dorsal fin is fringed with yellow. This fish is difficult to establish in the aquarium, and is initially rather shy. Once well at home, it can be rather aggressive unless kept with larger fish. It breeds quite easily, in typical Labyrinth fashion.

Colisa fasciata
(Giant gourami)

24-28°C (75-82°F)

A typical gourami, this comes from Southeast Asia and, despite its popular name, grows to only about 10cm (4in). In shape it is similar to C. *chuna*, but it is reddish-brown with a blue patch on the gill covers, and has blue diagonal streaks, divided by red bands, on the sides. The tail is speckled with red. This is a very hardy and highly prolific fish, breeds easily at the temperatures given above, and tolerates quite low temperatures for a short while.

Colisa labiosa

C. *labiosa* (Thick-lipped gourami) comes from Burma, and is sometimes confused with C. *fasciata*. It reaches only 8cm (3¼in), however, and the sides are marked with green and orange bars and have a lengthways blue stripe. The lips of the males are characteristically thicker. Care and breeding are as for C. *chuna*. This rather timid fish eventually becomes very tame.

Colisa lalia
(Dwarf gourami)

20-26°C (68-79°F)

This pretty little gourami from India is the most brightly coloured of the group. It can grow to 6cm (2⅓in), but is usually smaller. The colouring is crimson with narrow diagonal bars of metallic blue. Most of the head is a brilliant blue-green, and the fins' are mottled with blue and red. Compared with other *Colisa* spp., this is rather shy and delicate, and the young, being

proportionately tiny, are quite difficult to rear. It requires soft, acid water.

Ctenopoma acutirostris
(Spotted climbing perch)

23-27°C (73-81°F)

This large fish from the Congo region is a powerful predator. It grows to 15cm (6in) and has a powerful muscular body with a very large head and mouth. It is an attractive golden-brown colour, covered with large irregular brown spots. It feeds greedily on small fish, worms and pieces of meat, but does not usually bother fish too large to eat, although it can be aggressive with others of its own kind. It requires soft water.

Helostoma temmincki

Helostoma temmincki
(Kissing gourami)

21-28°C (70-82°F)

This large and rather ordinary-looking fish from Malaysia, Thailand and nearby islands grows to 30cm (11¾in), but in the aquarium seldom exceeds 15cm (6in). It is available in two colour varieties. The 'wild' type is silvery-green with indistinct lengthways stripes and a dark vertical bar at the base of the tail. The more commonly available variety is pearly pink with a slight metallic sheen. The chief peculiarity is its lips, which are greatly enlarged and can be turned back to produce an enormous disc-like mouth, with which the fish rasps away at algae on plants or rocks. It will also annoy large disc-shaped fish like *Pterophyllum* by 'kissing' their sides. This 'kissing' is one form of territorial display, and these gouramis frequently 'kiss' for prolonged periods, mouth-to-mouth.

Colisa lalia

Macropodus concolor

originally from Korea, China, Taiwan and Vietnam. It is very aggressive but very beautiful, and is one of the hardiest tropical fish available. Adults grow to 12cm (4¾in), and both sexes are beautifully coloured, although only males have the flowing lyre-shaped tail. The body is striped vertically with turquoise and red lines, and the head and front are speckled with black. The dorsal and anal fins are dark blue-grey, and the flowing tail orange. An albino variety is sometimes available. This fish breeds very easily, even in unheated tanks in a warm living room, and can cope with a wide range of temperatures, although the fry need warm conditions if they are to survive the critical changeover to air-breathing. Paradise fish are useful as well as pretty, in that they are among the very few types which will destroy Planarians — tiny harmless but unsightly flatworms which are often introduced inadvertently with live foods. They also destroy other aquarium pests like *Hydra*, which resemble tiny Sea anemones.

Despite their algal diet, they will eat anything offered but will seldom pick up food from the bottom. They breed only occasionally in the aquarium, scattering large floating eggs and taking no further interest in them other than as food. They are very hardy provided they are kept in soft, acid or neutral water. They do not tolerate chilling.

Macropodus concolor
(Black paradise fish)

20-25°C (68-77°F)

From Southeast Asia, this fish may be a subspecies of *M. opercularis*. It grows to 12cm (4¾in), and is very hardy and quite aggressive. It has an elongated body and, in the male, an exaggerated lyre-shaped tail. The body is blue, each scale being edged with dark blue. The fins are marked with light and dark blue, together with some orange-red markings. Like others of its genus, it will live in the community tank with other boisterous fish, but must be isolated for spawning, when it becomes extremely aggressive with even the largest tankmates. It spawns in typical Labyrinth fashion, making an elaborate bubble nest and having a spectacular courtship. It eats almost anything. Add 1 teaspoon of salt per 5 litres (1.1gal) of water.

Macropodus cupanus cupanus
(Spike-tailed paradise fish)

16-25°C (61-77°F)

This is a very peaceful Paradise fish from India and Sri Lanka, and grows to only 7.5cm (3in). It is light-brown, with the forward part of the body metallic-green, and has a large black spot at the base of the tail. Its popular name comes from the fact that the central part of the tail in males is extended to produce a large spike. This fish breeds easily, in typical Labyrinth manner.

Macropodus opercularis
(Paradise fish)

15-30°C (59-86°F)

Probably the 'original' tropical fish to reach Europe, the Paradise fish comes

Sphaerichthys osphromenoides
(Chocolate gourami)

26-30°C (79-86°F)

A popular but very delicate and short-lived shoaling fish from Malaysia and Sumatra, this grows to only 6cm (2⅓in). It is a typical gourami in appearance, but with the head and mouth up-tilted, presumably to help in surface-feeding. The body is rich chocolate-brown, with some metallic highlights, and the sides are marked with irregular creamy-white bars and blotches. The same colouring extends into the fins. There are few obvious differences between the sexes. This is a fish for the expert or specialist.

Trichogaster leeri
(Pearl gourami)

23-30°C (73-86°F)

A typical gourami from Southeast Asia, growing to 15cm (6in), but only slowly. Like all other members of the genus, it has a deep flattened body with large dorsal and anal fins, and

Trichogaster leeri

Trichogaster pectoralis
(Snake-skin gourami)

24-28°C (75-82°F)

A large species from Southeast Asia, growing to 25cm (9¾in), and only occasionally imported. It is hardy, and very peaceful despite its size. The colour is very variable, usually being greenish-olive with a heavy, dark lengthways stripe. The body is marked with irregular gold diagonal bars, giving the snake-skin effect referred to by the popular name. Once established it is very prolific, and is an excellent parent, so that arrangements must be made for sale of the young well in advance of breeding. It begins to breed at the comparatively small size of 8cm (3¼in).

pelvic fins elongated into long mobile sensory filaments. Mature *T. leeri* are very beautiful. They are olive-green covered with mother-of-pearl dots which extend over the dorsal and anal fins and the tail. Old males develop long, flowing dorsal and anal fins. There is a dark line extending from the snout to near the base of the tail. In mature fish, the throat, belly and forward part of the anal fin become brilliant red, and the colours are all intensified during breeding, which does not take place until the fish is at least a year old. They breed readily, in typical Labyrinth fashion, producing a bubble nest. Up to 2,000 eggs are produced in a single spawning. Very hardy and completely peaceable, *T. leeri* sometimes need protection from fast-swimming boisterous fish. They breed at the high end of their temperature scale.

T. microlepis (Moonlight gourami), from Cambodia and Thailand, is very similar. It grows to 15cm (6in), and is very shy and peaceful. It is slightly slimmer, and is bluish-silver all over, with clear fins, except for the thread-like pelvic fins, which in the male are red. Care and breeding are as for *T. leeri*.

Trichogaster trichopterus

Trichogaster trichopterus
(Three-spot gourami)

20-26°C (68-79°F)

Formerly very popular, but now eclipsed by more spectacularly coloured gouramis, *T. trichopterus* comes from Southeast Asia and grows to 15cm (6in). Shaped like *T. leeri*, it is pale olive with faint bluish bands. There is a large black spot on the flank, and another on the base of the tail; these, together with the eye, which is counted as the third 'spot', account for its popular name. The anal fin is edged with red. This is a rather aggressive fish, and breeds very easily, in typical Labyrinth fashion. Like the Paradise fish, it will clear the aquarium of *Hydra*.

Trichogaster microlepis

117

T. trichopterus sumatranus (Blue gourami) is a subspecies or cultivated mutant which has almost entirely replaced the original fish. It grows to 12cm (4¾in), and has lost the spots of the original. It is mid-blue with faint diagonal stripes. It must be allowed to spawn when in breeding condition, or the female will become egg-bound and, usually, die. Care and breeding are as for *T. leeri*. Another 'sport' is called the Cosby or Opaline gourami. It too is blue, and has dark blue marblings.

CATFISH

This is a very large and varied group of fish, found from most parts of the world with the exception of very cold regions, the Middle East, Australia and Papua New Guinea. Because the group is so varied, it is difficult to give a general description, but the most characteristic feature is the possession of sensory barbels, which may be very long, around the mouth. In some forms the mouth is modified into a sucker with which the fish feed on algae, or cling to stones to avoid being dislodged in fast-flowing waters. Many Catfish have an adipose fin like that of the Characins, but this may be absent. Their habitats vary from mountain streams to foul, stagnant tropical waters; some are capable of living in very severe conditions, or of withstanding prolonged drought by burying themselves in the mud for long periods. A few live in estuaries, and one or two are found in the sea. There is one European species, native to the Danube and since introduced to the UK and elsewhere. This fish, the Wels (*Silurus glanis*), grows to nearly 2m (6ft 6in) and is a powerful predator. Most other Catfish, however, are peaceful scavengers, grubbing about in the mud in search of food, although the smaller relatives of the Wels are active predators and not to be trusted with small fish. These predatory forms are usually very powerful swimmers but, like most of the group, are shy and nocturnal for much of the time.

With the exception of *Corydoras* spp., few Catfish are bred regularly in the aquarium. Among those that are, there is usually some form of parental care of the eggs or young. Most Catfish

Bunocephalus coracoideus

are imported and, as most of this 2,000-strong group are little known, it is as well to be wary when purchasing an unidentified type: it may well grow to an enormous size, with a matching appetite.

Acanthodoras spinosissimus
(Talking catfish)

22-25°C (72-77°F)

Also known as *Doras spinosissimus*, this 15cm (6in) fish comes from Amazonia. It is an effective scavenger, but will eat other fish. It spends the day buried in the gravel or hiding among the plants, and becomes active at night. The head is very large, and the shape is generally tadpole-like. The dorsal and especially pectoral fins have very powerful bony spines, as do the gill covers, and these are held stiffly erect when the fish is frightened. *A. spinosissimus* can often become inextricably tangled when being handled in a net. It is brown with white blotches on the sides. The popular name comes from the very loud grating sound it produces, using the swim bladder as a resonator, which can be clearly heard outside the aquarium.

Corydoras aeneus

It has been bred in the aquarium, but only very rarely, and no details are available.

Bunocephalus coracoideus
(Banjo catfish)

20-26°C (68-79°F)

This interesting Catfish from South America grows to around 12cm (4¾in). It is nocturnal and seldom seen, lying completely buried in the gravel for much of the time. These fish are bizarre-looking, with a flattened bulbous body and a long thin tail, with heavily spined and barbed pectoral fins. There are long barbels around the mouth, and the overall colour is brown with irregular light and dark patches. *Bunocephalus* are very industrious burrowers, sucking gravel in through the mouth and expelling it violently through the gills after extracting anything worth eating. In doing so, they can revitalize a biological filter which has become too tightly packed for efficiency, but they will also uproot plants. Tough and undemanding, breeding occasionally in a pit dug in the bottom and ignoring both spawn and fry, they are best kept in tanks with fine-grade gravel in which they can dig easily. They prefer neutral or alkaline, slightly hard water.

Several related species are also available.

Corydoras spp.

18-29°C (64-84°F)

There are very many different *Corydoras* species available. Their needs are all very similar.

C. aeneus (Bronze catfish) is the stereotype of the Catfish, the one which most aquarists think of when planning to introduce a scavenger fish to the tank. Like other members of the genus, it comes from South America; it is found also in Trinidad. It is a small shoaling fish, growing to 7.5cm (3in), and is exclusively a bottom-dweller. It is flattened underneath, and the upper surface is strongly arched. The body is covered with overlapping bony plates, which allow it to flex but protect it

Corydoras melanistius

from predators. The pectoral fins are stiffly spined and provide further protection; in the wild they are used as 'legs' to allow the fish to travel out of the water over mud banks. As in other *Corydoras*, the mouth is small and undershot, and fringed with small barbels. The fish is bronze with a metallic green tint. *C. aeneus* is an industrious scavenger, grubbing about in the gravel but seldom disturbing properly rooted plants. It is an air-breather, like others of the genus, and periodically rushes to the surface to take in a bubble of air, which is later absorbed from the gut. As would be expected, it can survive in very poor conditions, but does not appreciate neglect.

Corydoras **digging in gravel with sensory barbels.**

Corydoras all do best in neutral or alkaline water. They do not tolerate very acid conditions, or salt. They are not particularly easy to breed, or to sex: males are usually smaller than females, and have more pointed pelvic fins. They are usually spawned in trios of two males to one female, and should be kept in a tank containing plenty of

mulm, or very fine sand, together with rocks on which they can spawn. There is normally a prolonged courtship. They usually spawn when the temperature is raised to about 27°C (81°F) and then dropped to 18°C (64°F) at night, repeated as necessary until the eggs are deposited on rocks; the adult fish must be removed promptly, before they eat the spawn. Eggs hatch within 3-4 days. Careful hygiene is necessary to prevent bacterial damage to both eggs and fry in the mulm-laden water. The fry grow only slowly.

C. arcuatus (Arched catfish) is an Amazon Catfish growing to 5cm (2in). The body is ivory-white with a pearly tinge, and has a broad black band running from the snout, high along the sides to the tail, which may be speckled with dark spots.

C. elegans (Elegant catfish) is an Amazon Catfish growing to 6cm (2⅓in) and thriving in a shoal. Its body is mid-brown, with the forward part and dorsal fin marbled with dark brown; the rear has lengthways lines.

C. hastatus (Dwarf catfish) is a small, slim-bodied shoaling type from the Amazon which grows to only 3.5cm (1⅓in). It has an olive back and yellowish sides, with a pronounced lengthways stripe edged with gold. This pretty little fish often feeds in mid-water, and is consequently less flattened ventrally than the other bottom-feeding types. It is also quite active and not as nocturnal as other *Corydoras*, especially when kept in a small shoal.

Corydoras paleatus

C. julii (Leopard catfish) is a very active shoaling species from Brazil which grows to 6cm (2⅓in). Its silver-grey body is very short and plump. It is covered with a complicated network of black lines and speckles, and there is a silver-edged black line along the sides. The tail-fin is spotted with black, and the pointed dorsal fin is tipped with black.

C. melanistius (Black-spotted catfish) is a 7cm (2¾in) species from northern South America. A plump pinkish-grey fish, it has head, sides and tail covered with small black speckles. There is a prominent black band across the head, extending down through the eyes, and another black patch on the back, extending into the dorsal fin.

C. myersi (Myers' catfish) is an attractive species from South America which grows to 6cm (2⅓in) and does best when kept in a shoal. It has a typical *Corydoras* shape, but is brightly coloured, being orange or salmon-pink overall, with a very broad dark band running from the back of the head along the upper flanks to the tail. The fins are not coloured. This fish quickly loses its colour if water conditions are not to its liking.

C. nattereri (Blue corydoras), a shoaling Catfish from Brazil, grows to 6.5cm (2½in). Its body is light brown overlain by a bright metallic blue tinge, and pink underneath. There is a narrow black line along the sides.

C. paleatus (Peppered catfish or Leopard catfish) is a popular and very hardy species which grows to 8cm (3¼in) and thrives in a shoal. It is a plump, deep-bodied fish, coloured olive-green, with bold blue-green blotches and many small speckles on the sides. The fins, too, are speckled. There is a blue-green metallic sheen over the flanks.

C. punctatus (Spotted catfish) is a shoaling species from South America which grows to 6cm (2⅓in). It is very short and plump, with a pale beige body peppered with small brown speckles, which also cover the anal fin and tail. There is a large black blotch halfway up the dorsal fin.

C. pygmaeus (Pigmy catfish) is a shoaling Catfish from South America which grows to only 4cm (1½in). It is very similar in appearance to *C. hastatus* but is, like other *Corydoras*, a bottom-swimmer and very shy.

Etropiella debauwi

Etropiella debauwi

24-28°C (75-82°F)

These pretty little Catfish from Zaire will survive only in a shoal. They are constantly active and are not nocturnal, swimming continuously in mid-water. The 6cm (2⅓in) body is elongated and semitransparent, with three narrow blue-black lengthways stripes which extend right into the tail. They are very peaceful, but may eat smaller tankmates. It may be difficult to acclimatize them to dried foods. *E. debauwi* does not breed in captivity.

Farlowella amazonica
(Needle catfish)

20-24°C (68-75°F)

A peculiar elongated Catfish, from the Amazon region, which grows to 20cm (7¾in) but is usually much smaller. It is very slim, like a Pipefish (see page 128). The snout is pointed, with the undershot mouth positioned well back on the underside; this mouth is used to cling to stones and feed on algae. In the wild the fish frequents fast-flowing oxygen-rich streams, and it may be difficult to acclimatize it to the aquarium. It is brown or olive, and generally inactive. It must usually be given prepared vegetable food, such as porridge, which it eats greedily. It has bred in captivity on occasion, depositing its spawn on rocks. The males have bristles over the snout.

Kryptopterus bicirrhis
(Glass catfish)

20-27°C (68-81°F)

An actively swimming, shoaling fish from Southeast Asia, which swims in mid-water and will not survive if kept singly. Its long flattened body is transparent, with yellow and pink highlights, all the organs being squeezed into a silvery sac at the front. The anal fin is greatly elongated, extending along most of the length of the body. The dorsal fin is reduced to a single inconspicuous ray, and there is no adi-

Kryptopterus bicirrhis

pose fin. The fish has two very long, forward-pointing barbels. *K. bicirrhis* can seldom be persuaded to take dried food, preferring *Daphnia*. It is not known to have bred in the aquarium. It is very susceptible to white spot (ichthyophthiriasis).

Leiocassis poecilopterus
(Bumble-bee catfish)

22-25°C (72-77°F)

This large Catfish from Southeast Asia grows to 18cm (7in). It is very greedy, and will eat smaller fish if given the chance. It has an elongated slim body, a large flattened head, a deeply forked tail and a large, erect dorsal fin. It is velvety-black overall, with conspicuous cream bands across the body. It is nocturnal, and a very fast swimmer. It rests in a vertical position, leaning against a plant stem. It is not known to have bred in captivity.

Loricaria filamentosa
(Whiptailed catfish)

20-27°C (68-81°F)

This algae-eating Catfish from South America is one of the few types to spawn regularly in the aquarium. It has an elongated, flattened body, and the upper lobe of the tail is extended to a point. The mouth is undershot and modified into an efficient sucking organ, with which the fish industriously scours algae and other microorganisms from the plants. The fish is mottled olive-green over the body and fins. Breeding is Cichlid-like. The fry are quite large, and tadpole-shaped. They can be fed on cereal and freeze-dried Brine-shrimp, and grow rapidly.

Malapterus electricus
(Electric catfish)

23-30°C (73-86°F)

This bizarre fish, found in much of Africa, is noted for its ability to produce a powerful electric discharge with which it stuns its prey. It is hardly attractive, being a sausage-shaped creature up to 1m (3ft 3in) in length, although fortunately usually much smaller. It is pinkish-grey, flecked with black spots, and has a conspicuous vertical black bar just before its rounded tail. There is no dorsal fin. The eyes are so small as to be almost rudimentary, and the large mouth is surrounded by long barbels. It produces a current powerful enough to give a considerable jolt, and must be fed earthworms, strips of fish or meat, or small fish. *M. electricus* should be kept singly, and is not known to have bred in the aquarium.

Otocinclus affinis
(Dwarf sucking catfish)

20-25°C (68-77°F)

Probably the best scavenger for the community tank, this 4cm (1½in) fish and the related *O. flexilis* come from Brazil. They are slim-bodied, coloured olive-green with a bold black lengthways stripe. The underside is white or cream, and the tail is mottled with brown and has a black bar at its base. The small sucking mouth is well beneath the head. These fish are nocturnal and extremely active and effective browsers on algae, but will not damage even delicate plants. They must receive adequate amounts of vegetable material in their diet; in an algae-free tank, vegetable supplements

Loricaria filamentosa

Otocinclus affinis

must be given. They breed like *Corydoras*, attaching their eggs to stones. Feeding the tiny young is a problem, as their mouths are very small.

Pimelodella gracilis

18-25°C (64-77°F)

A very active and voracious shoaling Catfish, not to be trusted with smaller fish, this comes from South America and grows to 15cm (6in). It has an elongated body with a very large adipose fin. Its head is flattened, and the barbels around the mouth may be at least half the length of the body. The body is greyish-brown, with a darker lengthwise stripe. *P. gracilis* will not bother fish which are too large to eat. It is almost entirely nocturnal, and is not known to have bred in the aquarium.

Plecostomus punctatus
(Sucking catfish)

20-25°C (68-77°F)

Known also as *Hypostomus punctatus*, this is a large and robust Catfish from South America, growing to 30cm (11¾in). It is an algae-eater, and has a very large and efficient sucker mouth with which it may suck clean through delicate leaves such as those of *Aponogetom*. The body is flattened under-

neath, and has large fins, usually carried stiffly erect. It is olive-green with black speckles and indistinct lengthways stripes. It eats anything offered, but must have adequate vegetable material. Territorial but peaceful, and largely nocturnal, it tends to uproot plants and disturb all but the largest tanks due to its bulk and blundering swimming habits. It is not known to have bred in captivity.

Sorubim lima

Sorubim lima
(Shovel-nosed catfish)

20-25°C (68-77°F)

This peculiar-looking Catfish from South America grows to 60cm (2ft) in a large tank. It is extremely elongated, with a long, slim flattened head. Very long and conspicuous barbels surround the mouth. The colouring is greenish-grey above, white below, and there is a broad black band along the sides and into the lower lobe of the tail. This fish is an active predator, but does not

bother fish too large to swallow. It has a peculiar resting pose on plant stems, either head-down or head-up. It is not known to have bred in captivity.

Synodontis angelicus

20-26°C (68-79°F)

A large Catfish, growing to 20cm (7¾in), from West Africa and the Congo. It is deep-bodied, shaped rather like *Corydoras*, and is beautifully coloured. The body is deep purple covered with small yellow or pinkish spots, and the fins are barred with purple; the colours are most intense in the young. It is very peaceful and shy, and almost completely nocturnal, resting during the day, usually in an upright position behind the plants. It eats almost anything, and is peaceful although territorial. It has not been bred in the aquarium, and is extremely (and unjustifiably) expensive.

Synodontis nigriventris
(Upside-down catfish)

22-28°C (72-82°F)

A fascinating shoaling Catfish from Zaire which grows to 9cm (3½in). It is of great interest due to its habit of swimming on its back. Similarly, the normal type of colouring is reversed: the belly is dark brown and the back a light mottled brown. It feeds in mid-water, grazing on the undersides of leaves, although it can happily 'invert' itself and feed normally from the bottom. It eats anything offered and is very peaceful, although it may irritate other fish by nibbling at them. Like *S. angelicus*, it has strong spines in the

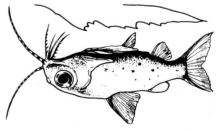

Synodontis nigriventris, swimming upside-down while feeding. Note reversed coloration.

Synodontis nigriventris

fins, and must be handled carefully if it is not to be entangled in a net. It breeds occasionally in the aquarium, depositing its eggs on plant leaves and guarding the spawn.

Several other species of *Synodontis* are available apart from the two mentioned here, and some share the upside-down habit. Beware that you do not purchase one of the larger species: they can grow to 60cm (2ft) or more.

LOACHES

Loaches are members of the Cobitidae family, found throughout Europe and Asia and occasionally in North Africa. They are timid scavengers with barbels around an unusually small mouth. Most have an elongated body, and they are scaleless, or at best have only rudimentary scales. Loaches usually inhabit fast-moving streams, and protect themselves from the current by hiding among stones or burying themselves in the gravel. They have high oxygen requirements, and many species obtain extra oxygen by taking in bubbles of air through the mouth and expelling the waste gases via the vent. Loaches are frequently sensitive to the alterations of atmospheric pressure preceding weather changes, becoming restless, and the Weatherfish (*Misgurnis fossilis*) has been kept as a living barometer for centuries.

Loaches are omnivorous, eating anything offered, and thriving on *Tubifex* and chopped earthworms; they find it difficult to catch swimming prey such as *Daphnia*. They burrow continually in the gravel, looking for food, but only the large species will disturb the plants. They very seldom breed in the aquarium.

Probably because of their scalelessness, Loaches are prone to *Ichthyophthirius* disease (white spot), as well as skin ulcers, which are possibly caused by some dietary deficiency.

Acanthophthalmus semicinctus
(Coolie loach)

25-30°C (77-86°F)

A pretty and popular Loach, growing to 8cm (3¼in) and originating in Malaysia; very similar species are found in Sumatra, Java and Borneo. The body is very slim and wormlike, and is fleshy pink. There are 12-15 thick, dark-brown or blue-black vertical bars on the sides. The dorsal fin is set well back near the tail, and all the fins are colourless except for the tail, which has a dark vertical bar. Beneath the eye there is a large spine which is normally folded away into a socket, being erected only when the fish is frightened. Females are fatter than males, and in breeding condition become very bloated. Breeding is not well understood. This little fish is totally peaceful, and is a very effective scavenger. It will bury itself completely in fine gravel, or hide among the plants, emerging only at night.

Acanthophthalmus semicinctus

Botia spp.

25-30°C (77-86°F)

B. horae (Skunk loach or Cream loach) is a large Loach from Thailand, growing to 10cm (4in); it is a typical *Botia*. It has a powerful stocky body with a pointed head and a large deeply forked tail, all of which features combine to make *Botia* powerful swimmers. They are all extremely difficult to catch in a well planted tank.

The body of *B. horae* is cream or beige, with a bold brown stripe running along the back from the snout to the tail; there is also a dark vertical bar across the base of the tail. Like other *Botia*, it has a very large retractable spine beneath the eye, and this can cause a painful wound when you are handling the fish in a net. Like the other species, it shoals in small groups, and often hovers in mid-water making a curious fluttering movement. *Botia* do not like well aged water, and a proportion should be changed regularly. They have not bred in captivity.

B. hymenophysa (Tiger loach) is a large Loach from Southeast Asia, reaching 20cm (7¾in) or more, but slowly. It is aggressively territorial, and often rushes at other fish to drive them away, although it cannot cause serious damage. It is a typical *Botia* in shape, and is yellow-brown in colour with many narrow dark-brown vertical stripes, which also cover the dorsal and anal fins and the tail.

Detail of Botia, *showing spine beneath the eye.*

B. macracantha (Clown loach) is by far the most popular of the *Botia* Loaches. It is bright yellow with three very dense, wedge-shaped black bars on the side; the last of these bars runs through the dorsal and anal fins. The fins and tail are bright crimson. This is the largest Loach kept in the aquarium, growing to 30cm (11¾in), but it seldom reaches this size in captivity. When first imported it is very delicate and prone to disease, but once established it is very hardy. It is not particularly nocturnal, and has the odd habit of swimming in a shoal with similarly striped fish, especially *Barbus tetrazona* (see page 77).

B. sidthimunki (Dwarf loach), a small shoaling species from Thailand, grows to only 3cm (1¼in). It is very active and not especially nocturnal, and swims in the middle water as well as scavenging on the bottom. The body is creamy white, with the back marbled in dark brown. A pretty and inoffensive fish, it is well suited to the community tank, although it sometimes nibbles harmlessly at larger fish.

B. striata (Tiger loach) is a large species of *Botia*, growing to 10cm (4in), from Southeast Asia. It is entirely covered with narrow brown stripes which run right round under the belly and over part of the tail. Unlike the other large *Botia*, it swims a great deal in mid-water, and often perches on leaves. It is not exclusively nocturnal, and is quite peaceful.

MISCELLANEOUS FRESHWATER FISH

Anableps anableps
(Four-eyed fish)

22-25°C (72-77°F)

This very odd fish from South America grows to 25cm (9¾in) or more. It is elongated and golden-brown, with several lengthways, branching, dark stripes along the sides, and a rounded tail. It is remarkable for two quite separate reasons. Firstly, its eyes are modified into a figure-of-eight shape. It lies on the surface, with its eyes half under and half above the surface, with the upper part on the lookout for flying insects or enemies, while the lower part simultaneously looks under the water.

The two-part eye of Anableps *enables it to look through both air and water.*

Its other peculiarity is that its sex organs are right- or left-handed; that is, a male with a right-handed gonopodium (see page 22) can mate only with a female whose sex organs open to the left, and vice versa. These fish are live-bearers, reproducing like the Guppy (see page 103), and produce a few very large fry. They feed entirely on the surface, and are powerful leapers. Adequate swimming space must be provided, with plenty of floating plants. Add 2 teaspoonfuls of salt per 5 litres (1.1gal) of water.

Anableps anableps

Badis badis

20-27°C (68-81°F)

A small, retiring fish from India which, while unrelated to Dwarf cichlids, shares many of their characteristics. It grows to 8cm (3¼in), and has a large dorsal fin with sharp spines. The colour is extremely variable: at different times the fish is yellowish-brown, nearly black, or reddish, often marked with lozenge-shaped spots. When ready to breed, it becomes aggressively territorial, and usually selects a cave or upturned flowerpot as a spawning site. The female can be removed after spawning, and the male will guard the eggs and fry. The young fish must be given infusoria until they are large enough to cope with newly hatched Brine shrimps.

Brachygobius xanthozona
(Bumble-bee goby)

24-28°C (75-82°F)

A pretty Goby from Java, Borneo and Sumatra, growing to only 5cm (2in). It is fairly peaceful, but may nip the fins of slow-moving fish, being fearless and territorial. It and several related species have a stocky, plump body with a rounded tail. The pelvic fins, as in other Gobies, are fused to form a sucker with which the fish can cling to plants or the tank sides. The body is bright yellow, crossed by four broad black bands, and the dorsal and anal fins are also black. This is an inactive fish which often perches on the plants, and prefers to eat live foods. It does best in brackish water, with sea-salt added at a rate of one teaspoonful per

Brachygobius xanthozona

Badis badis

5 litres (1.1gal). They can be spawned in a small group in water which is hard yet acid. The fish pair off and spawn in an upturned flowerpot, depositing eggs over several days. The male then drives the female away, and she should be removed. He guards the spawn, removing fungussed eggs and fanning the remainder with his fins. He will not harm the newly hatched fry, which can be fed on infusoria and fine dried food.

Chanda ranga
(Indian glassfish)

20-25°C (68-77°F)

A small shy fish from Southeast Asia, growing to 7cm (2¾in), and formerly known as *Ambassis ranga*. It has a flattened, deep shape and spiny fins, with an overall yellowish cast to its transparent body, within which the spine can be clearly seen. The internal organs are contained in a silvery sac in the abdomen. There are some faint vertical bars on the sides, and the dorsal fin is divided into two distinct sections. The dorsal and anal fins are edged with blue; this is more pronounced in the male. These are brackish-water fish, and 2-3 teaspoonfuls of sea-salt per 5 litres (1.1gal) should be added to their water. They are happiest in a shoal, and take only

live foods. They will breed in shallow water, depositing their eggs into the roots of floating plants. The tiny eggs are adhesive, and hatch quickly. Neither eggs nor fry will be eaten by the parent fish. The young are difficult to raise, eating only tiny Rotifers and *Cyclops*.

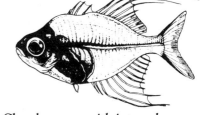

Chanda ranga, *with internal organs packed in a transparent membrane.*

C. wolfi is very similar to *C. ranga*. Found in Thailand, Borneo and Sumatra, it grows to 10cm (4in). The body is silvery with a brilliant silver lengthwise line. It is territorial, but seldom aggressive.

Dermogenys pusillus
(Malayan half-beak)

20-30°C (68-86°F)

An unusual live-bearing fish from Southeast Asia, which grows to 7cm (2¾in). *D. pusillus* are shoaling fish, and males often fight viciously at breeding time. They resemble tiny Swordfish, but with only the lower jaw extended into a point, and they feed exclusively on the surface, preferring live foods. They are brown, although males develop a red tinge around the head and beak. They breed like other live-bearers, but require prolonged conditioning and even then produce few live young. They do best in hard brackish water, of neutral pH, containing sea-salt at a rate of one teaspoonful per 5 litres (1.1gal). The young, nearly 1cm (½in) long at birth, must be fed on very small living foods.

Eigenmannia virescens
(Green knifefish)

22-28°C (72-82°F)

A very shy nocturnal fish from South America, growing to 45cm (17¾in) but usually much smaller. It has an elongated knife-like body and very small eyes. The anal fin is enormously long, running almost the whole length of the body. There are no dorsal, pelvic or tail fins, and the fish is propelled forwards or backwards by rippling movements of the anal fin, the body itself being held straight and stiff. The body is pinkish brown with green highlights. These hardy territorial fish should not be kept with aggressive tank-mates, which may nip the long pointed tail. They prefer to eat live foods. They are not known to have bred in captivity.

Gnathonemus macrolepidotus

24-28°C (75-82°F)

A fascinating and very odd fish from West Africa which grows to 15cm (6in). It has a long flattened body, with a slim base to the deeply forked tail. The jaw is thrust forward like a bulldog's, but the mouth is quite small. The fish is pinkish-grey all over, and there is a thick coating of slime on the body. These fish are shy and territorial, being aggressive to their own kind but peaceful with other species. They have electric organs with which they can sense their surroundings and find food in the very dark waters in which they

Gynochanda filamentosa

live in the wild — they do not produce electric shocks! They have a very large brain in proportion to their size, and seem highly intelligent, often playing with a piece of leaf or a pebble. Many will take food from the hand. They are undemanding and hardy, if kept in soft acid water in a tank with plenty of hiding places. They will not withstand chilling, and have not bred in the aquarium.

Gnathonemus macrolepidotus, *showing 'bulldog' jaw.*

G. petersi (Elephant nose) is very similar, and is also from West Africa. While the body shape is the same, the lower jaw carries a fleshy protuberance

2-3cm (¾-1¼in) in length, and of uncertain function. The body is black, and there are two creamy crescent-shaped lines connecting the dorsal and anal fins. A shyer fish than G. *macrolepidotus*, it grows to 20cm (7¾in). It has not yet been bred in captivity.

Gnathonemus petersi

Gynochanda filamentosa

22-27°C (72-81°F)

This is very similar to *Chanda ranga* (see page 00), and grows to 5cm (2in).

It is found in Malaysia. While it has the same general shape and transparent body as *C. ranga*, it has enormously elongated fin rays in the near part of the dorsal fin and in the anal fin. Care and breeding are as for *C. ranga*, but tank-bred specimens do not develop the extended fin-rays.

Macrognathus aculeatus
(Spiny eel; Arrownose)

22-28°C (72-82°F)

This curious eel-like fish from Southeast Asia grows to 30cm (11¾in), but is usually smaller. It has a long pointed snout, with a flexible proboscis carrying barbels which it uses to locate its food. The body is mottled brown, with darker marblings on the back. There are some conspicuous 'eye spots' on the rear half of the body. The dorsal and anal fins are long, and the tail is very small. The forward part of the dorsal fin is reduced to a series of small spines. This fish spends most of the day buried in the gravel, emerging at night to forage for food. It consumes large amounts of *Tubifex*, or any other food offered. It is not bred in the aquarium. It prefers water to which 1 tsp of salt has been added per 5 litres (1.1gal).

Macrognathus aculeatus

Melanotaenia maccullochi
(Dwarf rainbow fish)

20-26°C (68-79°F)

A hardy shoaling fish from northern Australia which grows to 8cm (3¼in). It has an elongated oval body, and is an active swimmer. The body is yellowish-green, darker on the back, and the sides are marked with seven thin, dark-brown horizontal lines

Melanotaenia nigrans

separated by gold bands. There is a red patch on the gills. This fish breeds very easily, scattering eggs that adhere among the plants; the parents should then be removed to prevent them eating the eggs. The young are easy to raise on commercial dried fry-food. This fish prefers hard alkaline water.

M. nigrans (Australian rainbow fish) is similar, but grows to 10cm (4in), and comes from southern Australia. It is green with yellow and red lengthways stripes, and has bright metallic tints on the sides, which reflect green, blue and purple.

Microphis smithi
(Large freshwater pipefish)

22-28°C (72-82°F)

A Pipefish from West Africa, growing to 20cm (7¾in), this has a typically eel-like shape, with a head like a Seahorse's and a tiny upturned mouth with which it eats only small live foods like *Tubifex* and *Daphnia*. The body is armoured with jointed plates, and all the fins are of reduced size except the dorsal, which produces most of the

Melanotaenia maccullochi

propulsive action. The fish is golden-brown, with a short dark-brown stripe through the snout and eye. As is typical of its group, the males incubate the young in a large pouch, and 'pregnant' males become very fat. It does not actually breed in captivity, but 'pregnant' males are often imported and give birth in the aquarium. The young are difficult to rear. It requires sea-salt to be added to the water.

Monocirrhus polyacanthus
(Leaf fish)

22-26°C (72-79°F)

Displaying probably the best camouflaging abilities of all aquarium fish, this comes from South America and grows to 9cm (3½in). It looks very convincing as a drifting leaf, both to escape predators and to allow it to move slowly up on unsuspecting small fish, which it engulfs with its enormous extensible mouth. It has a deep flattened body, and inconspicuous transparent fins. The body is marbled in various shades of brown, like a rotting leaf, and the illusion is completed by a 'stalk' on the pointed chin. It lives only on fish, and must be kept in very soft, acid water. It breeds like a Cichlid. The young feed immediately on Daphnia and Brine shrimps.

Pantodon buchholzi

Pantodon buchholzi
(Butterfly fish)

23-30°C (73-86°F)

An interesting fish from West Africa which is able to leap out of the water and glide. It grows to 15cm (6in), and has a broad, squat body with a very large upturned mouth for surface-feeding. The pectoral fins are very large and winglike, and the pelvic fin-rays are extended like fingers. The tail is pointed. The body is light brown overall, with darker marbling and a silver belly. This fish is difficult to acclimatize to anything other than live food, and will eat only on or near the surface: floated mealworms are probably easiest. It will breed, provided the fish can be properly conditioned; they deposit large masses of floating eggs among surface plants. The eggs hatch only slowly, and the young are extremely difficult to feed.

Syngnathus pulchellus
(Dwarf pipefish)

22-26°C (72-79°F)

This small Pipefish from West Africa grows to only 15cm (6in), and is very slim. Its body is golden-brown. Care is much as for Microphis smithi (see page 00), but this fish will live only in hard, alkaline water to which seawater has been added, and is not known to have bred in captivity. 'Pregnant' males usually abort their young when disturbed.

Telmatherina ladigesi
(Celebes rainbowfish)

24-28°C (75-82°F)

A very active shoaling fish from the Celebes. It has an elongated body which is silvery-yellow with an iridescent sheen and, on the rear part, a blue lengthwise line. It has two dorsal fins, of which the first is small; however, in the male the second fin has greatly elongated fin-rays, as does the anal fin. Dorsal and anal fins of both males and females are bright yellow with black edges. This coloration develops only when the fish are kept in hard alkaline water with 1 tsp of sea-salt added per 5 litres (1.1gal) of water. Frequent water-changes are beneficial. The fish breed easily, depositing adhesive eggs on floating plants. The eggs hatch in about 10 days.

Tetraodon spp.

22-26°C (72-79°F)

T. fluviatilis (Freshwater puffer or Green pufferfish) is a very active and fairly aggressive Pufferfish found in brackish water in Southeast Asia; it grows to 15cm (6in). It has a short rotund body and large mobile eyes. With its powerfully beaked mouth it can crush and eat snails as well as biting pieces clean out of slow-moving

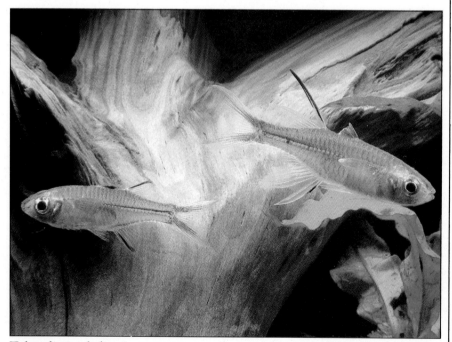

Telmatherina ladigesi

Toxotes jaculator

flying insects. It can unerringly extinguish a lighted cigarette held over a darkened tank, and can bring down even a large bluebottle. The size and power of the jet are proportional to the size of the fish. *T. jaculator* comes from the coastal regions around the Indian Ocean and parts of the Pacific, and is strictly a brackish-water fish. It grows to 20cm (7¾in), but is usually smaller. Although it lives in shoals it is rather quarrelsome. The body is deep and muscular, with a large head and mouth. The dorsal and anal fins are set well back. It is silver overall, and darker above, with a series of broad black bars on the sides. It is not known to have been bred, and in the wild is thought to migrate to the sea for spawning. Salt must be added to the water at a rate of one teaspoonful per 5 litres (1.1gal).

Xenomystus nigri (African knifefish)

25-28°C (77-82°F)

A popular and inoffensive Knifefish from East and West Africa, this grows to 20cm (7¾in) but is usually smaller. It has a teardrop-shaped body and no dorsal or pelvic fins, but has a greatly elongated anal fin which propels it forwards or backwards very rapidly. It is pinkish-grey or sometimes nearly black, and is largely nocturnal. A shy fish, it hides behind rocks or plants for much of the time. It is best kept singly or with several of its own kind — a pair will fight — and is not to be trusted with small fish. It has not bred in the aquarium. Keep in soft, acid water and feed on live foods when possible. If kept in a dimly lit and well planted tank, this fish will become very tame.

fish. The fins and tail are small and weak, and the fish propels itself by a rowing action of the pectoral fins, so that it is very agile but not fast-moving. Its upper parts are yellow or greenish-gold, covered with large round black spots, and it is white below. Like other Puffers, it will inflate itself like a ball if frightened, but should not be tormented into doing this as shock can kill it. It must be kept in hard brackish water, or it will develop fungus which will quickly prove fatal; add 2 teaspoonfuls of sea-salt per 5 litres (1.1gal) of water. It breeds in large tanks, behaving like a Cichlid, with the male guarding the eggs. It is an acceptable community fish among large, robust fish.

T. palembangensis is very similar to *T. fluviatilis*, but grows to 20cm

(7¾in); it comes from Southeast Asia, and is very aggressive. It is bright gold with a white belly, and is heavily marbled with dark brown streaks and blotches. Care is as for *T. fluviatilis*, but without the added salt. It has not bred in the aquarium.

T. somphongsi (Thai puffer) is an aggressive Pufferfish from Thailand which grows to only 7cm (2¾in). This fish is even plumper than other *Tetraodon* species, and is coloured quite differently. The body is cream and brown; the fins are red and blue; and the eye is red. This fish seldom inflates when scared, but can erect a crest on its throat as a threat display. It is aggressive with its own kind, and is a fin-nipper; it is much bolder than other Pufferfish. Some sea-salt must be added to the water. It has been bred occasionally, and does so like *T. fluviatilis*.

Toxotes jaculator (Archerfish)

25-30°C (77-86°F)

This extraordinary fish is well worth keeping for its appearance and its habit of spitting jets of water to knock down

Tetraodon fluviatilis

Xenomystus nigri

PART THREE

THE MARINE AQUARIUM

It is wise to learn the rudiments of fish-keeping with the much tougher and cheaper freshwater types before moving on to the marines, which are a more serious challenge. However, it is possible to start off with marines if you take especial care to understand their requirements and, preferably, have access to the advice of an experienced aquarist or very understanding dealer.

Virtually all marine fish kept in the tropical aquarium are from coral reefs — although a few come from brackish coastal waters. This is fortunate because, although it can be difficult to recreate the exact conditions of a reef, once you have done so you will have an environment in which almost any marine fish can be kept.

Coral reefs have been described as 'the most stable environment on Earth'. The oxygen level of the water is stable and, because reefs are found only in the tropics, water temperatures are usually constant. Light levels are very high, as the coral grows only in shallow water beneath a fierce tropical sun. And, as the reefs are constantly flushed with water thanks to ocean currents and tides, the normal waste products of fish life, such as nitrates and carbon dioxide, are present in immeasurably small amounts.

It is because this natural environment is so stable that marine fish may be difficult to keep. The fish are not adapted to cope with any significant environmental variations — unlike freshwater fish.

LEFT: *In general, marine fish are more gaudily coloured than freshwater fish, and those whose natural habitat is the coral reef, have little protective camouflage. Few are more brightly coloured than the Surgeonfish,* Paracanthurus hepatus.

THE FISH AND THEIR HABITAT

Seawater contains a very large amount of dissolved salts; about 35g per litre (about 5½oz/gal), or 3.5 per cent by weight. The mixture of salts is immensely complex; some of the most common constituents, in descending order of amounts, are sodium chloride (common salt), magnesium chloride, magnesium sulphate (Epsom salts), calcium carbonate (chalk), and potassium and sodium bromides, and there is a huge range of other substances, some in very minute amounts. For many years marine fish-keeping was hampered by the need to use natural seawater (which had to be purified and stored for use) because artificial salt mixtures proved unsatisfactory. Now, however, the significance of the tiny amounts of 'trace' elements in seawater has been largely understood, and 'sea-salt' is available for mixing with tap water to produce an excellent synthetic seawater in which all marine fish can thrive.

Another important characteristic of seawater is its alkaline pH, usually maintained at around 8.0-8.3. This is because, on a reef, various chemical reactions interplay to produce a system which is, in technical terms, 'buffered' — that is, which strongly resists

ABOVE: *Like its relatives, the Surgeonfish,* Acanthurus leucosternon, *has a sharp, scalpel-like blade at either side of the root of its tail. It uses this as a means of both defence and attack, and must be handled with caution. Unlike many marine fish, Surgeonfish retain their colouring throughout life, changing very little between juvenile and adult forms.*

chemical changes, and tends to return conditions automatically to 'normal' after any change. Carbon dioxide gas, produced as a waste product by animals, dissolves in water to produce a weak acid, which tends to make the pH acidic. However, in nature, huge amounts of algae reduce the carbon dioxide to insignificant levels, and so prevent the acidification. In addition, the coral skeletons are largely composed of calcium carbonate, which dissolves in the water to form an alkaline solution. The same sort of situation applies to the presence of organic wastes, and especially those containing nitrogen, which are present in seawater in only minute amounts. In the unnatural conditions of the aquarium, however, unless care is taken both pH and nitrogen levels can fluctuate, since the buffering action of the ocean is absent.

For all these reasons, successful marine fish-keeping requires frequent monitoring of conditions to detect any unwelcome trends away from the 'normal', and to head off any problems. In practice, once the tank has been properly established, this means only a few minutes' work each week.

ABOVE: *The juvenile coloration (shown here) of the Imperial or Emperor angelfish,* Pomacanthus imperator, *is totally diferent from that of the even more brightly coloured adult, shown on page 16.*

SPECIAL REQUIREMENTS FOR THE MARINE AQUARIUM

A golden rule for the marine aquarium is: *never let any metal near seawater*. As anyone with experience of boating or sea-fishing can confirm, seawater is immensely corrosive, and metals like aluminium are attacked by it immediately. Dissolved metals are extremely poisonous to nearly all forms of marine life, so it is never worth taking a chance, even with supposedly 'safe' metals like stainless steel.

ABOVE: *The Powder blue surgeon,* Acanthurus leucosternon, *requires large amounts of algae or other vegetable material in its diet.*

THE TANK

As with freshwater fish, a modern all-glass tank is ideal for marine fish, and there is no point in trying to use other types. Metal-framed aquaria are obviously too hazardous, and all-plastic tanks, although initially attractive, soon become scratched and discoloured. Remember that, the larger the tank, the more stable will be the habitat it contains. Moreover, because of their high oxygen demands, marine fish cannot tolerate any degree of crowding. Except for tiny fish, a tank of about 75×50×30cm (30×20×12in) should be the minimum, and a tank about twice this size is preferable. The tank should be deep, as marine fish do not usually live only at the surface, and spend as much time swimming vertically up and down as they do swimming along the tank.

The tank can be installed as for freshwater aquaria (see page 51). When you position it, remember that any spilled seawater will cause more damage to carpet or furnishings than tap water, so be very sure that you can fill or empty it without risk of domestic damage.

A close-fitting glass cover is essential. Not only will it prevent fish from jumping out (although marine fish are less likely to do this than freshwater fish), but — most importantly — it will reduce evaporation of the water, which would cause drastic increases in salinity.

It is obviously impossible to avoid the use of metal in the lighting hood, but great care must be taken to ensure that any condensation cannot drip back into the tank. Use of fluorescent tubes is very important, as these can provide the bright light, rich in ultraviolet, which the fish need for health, and under which their colours can best be seen. Use the largest single fluorescent tube you can fit into your lighting hood. As a rule of thumb, it is normal to allow 30 Watts per 900cm^2 (140sq in) of the tank's surface area (length × breadth). There is little harm in having too much light: it is unlikely to be more intense than that in the natural habitat of the fish, and will cause algae to grow; marine fish graze on algae,

ABOVE: *The Dwarf lion fish,* Dendrochirus brachypterus, *is the smallest of its family and spends most of its time perched on the coral.*

ABOVE: *The juvenile and adult Wrasse,* Coris gaimard, *differ so greatly that it is difficult to believe that they are the same fish. This is an adult.*

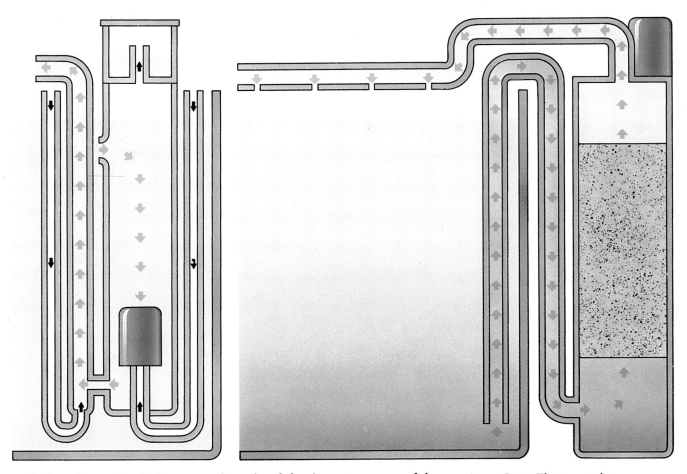

and the algae also help neutralize the fishes' toxic wastes. Most aquarists prefer to use the special horticultural tubes sold under various brand names, which not only encourage algal growth but also greatly intensify the colours of the fish.

The marine tank can be positioned where it will receive a reasonable amount of natural light (but not direct sunlight). Once again, this additional light improves growth and will not disturb the fish.

ABOVE LEFT: *The protein skimmer removes protein waste which builds up in the tank water. Bubbles from an aerator produce foam, which carries the protein with it into a reservoir at the top, where it can be removed.*

ABOVE: *The external power filter is an important device that pumps water from the tank, through a very fine and efficient filter, and back into the tank.*

FILTERING SYSTEMS

Filtration is obviously essential. There are various schools of thought among marine aquarists, and many experts have extremely powerful and expensive filters which provide absolute cleanliness without the need for 'biological' or subgravel filters. For most of us, however, these filters are the most useful and cost-effective types, and provide good and consistent results.

The biological filter is exactly like that used in the freshwater aquarium, usually consisting of a perforated or slotted plate installed beneath the gravel, with a bubble airlift which produces a powerful current down into the gravel carrying debris to be broken down by bacteria. It is important that the airlift be as powerful as possible, to create an adequate water-flow. There is a further very

important function of this type of filter in the marine aquarium, as the bacteria which develop in the gravel bed remove or detoxify the breakdown products of the fish wastes, and so maintain the 'buffer' which is so important in stabilizing water conditions.

When a biological filter is used, at least 8cm (3¼in) of gravel must cover it. This is not ordinary builders' gravel but usually coral sand, composed almost entirely of calcium carbonate and formed from the crushed skeletons of the coral animals. It may be very fine, or can be in coarsely crushed lumps of about 0.5cm (¼in). Some aquarists use crushed cockle-shells, which are local and cheaper, and work just as well. All these materials are slightly porous, and contain cavities in which the bacteria lodge, so that the gravel bed can contain many more bacteria than it would if composed of nonporous stone. The more bacteria, the more effective will be their 'buffering' action.

The only drawback to this orthodox type of filter is that large

food particles may lodge in it and produce excessive amounts of waste as they decay. For this reason, power filters are usually used in addition. The power filter is expensive, but pays for itself many times over. It usually consists of a large canister containing a polyester filter medium together with activated charcoal. On top of the canister is a powerful electric pump. The filter draws water from the tank bottom through a plastic pipe and forces it through the filter canister. All solid debris is removed, and the activated charcoal chemically breaks down some organic waste materials which are not removed by biological filters — these are the substances which cause the water in an old-established tank to become slightly yellowish. In time, bacteria become established in this filter medium, making it doubly effective. The pump is very powerful; a size should be selected which is capable of shifting all the water in the aquarium at least three times every hour.

The output from the power filter is a powerful jet which is directed at an angle beneath the water surface, so that it encourages water circulation and dislodges food particles which may have lodged in the coral.

Because the water leaving the pump is clean, it can be used in conjunction with a biological filter to prevent large particles of debris lodging in the filter bed of gravel. This is the process called 'back-filtration', where the water from the power filter is pumped down *under* the gravel and emerges into the tank through the gravel surface. This technique avoids the packing-down of gravel which occurs when a biological filter has been in use for a long while.

Other types of filter can be used, such as corner filters or outside types, as described on pages 37-40. The normal outside filters are not very practical, unless they have a tightly fitting cover, as the constant bubbling will otherwise cause rapid water evaporation, so that the filter and any items near it soon become encrusted with salt.

In addition to filters, aeration stones are usually fitted. It is scarcely possible to produce too high an oxygen level for reef fish, which also enjoy the constantly moving water.

A further, related piece of equipment is the protein skimmer (see pages 141-2).

ABOVE: *The blue spot near the tail of the Blue-faced angelfish,* Euxiphipops xanthometopon, *is possibly intended to look like an eye, and therefore confuse a predator. The rest of the fish, however, seems designed to look as conspicuous as possible, even among the bright colours of the reef.*

LEFT: *The Sea-horse,* Hippocampus kuda, *is the easiest of its family to keep, as it can eat larger pieces of food than its smaller relatives. Sea-horses are inactive, and cling to coral or sea whips for most of the time.*

ARTIFICIAL SEAWATER AND SETTING-UP

Because you will need to mix commercially prepared 'sea-salt' with large amounts of tap water, it is advisable to acquire a large, new, plastic dustbin in which the materials can be mixed. However, you will not need to do this immediately, because the process can be started in the tank.

First, calculate the volume of your tank (length × breadth × depth, in centimetres or inches, remembering that 1 litre =

1,000cm³ and 1 gal ≃ 275in³). You will then be able to purchase the appropriate amount of special salt compound. (The volume of the gravel or coral can be ignored at this stage.) Use *only* salt compounds specially prepared for aquarium use, not ordinary salt or sea-salt sold for cooking purposes.

Install the heater and thermostat, and a suitable thermometer, as described on page 32 (remember: no exposed metal parts). Fill the tank with normal cold tap water which has been allowed to run for a few minutes to remove any water which might have been contaminated with copper dissolved from the pipes. Pour the water into the tank from a plate or bowl, to avoid disturbing the gravel. The tank can be filled to within 4cm (1½in) of the top.

Switch on the heaters and air pump and, over the next 24 hours, check that the temperature has established itself at 24-26°C (75-79°F). Meanwhile, the aerator will have driven off dissolved toxic chlorine gas. Adjust the thermostat if necessary to get the temperature right. The sea-salt can now be added gradually. There will be a chart or table with the salt, giving the amounts required per litre or gallon of tap water, and you must adjust this according to the volume you have calculated. Don't put in the full amount: hold back about 10 per cent. Stir the water thoroughly as you add the salt, and leave it for another 24 hours to dissolve properly.

Now you will need a simple hydrometer, to check the salinity accurately. This is a floating device which gives a reading of the density, or specific gravity (SG), of the water. Pure water has an SG of 1.00, while the SG of natural seawater is 1.020 to 1.025, at a standard aquarium temperature of 25°C (77°F). In the aquarium, there is some benefit in keeping the SG low to discourage parasites and other disease-producing organisms, and 1.020 is about the right figure to aim for (for the more specialized needs of marine invertebrates, an SG of 1.025 is better). If you find that the SG is too low, stir in more salt gradually until you have achieved the proper level. It is easiest to make these fine adjustments if the salt is dissolved in water first and then added as a concentrated solution. If you have miscalculated and made the water too salty, remove some and replace it with fresh water until you have the correct SG.

MATURING THE TANK

Before adding the fish, there are a few essential procedures to check. To break down the waste products of the fish, a huge population of bacteria must be built up in the gravel, without allowing them to reach toxic levels. These wastes are broken down by the bacteria first into nitrites, which are highly poisonous, and then into harmless nitrates. There are two means of achieving the proper bacterial population, and with each you will need to use a nitrite test kit. This is a special dye which you add to a sample of aquarium water; nitrite levels are indicated by colour changes.

Method 1 Use a commercial maturation kit, which has fluid which is dripped into the tank in measured amounts. It contains both bacteria and nutrients. Use the nitrite test kit over a few days until nitrite levels drop from 12-15ppm (parts per million) to 0ppm. Now a few small fish can be added.

Method 2 This depends on a friendly aquarist or dealer. Add a large scoop of gravel, complete with millions of bacteria, from a well established marine tank to the new tank. Carry out the nitrite test as before.

The size of the population of nitrifying bacteria which develops depends on the amount of nutrients produced to feed them — that is, on the number of fish in the tank. It is therefore not possible to add all the fish at once: they must be introduced only a few at a time. It is sensible to add at first only small cheap fish, known to be tolerant of nitrites. *Dascyllus* are commonly recommended, but even more satisfactory are brackish-water or harbour-living fish like *Scatophagus* or *Monodactylus*, which can tolerate conditions that would kill most other marine fish.

Keep checking nitrite levels — daily for the first couple of weeks and then at weekly intervals. Increasing nitrite levels are a sign of an overpopulated tank, or of some drastic problem such as an undiscovered dead fish.

DECORATING THE TANK

Coral is the most natural material for decorating the tank, and can be bought from marine specialists. It is the limy skeletons of tiny anemone-like creatures, and although it will have been cleaned it will still contain organic matter which can foul the water very quickly. Soak all coral in a strong solution of bleach — one cupful per 5 litres (1.1gal) — and leave it for at least a week, repeating the process with fresh bleach for another week. Then soak it for several days in fresh water until all trace of the chlorine smell is removed. Only now is it clean enough for use.

Coral is usually white, and comes in many forms. There is a dark red type called organ-pipe coral, which is very useful as it can be easily cut or chipped into caves in which fish can hide, or shaped to conceal heaters. Another type grows in heavy sheets and slabs, and is pale blue. Coral of any other colour is dyed, and must not be used. Do not use sea-fans or sea-whips, which are rubbery corals which gradually break down in the tank. Stone can be used in the marine aquarium, limestone or York stone being the most useful.

You can construct a coral reef in the tank by cementing individual blocks of coral together with silicone adhesive. However, it is best to leave corals or rocks loose so that they can be shifted to allow proper cleaning of the tank. You may have other good reasons for moving the coral, such as to break up territories held by aggressive fish when you introduce new tankmates.

You can buy so-called 'living rock' — stones complete with an encrustation of living plants and animals. Unfortunately, it can only be used in a mature aquarium, where water conditions have become established. It will then be welcomed by the fish, who will very quickly chew off all traces of any edible organisms.

PROTEIN SKIMMERS AND OTHER HI-TECH EQUIPMENT

In a well established tank there is a gradual build-up of waste material which is not easily broken down by bacteria. This is in the form of albumin, a protein found in egg-white, and can be recognized when foam develops on the water surface, and the bubbles seem to

persist. This is a greasy film of protein and bacteria. The characteristics of this foam serve to help remove it. A simple device called a protein skimmer can be used occasionally. Powered by a bubble airlift, the skimmer is suspended in the tank. An aeration stone at its base produces foam, which can be removed (see page 34).

Another device used by some aquarists is an ozonizer, which generates ozone and diffuses it into the tank water. This has an antiseptic action, killing bacteria and other organisms, and also speeding the breakdown of nitrites. If used to excess, however, it will kill the beneficial bacteria in the filter bed, and, as ozone is an irritant, may damage the fish. This is an expensive device and needs to be used very carefully if it is to give good results. Some aquarists use an ozonizer instead of a biological filter.

A similar device is the ultraviolet sterilizer, which draws tank water through a powerful source of ultraviolet radiation, killing micro-organisms. This does not damage bacteria in the filter bed,

All of these beautiful, flower-like organisms are invertebrates. Most are corals or anemones; some are worms and molluscs. Unfortunately, they are not easy to keep, and many would be eaten by the fish.

but probably does not kill many disease-producing bacteria either, as they are exposed to the radiation for only a short time.

Yet another hi-tech gadget is the diatom filter, used in conjunction with a high-output power filter. It is a special filter cartridge containing a material consisting of the skeletons of Diatoms, which are microscopic marine organisms. It is so efficient that even single-celled parasites can be filtered out of the tank water, but because of its tremendous efficiency the filter medium becomes blocked very quickly, and the system needs constant maintenance.

For the average aquarist, a biological filter and an ordinary power filter are quite sufficient for effective filtration, and require the minimum of upkeep.

WATER MAINTENANCE

You should buy, as well as a nitrite test kit, a pH test kit. This is used in the same way, measuring the pH of water samples by their effects on coloured dyes. The kit will contain acid and alkaline solutions which can be used to adjust the pH to the optimum 8.0 to 8.3 level. Once the tank is properly matured, pH seldom varies much, but it may become more acidic in a long-established tank. To avoid such problems, it is sensible to change 25 per cent of the water every two months, replacing it with water (of the proper SG) prepared in your plastic dustbin.

Maintain clinically clean conditions, removing every scrap of uneaten food or debris. Algae will grow on the coral and glass, and need not be removed unless they become too unsightly. Alternatively, reduce the lighting level a little or shorten the period of artificial lighting each day.

INTRODUCING THE FISH

Initially, fish are introduced exactly as with freshwater fish (see page 42). In an established tank, newcomers will probably be attacked, so feed your old fish well and shift some of the coral around. The previous occupants will be so busy squabbling with each other over establishing new territories that they will ignore the newcomers.

Seawater has much less capacity to hold dissolved oxygen than does freshwater, so proportionately fewer fish can be kept in a given size of tank. Just how many fish can be kept in one aquarium? The traditional formulae — so many centimetres of fish per litre of water — do not work, because individual fish have different tolerances for crowding. On average, each medium-sized fish needs probably 5 to 6 litres (1.1-1.3gal) of water in a properly kept aquarium. This will not allow much scope for survival if anything goes wrong, however. In addition, you must consider the lifestyle of the fish. Generally, small territorial fish like *Dascyllus*

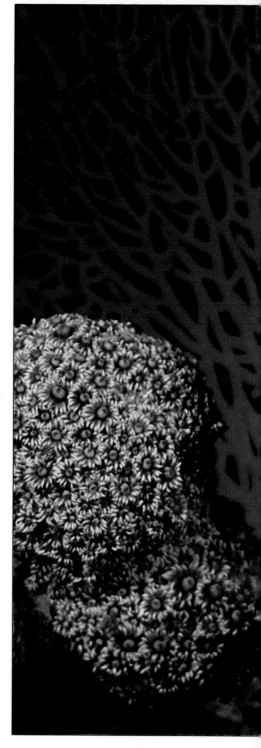

can tolerate some overcrowding, as can inactive fish like Groupers. Fast-swimming fish, however, need more space, as do nervous, highly strung fish like Butterfly fish and Surgeonfish. It is only common sense to study each fish carefully in the dealer's tank, and to find out as much as possible about it before committing yourself to buying it. Always get the dealer to demonstrate that the fish is feeding properly before you purchase, especially with temperamental fish like Butterfly fish.

ABOVE: *The Pearlscale butterfly fish,* Chaetodon chrysurus, *is typical of its group, being very beautiful, but difficult to establish and a very temperamental feeder. It is more uncommon than other Butterfly fish.*

143

INVERTEBRATES AND PLANTS IN THE MARINE AQUARIUM

It is very tempting to try to reproduce in the aquarium a living reef inhabited by a cross-section of all the available forms of life. This can be done, but in practice it is difficult — for a variety of reasons.

Living coral is available from dealers, complete with the flower-like polyps which emerge at night to feed on plankton. Many very large Sea anemones also feed on plankton, and these are frequently offered for sale. Yet another form of plankton-eater is the Tube-worm; this produces a horny tube, growing vertically up from the sand, from which the head of the worm emerges like a brightly coloured flower to sieve plankton from the water. All of these organisms are beautiful, and can be kept successfully in the aquarium. Yet it is not possible to provide the huge amounts of living plankton they require: the filtration system does an excellent job of removing plankton. They can only be fed by switching off the filters while stirring ground clam or shrimp into the water, and then switching the filters on again a little while later. However, in such conditions sooner or later water fouling is inevitable. The only truly successful way to keep these creatures is in a separate invertebrate tank, with only minimal filtration, and where there are no fish to attack the vulnerable invertebrates. Corals are an exception, and many types subsist on nutrients produced by algae living within their tissues. All they demand is very strong light, sufficient to keep the algae healthy.

A few large anemones are available which feed on chunks of meat or fish, just as do those in our rockpools. These are generally tougher and easy to feed, and, since they have stinging cells on their tentacles, most fish leave them well alone.

Molluscs of several types are available. Scallops and their relatives are bivalves (they have two shells joined by a hinge), and most swim by clapping their two shells together, lying on the surface of the gravel most of the time. They are filter-feeders, and are as difficult to feed as the other creatures we have just described.

Various other molluscs, such as Sea snails and Sea slugs, are similar to their terrestrial relatives but often very beautifully coloured. Some can be kept easily, feeding on lettuce or on pieces of fish, but most have very specialized diets. The Octopus is also a mollusc, but is very delicate and difficult to establish, and has an astonishing ability to climb out of the most tightly covered tank. Even a large Octopus can force itself through a 1cm (½in) gap!

The Crustacea are the most practical invertebrates for the aquarium; they include Shrimps, Lobsters and Crabs. Some are

ABOVE: *Fan worms live in leathery tubes, and extend their long, waving tentacles to sift plankton from the water. They retract swiftly into the tube, if disturbed.*

ABOVE: *Shrimps are the most practical invertebrates to keep, since they are relatively hardy, and also easy to feed. They may be eaten by large fish, however.*

ABOVE: *Clownfish thrive if kept with large anemones, in which they normally live. The anemones must be checked carefully every day, as they foul the water quickly if they die.*

ABOVE: *Long-tentacled anemones, though decorative, can catch and eat small fish; they should, therefore, be used with caution in the average marine tank.*

quite tough enough to live in a tank with fish — some will eat the fish! Most interesting of all are the Cleaner shrimps, which are of various brilliant colours and are highly territorial. They establish a 'shop', which fish visit to have the Shrimps clean parasites and dead tissue from their surfaces, and even from the insides of their mouths and gills. Cleaner shrimps are seldom eaten — even by very large fish which normally eat other Shrimps and their relatives.

Hermit crabs are amusing and bold invertebrates for the tank. They need a good supply of spare shells into which they can climb as they grow.

Yet another class of invertebrates are the Echinoderms, including Sea urchins, Sea cucumbers, and Brittle stars, All are scavengers, and all are difficult to keep for any length of time. They share with other invertebrates a tendency to disintegrate: they foul the tank very rapidly should they die.

Probably the biggest difficulty with invertebrates is their sensitivity to compounds containing copper, the basis of many drugs used to treat the most common infections of fish. This poses a problem if disease breaks out in a tank where invertebrates and fish are being kept together.

Algae grow copiously in marine aquaria. Most are encrusting types, forming a film over the glass and coral, and these are grazed eagerly by the fish. The larger tropical algae, popularly known as seaweed, can also be kept in the marine aquarium, but are not easy to maintain. There are several attractive types, notably *Penicillus* or Merman's shaving brush, which is best described by its popular name; *Ulva*, which grows in lettuce-like sheets; and *Caulerpa*, which resembles British seaweed in shape. All are dark green in colour, although there are also some red algae. The main problem with algae is that they do not survive chilling or even being lifted out of the water. This is because they have no solid framework, and their cells are easily ruptured. If a damaged alga is placed in the tank the ruptured cells decay very rapidly. If you can obtain algae in good condition, and give them sufficient light, they will grow very rapidly, spreading by means of runners across the gravel surface. They perform a very useful function in using up the waste products of the fish, but are something of a timebomb, waiting to go off as soon as something goes wrong with water conditions in the tank, and decaying with frightening speed. They are best avoided, except by the expert who has spare tanks available in case of emergency.

FOODS AND FEEDING

Unless you have purchased particularly temperamental fish, food and feeding are seldom a problem in the marine aquarium. Most marine fish eat anything that looks remotely edible. There are some picky and specialized feeders, notably among the Butterfly fish, and their requirements are discussed under the relevant species names in the Directory.

There is a seemingly endless list of suitable food for marine fish. Here are some of the most useful.

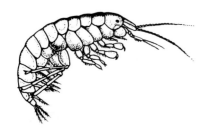

Brine shrimp

Brine shrimps are the universal food, usually given as freeze-dried or deep-frozen shrimps, and eaten greedily by most fish. For small and picky eaters, like Seahorses, it is necessary to raise live Brine shrimps; while this is easy it is also time-consuming. Culture instructions for Brine shrimps are given on page 68.

Dried foods are available, containing all the nutrients needed by fish. They are particularly relished by omnivorous or herbivorous fish, but are seldom consumed by fish which normally feed on live foods.

Fish, shrimp, crabmeat, earthworms and many other meaty materials will be eaten by most fish. Large chunks of fish or meat should be suspended on a thread and the uneaten parts removed after feeding. Frozen shrimp-tails are particularly useful, as are Scallops, which should be chopped finely before use. Fish will eat any dead organism they can find, so it is worth experimenting with small amounts of any promising material.

Shrimps are sometimes available live from dealers, and these are eaten eagerly by larger fish. They can, however, introduce infection, especially worm parasites, and many aquarists prefer not to take a chance. Freeze-dried shrimps are also available, and are perfectly safe.

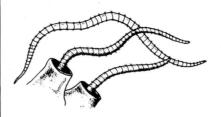

Tubifex

Tubifex is relished by most fish, but should never be given fresh, as the bacteria it contains will cause problems. The freeze-dried form is well accepted.

Vegetable material is an important part of the diet of many fish. Any vegetable matter offered should be chopped finely, and any uneaten excess removed quickly. Suitable vegetable foods include lettuce, spinach, many freshwater plants and well soaked oatmeal. This type of food is essential for the health of Surgeon-fish and many others.

GENERAL POINTS

Give your fish as much variety as possible in their diet. They can soon become so dependent on one type of food that they will starve rather than take any alternative, and this can be a particular problem with 'seasonal' foods. In addition, a varied diet is more healthy and will ensure that the fish get all the nutrients they need, including trace elements and vitamins that may not be present in a single type of food source.

Newly caught fish are often reluctant to feed, but most can be tempted with live Brine shrimps. Large predatory fish like Groupers normally feed only on live fish and Crustacea, and may be very reluctant to take dead foods. They can usually be tempted if you tie a shelled shrimp loosely to a thread and jiggle it realistically in front of the fish's lair. Usually, once they have got used to the idea, these formerly reluctant eaters will churn around eagerly on the surface at the first hint of feeding-time.

The key to healthy feeding for marine fish is 'little and often'. Be very careful not to let pieces of fish and shrimps drift away under rocks or cracks in the coral, where they cannot be reached by your specimens, as they will rapidly cause fouling of the water.

DISEASES

Marine fish are just as prone to infection as other animals, and in a marine environment treatment can pose some special problems. In recent years, antibiotics have become freely available to treat many infectious diseases of marine fish. Most are very effective, but remember: they kill *all* bacteria, even those in the gravel bed responsible for detoxifying nitrogenous wastes. The death of these causes almost immediate breakdown in the tank ecology. Treatment with antibiotics or most other drugs must therefore take place in a special hospital tank, bare of gravel. This poses its own problems, as the water must be changed frequently to prevent the build-up of toxic wastes. Here is one of the few real applications of ozonizers, which can perform the task usually carried out by the bacteria in the biological filter. Most drugs must be used at near-toxic levels to achieve proper control of disease, and it is absolutely essential to follow the directions religiously, especially when mixing up the drug.

The following are the most common diseases that affect marine tropical fish.

Bacterial diseases. Outbreaks of these usually follow some stress or injury. They may show up in a variety of ways, usually as red sores or swellings on fins and body. Bacterial diseases are easily controlled with broad-spectrum antibiotics.

Fungal diseases. These seldom affect marine fish, but those causing cotton-wool-like growths can be controlled by drugs containing copper (toxic to invertebrates). Internal fungal infections may occur, and these are not treatable. Infected fish are best destroyed.

Lymphocystis. A viral disease which causes large cancer-like growths, usually on the fin. It cannot be treated, but the affected part of the fin can be cut away with sharp scissors and the remaining stump painted with acri-

White spot

flavine solution to sterilize it. The fin will usually regenerate slowly.

Oodinium. The most common infection of all, oodinium covers fish with tiny yellowish to grey speckles that eventually form a film over the whole body. It also attacks the gills, and it is this which causes the most damage. The first signs of infection are often rapid and exaggerated gill movements as the fish breathes. The *Oodinium* organism is probably already present in many tanks, and breaks out as a disease only when fish are weakened or stressed in some way. It is sensible to quarantine new fish and to dose them

Popeye

with a proprietary oodinium treatment before introducing them to the community tank.

Popeye. Bulging eyes are common in certain types of fish, such as Clownfish, Triggerfish and Groupers. The condition is symptomatic of other disorders, and often clears up spontaneously. Popeye often responds to a partial change of water.

Swim-bladder problems. These cause affected fish to float helplessly or sink to the bottom. Swim-bladder problems are symptoms of disease rather than diseases in their own right, and may clear up if the underlying conditions can be cured. If not, the fish should be destroyed.

White spot. A disease caused by a parasite related to that causing *Ichthyphthirius* disease in freshwater specimens, and producing similar white cysts over the fish. It is fairly easy to treat, using the drugs used to control oodinium.

DIRECTORY OF MARINE FISH GROUPS

The symbols at the head of each entry are as used in the Freshwater Directory (see page 72) although, for obvious reasons, no temperature ranges are given.

BUTTERFLY FISH

The Butterfly fish, the Chaetodontidae family, are typical reef dwellers of tropical seas. All are comparatively large fish, with deep flattened bodies. They have spiny dorsal fins which are used in self-defence, but they are seldom really aggressive except with members of their own species, with whom they squabble over territories. Most have a small beak-like mouth adapted to picking food out of the crevices in coral and between stones. Some have a very highly specialized diet, grazing on specific types of coral polyps, and are very difficult to feed in captivity. Most Butterfly fish are peaceful community fish requiring temperatures of about 27°C (81°F) and a salinity of at least SG 1.025 (that is, a higher temperature and salinity than normal). Very

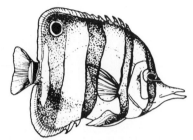

Butterfly fish, showing dorsal spines.

small specimens are extremely delicate, and it is best to purchase large ones, although even these cannot be regarded as hardy. They are, however, very bold, and are always active. Give plenty of vegetable material as well as the usual live or freeze-dried foods, and watch to make sure that they get their fair share of the food. They can only cope with finely chopped food or small live foods. Butterfly fish have not been bred in captivity.

Chaetodon spp.

There are many species of *Chaetodon* offered for sale. Most are difficult to feed and short-lived in the aquarium.

Purchase only those species which you know to be relatively hardy.

C. auriga (Threadfin butterfly fish, or Golden butterfly fish) is a very common Butterfly fish from the Indian and Pacific Oceans, growing to 22cm (8²/₃in) or more. Hardy for its type, it is ideal for the beginner. The body is typical of the group, being flattened and disc-like with a pointed snout. The front part is pearly grey, the rear part brilliant orange-yellow. The dorsal fin is prolonged into a point, and has a conspicuous black spot and a black edge; a black line runs from the beginning of the dorsal fin down through the eye. Two sets of purplish lines intersect at an angle around the centre of the body. This fish is relatively greedy, enjoying Brine shrimps and most proprietary flake foods.

C. bennetti (Bennett's butterfly fish) is a typical Butterfly fish from the Indo-Pacific; it grows to 15cm (6in). Its disc-like body is almost exactly round, with a shorter snout than most fish of the genus. The body and fins are bright yellow, with a black line running vertically through the eye. Two metallic blue lines run diagonally from the gills towards the anal fin, and there is a very large black 'eye spot' on the flanks, ringed by blue. This is a very active fish, but a picky eater.

Chaetodon chrysurus

C. chrysurus (Pearl-scale butterfly fish) is an uncommon but very beautiful fish from the Indo-Pacific region, growing to 15cm (6in). It is more elongated than most Butterfly fish, and very distinctively coloured.

Chaetodon auriga

Chaetodon collare

The large scales are pearly, edged with dark blue. There is a dark vertical stripe through the eye; the rear of the body, including parts of the dorsal and anal fins and the tail, are bright orange, edged with dark blue. A broad white stripe crosses the base of the tail. The dorsal fin has conspicuous yellow spiky rays. These fish are uncommon even in their native habitat, and are consequently expensive. Unlike many Butterfly fish, they live peaceably in pairs.

C. collare (Pakistan butterfly fish) is a 16cm (6¾in) species, common around the eastern part of the Indian Ocean and Sri Lanka. It is robust and fairly easy to acclimatize to captivity. The body is of typical shape, and is a rich chocolate-brown, with each scale having a golden centre. The head is boldly marked in black and white, and the dorsal and anal fins are fringed with purplish-red. The tail is red, with a blue edge and a transparent tip. The broad white stripe across the head is the most distinctive feature. Relatively hardy, but aggressive with its own and related species.

C. ephippium (Saddle butterfly fish, or Black-back butterfly fish) grows to 20cm (7¾in) or even more in a large tank, and comes from the Indo-Pacific region. It has a long pointed snout, but is otherwise typical of its genus. The body is pearly beige with a yellow throat and belly and a fine black stripe through the eye. There is a very large black saddle-like patch, bordered in white, covering the upper rear part of the body and rear of the dorsal fin. The rims of the dorsal and anal fins are bright yellow, edged with black. This fish is peaceful but temperamental, and often hard to persuade to feed properly. It requires large amounts of vegetable food.

Chaetodon ephippium

Chelmon rostratus

A beautiful and distinctive fish from the Indo-Pacific, growing to 17cm (6¾in). It is aggressively territorial, and can destroy invertebrates like Tube-worms. The snout is very long and tubular, enabling the fish to pick food out of cracks in the coral. The body is distinctively coloured: brilliant silver with four conspicuous vertical orange stripes edged with black. There is a large black 'eye spot' on the upper hind part of the body, and the dorsal and anal fins are fringed with orange at the rear. Though difficult to acclimatize — it may need tempting with live Brine shrimp — it will usually, once acclimatized, eat dried food, and may take food from the fingers.

Chelmon rostratus

Forcipiger flavissimus
(Yellow long-nosed butterfly fish)

Most distinctive of all the group, with a comically long snout, this fish comes from the Red Sea and Indo-Pacific, growing to 18cm (7in). The body's brilliant chrome-yellow extends over the dorsal and anal fins. The upper part of the head is dusky black; the lower portion and throat are white. The tail is transparent, and there is a large black spot near the rear edge of the anal fin. The large spines of the dorsal fin are carried stiffly erect. This fish is quite hardy once acclimatized and feeding well. It cannot cope with large foods, but will pick away at almost anything offered. Not to be trusted with any but hard-shelled invertebrates.

Forcipiger flavissimus

Heniochus acuminatus
(Wimple fish; Poor man's Moorish idol)

Toughest of all Butterfly fish, despite its exotic shape, this comes from the Indo-Pacific. It grows to 25cm (9¾in), and is an active shoaling fish which wanders away from the reefs into open waters. The body is typical, but the front part of the dorsal fin is enormously extended and swept back in a scimitar-shape. The colour is pearly-white, with two broad and conspicuous vertical black bands; the rear of the dorsal fin and the tail are bright yellow. It is a greedy feeder, and is unusual in living peacefully with other fish of the same species. Do not keep it with fin-nippers; they often damage the flowing tip of the dorsal fin.

WRASSE

The Wrasse or Labridae family is a very large group containing at least 600 species. All have characteristically elongated and muscular bodies and propel themselves by a rowing action of the pectoral fins; the tail is used for steering.

Wrasse diving beneath gravel.

They have very sharp, powerful teeth, and make short work of invertebrates like Shrimps and molluscs. The smaller species bury themselves in the sand at night; if kept in tanks with a coarse gravel bed, so that they are unable to do this, they will not thrive. Newly introduced fish may hide for several days beneath the sand. Some large Wrasse have the disconcerting habit of sleeping, lying flat on their sides on the tank bottom. A few secrete every night a mucous coat which completely covers the body. They are omnivorous and are greedy feeders, often churning up the gravel while seeking food. Many build

Heniochus acuminatus

Bodianus pulchellus

nests, and the males brood the young; they are not known to breed in captivity.

Wrasse are generally hardy and long-lived, though very nervous for the first few days in a new tank, and at this time they should be disturbed as little as possible.

Bodianus spp.

B. pulchellus (Cuban hogfish), a beautiful and very hardy fish from the Caribbean, comes from deep waters — about 20m (66ft) — and is therefore both scarce and expensive. This is a pity, as it is one of the best marine tropicals available. It grows to about 20cm (7¾in), and is unusual in being a brilliant pink. A white streak on the throat extends back along the flanks. The rear of the flowing dorsal fin and the upper part of the tail are bright lemon-yellow. Fairly peaceful if kept with similar-sized tank-mates, this fish eats most things, although initially it may need to be tempted with more exotic foods, such as fresh Squid or roe.

B. rufus (Spanish hogfish) is potentially a very large fish, up to 60cm (2ft), but remains much smaller in the aquarium. From the Caribbean, it is a deepwater fish. The young are particularly brightly coloured; the upper front two-thirds of the body is a magnificent purplish-red, and the rest of the body and the fins are bright yellow. These colours fade to a purplish-brown in large fish. Like *B. pulchellus*, this fish is a cleaner while young, removing parasites from larger fish. It is a clumsy, blundering swimmer.

Coris spp.

C. angulata (Two-spot wrasse) is scarce but beautiful. From the Red Sea and the East African Coast, it grows to over 1m (3ft 3in), but is usually much smaller. As with many Wrasse, the juvenile colouring is entirely different from that of the adults, which are dark green. The young are pearly white, the front of the body being dotted with black spots. The fins are marbled in black, and the dorsal fin has two large black 'eye spots'. On each side, near the back, are two very large

Bodianus rufus

brilliant orange-red spots — hence the fish's popular name. As the fish ages, a fleshy lump develops on the forehead. This fish is very likely to dive beneath the sand when scared.

C. gaimard (Clown wrasse or Red wrasse) is a medium-sized Wrasse from the Indian Ocean; it grows to about 40cm (15¾in) and goes through very drastic colour changes as it does so. The juvenile colouring is bright orange with wedge-shaped white bars, edged with black, and a white tail. As the fish reaches 10cm (4in) or so, the black areas increase in size until, in adults, the body is dark bluish-purple, covered in pale blue dots, with a yellow tail. The head is covered with blue wavy lines. This fish is very nervous, and may die from shock on being moved to a new tank unless special

Coris angulata

precautions are taken: cover the tank and keep it in darkness for at least 24 hours to give the fish a chance to get used to its new home. It will often dive under the sand when scared.

Coris gaimard

Gomphosus coeruleus
(Beakfish; Birdmouth wrasse)

An odd elongated fish from the Indo-Pacific, this has a prolonged snout like a bird's beak. It grows to 30cm (11¾in) and is a magnificent blue-green with an iridescent speckle on each scale and a yellow tip to the tail. It is a very speedy, active fish, needing plenty of room, and is extremely hardy. When small it is a cleaner fish.

Gomphosus coeruleus

colour varies wildly during growth. Adult males have a metallic blue head, followed in order by a black stripe, white stripe and another black stripe, with the rear half of the body bright yellow-green. Females are less colourful. Young fish act

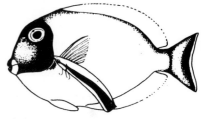

Labroides dimidiatus, *cleaning the gills of a Grouper.*

as cleaners. This species is very active, and is sensitive to changes in water chemistry: it benefits from frequent changes of part of the tank water, and will not tolerate measurable levels of nitrites.

T. lunare (Moon wrasse or Lyretail wrasse) is a very active fish from the Indo-Pacific and Red Sea, growing to 30cm (11¾in). It is a brilliant blue-green, with a purplish head which has numerous pink wavy lines. Each scale has a distinct red mark. The tail is green, with a large yellow central patch, and the dorsal and anal fins are marked with blue and yellow. It is hardy, resists most diseases, and retains its brilliant colouring into maturity. It swims very quickly, and is difficult to catch in a net.

Labroides dimidiatus
(Cleaner wrasse; Blue streak)

A small Wrasse, with numerous sub-species, from the Indo-Pacific and Red Sea, this grows to 10cm (4in). Juveniles are blue with a dark stripe, and adults white with a conspicuous lengthways black stripe and a brown back. A narrow black stripe runs from the anal fin to the tail. Very elongated and slim, this fish is a very effective cleaner, and may pester large, slow-moving fish like Boxfish. It is rather delicate and difficult to acclimatize, and will not tolerate freshly made-up 'seawater' or water with any trace of nitrites.

Labroides dimidiatus

L. quadrilineatus (Four-lined wrasse) is extremely similar and grows to about 15cm (6in). Found in the Red Sea, it is sooty or dark blue, with two bright blue lengthways stripes. The tail has a white edge. Hardier than *L. dimidiatus*, it eats dried foods readily.

Thalassoma spp.

T. bifasciatum (Bluehead) is a slim wrasse from the Caribbean and tropical Atlantic, growing to 15cm (6in). Its

Labroides quadrilineatus

Thalassoma bifasciatum

Thalassoma lunare

T. parvo (Peacock wrasse) is very similar to *T. lunare*; it is found in the tropical Eastern Atlantic and the Mediterranean. The body is light metallic green, crossed by broad orange-and-blue stripes. The head is pink and blue, and the dorsal and anal fins are metallic blue. The lyre-shaped tail is marked in red and blue. Many colour variations occur, depending on the source of the fish. As would be expected from its northerly habitat, this Wrasse tolerates

Thalassoma parvo

lower than usual temperatures — 18-22°C (64-72°F). It is hardy and peaceful, but cannot withstand high nitrite levels.

DAMSELFISH

These fish are members of the important Pomacentridae family; the other major members are the Clownfish. Damselfish are extremely popular — and rightly so: they are very cheap and extremely hardy. In a way, they are the marine equivalent of the Guppy: ideal for the budding marine aquarist. They eat almost anything, and are small even when fully grown, tolerating a reasonable amount of overcrowding. Because they are quite tolerant of nitrites in the water, they are often used as part of the conditioning process for a newly set-up aquarium, providing the nitrogenous wastes on which the bacteria in the gravel bed will feed.

They are among a select few marine fish which are regularly bred in the aquarium, and many generations of some of the more common species have been tank-raised. Breeding is exactly as for Cichlids (see page 105). It is difficult to rear the young, which are generally too small to take the usual live foods.

There is one major disadvantage with these apparently exemplary fish: they are extremely territorial and aggressive, especially to fish newly introduced to the tank. It is essential to break up the terri-tory by shifting rocks and coral to give new fish a chance. Unfortunately, some adult Damselfish are too aggressive to be kept with any other fish. The classification of this group of fish is doubtful, and they may be sold under several different names. In general, however, their habits are similar.

Abudefduf assimilis
(Blue devil; Blue damsel)

This brilliantly coloured little fish comes from the western Pacific and Philippine region, and grows to about 8cm (3¼in). It is a brilliant blue and, unusually, adults are as brightly coloured as the juveniles. In males the colour is more intense, and the tail and anal fins are dotted with black. Best kept in a small shoal, where they will concentrate on squabbling with each other rather than with their tank-mates. Unfortunately, the name 'Blue devil' is apt: they have a nasty disposition. On the credit side, they are always cheap and readily available.

Abudefduf assimilis

Abudefduf oxyodon
(Black neon damsel; Emerald perch)

This beautiful fish from the Indo-Pacific grows to 11cm (4⅓in). It is a deep velvety blue, with a transverse yellowish white bar across the middle of the body. The head is crossed by diagonal metallic blue lines, and there are further lines in the dorsal fin. These colours fade as the fish matures. A solitary and uncommon fish, *A. oxyodon* is always expensive. It will not tolerate similar Damselfish in a community tank and is more sensitive to water conditions than most of this group.

Abudefduf oxyodon

Abudefduf saxatilis
(Sergeant major)

An extremely common and very hardy fish found almost worldwide in tropical regions, this grows to 16cm (6⅓in) and is attractively but not brightly coloured: white below, and yellowish over the rest of the body, with five bold vertical black bars. These fish are extremely aggressive, which is a pity as they are very easy to keep and spawn regularly in the aquarium. During breeding, the male turns deep blue.

Abudefduf saxatilis

Chromis spp.

17-21°C (63-70°F).
C. caeruleus (Blue-green chromis) is a pretty, brilliant blue-green fish from the Indo-Pacific and Red Sea and grows to 10cm (4in). It is fairly peaceful, and a very active fish. It should be kept in a shoal, and will swim relatively near the surface, preferring to stay in the current from a filter or aerator. It feeds well on dried foods, and will not usually bother invertebrates. It is thought to spawn in masses of filamentous algae, with the male guarding the eggs, but this has not been achieved in the aquarium.

Damselfish spawning on a rock.

C. chromis (Blue damselfish or Brown forktail) is a very common Mediterranean and Atlantic fish, growing to 12cm (4¾in) and found in huge shoals. The juveniles are an intense blue, but above 2.5cm (1in) they become golden-brown, with darker-edged scales. There is a white patch on the tail, making it appear very deeply forked. These fish must be kept in a small shoal. They are known to breed in Cichlid fashion, but this has not been achieved in the aquarium. Very peaceful, they prefer cooler temperatures than truly tropical fish.

Dascyllus spp.

D. aruanus (Humbug damsel) are attractive but extremely aggressive 8cm (3¼in) fish from the Indo-Pacific. They are highly territorial, and a small group

Chromis caeruleus

154

will quickly stake out the whole tank, making the life of other fish a misery. The very deep body is white, crossed by three very bold black bars; the tail is white. Females have a white spot on the forehead.

Dascyllus aruanus

D. melanurus is exactly the same, but has a black tail. It breeds easily in the aquarium, and the young may live in Sea anemones, as with Clownfish.

D. carneus (Dusky damsel or White-tailed damsel) is an 8cm (3¼in) fish from the Indian Ocean. It is not brightly coloured. The body is greyish with a violet sheen and two indistinct vertical dark bars. There is a large white spot on the shoulder, which fades if the fish is not thriving. Aggressive, this fish is best kept singly.

Dascyllus trimaculatus

D. trimaculatus (Domino damselfish or Three-spot damselfish) is the most rotund Damselfish. It comes from the Indo-Pacific and Red Sea, and is always available cheaply, being regularly tank-bred. It grows to 12cm (4¾in) or a little more. Juveniles are velvety black with one conspicuous white spot on the top of the head and one on each flank. The black fades to grey as the fish matures. This fish is very bold and tame, but highly aggressive with other fish. It breeds very easily.

Calloplesiops altivelis

GROUPERS

The Groupers are a family of large fish, the Serranidae, found in temperate and tropical waters. Many are vast and quite tame. In the aquarium, most are sedentary, hiding for most of the time but rushing out occasionally to engulf food with their huge mouths. Only a few are small enough to keep in the aquarium; they are very peaceful and do not bother fish too large to swallow. They are generally very hardy and tolerant of poor conditions. All Groupers have a stocky, very powerful body with spiny fins, and tend to wedge themselves immovably into caves in the coral when frightened. Due to their size, they have not been bred in the aquarium. All will feed on strips of fish or meat, once they have been acclimatized to this type of 'artificial' diet, although they prefer live fish and shrimps.

Calloplesiops altivelis
(Comet grouper; Blue-spotted longfin)

This lovely fish from the Indo-Pacific grows to 20cm (7¾in). It has a short, stocky, dark-brown body, and very large, flowing dorsal and anal fins and tail. The pelvic fins are long and pointed. The body and fins are peppered with small sky-blue spots, and on the rear of the dorsal fin is a black 'eye spot' edged with white and yellow. Shy at first, this fish becomes very bold and will feed from the fingers. The huge fins are often spread stiffly, like those of the Siamese fighting fish.

Grouper feeding, showing large, extendable mouth.

Cephalopholis miniatus

Chromileptis altivelis

Cephalopholis miniatus
(Jewel bass)

From the Indo-Pacific region, this fish grows to 30cm (11¾in) or more, and is very secretive — a pity, because it is brilliantly coloured. It is bright orange-red and covered with small metallic blue spots. It has a huge mouth and can swallow fish up to half its own size.

Chromileptis altivelis
(Pantherfish; Polka-dot grouper)

Probably the best known Grouper, this fish of the Indo-Pacific grows to 50cm (20in), but is usually smaller. It is more elongated than most of the family, and has a noticeably smaller head. The fins are large and spreading. The body is a pale pinkish grey, and both fins and body are covered with large round black spots; these are proportionately larger on young fish, but are still present on adults. It is not very aggressive, and has a comparatively small mouth. Unlike most of its relatives, it spends the majority of its time in open water, swimming very gracefully and becoming extremely tame. It is very hardy.

Gramma loreto
(Royal gramma; Fairy basslet)

This fish from the Caribbean is not in fact a Grouper, but is closely related. It grows to only 6cm (2⅓in), and is among the most brightly coloured of all fish. The front half of the body is vivid violet, and the rear bright orange-yellow. There is a large black spot on the dorsal fin. A shy, solitary fish found in fairly deep water, it is consequently quite expensive. It has the odd habit of keeping its belly against any nearby surface, and so is often found swimming upside-down near the roof of a cave in the coral. Although shy, it is territorial with its own species. It occasionally spawns in the aquarium, constructing a nest with pieces of coral and algae. The fry have proved very difficult to rear. *G. loreto* does not tolerate acid water or nitrite contamination. A picky feeder, it may go

Gramma loreto

hungry in a tank with greedy fish. It is highly recommended, provided it is well cared for.

Grammistes sexlineatus
(Six-lined grouper; Gold-stripe grouper)

From the Indo-Pacific, this Grouper grows to 25cm (9¾in). It has a very stocky body and an extremely large mouth; it can swallow fish nearly as large as itself. The body is dark-brown with several lengthways yellow stripes, the number of which increases as the fish grows. Extremely hardy and long-lived, it has one serious drawback: when frightened it produces poisonous mucus which kills not only tankmates but the Grouper itself, and it should not, therefore, be pursued around the tank with a net but persuaded to enter it more peacefully. These fish become very tame, but must be trusted only with larger fish.

Grammistes sexlineatus

ANGELFISH

The Angelfish, or Pomacanthinae, form a subfamily of the Chaetodontidae, to which belong the Butterfly fish; there are many similarities. Angelfish differ mainly in being thicker-bodied and having a sharp spine on the lower edge of the gill cover. Most are large and magnificently coloured, and they are very strongly territorial, being particularly aggressive towards members of their own species. They are very active and bold, but require adequate hiding

Centropyge argi

places behind the coral in order to feel secure. More than most marine fish, they need a highly varied diet with a large proportion of vegetable matter, but many are reluctant to start feeding and even large Angelfish can be driven away from food by smaller but greedier tankmates. They are characterized by a very marked variation in juvenile and adult colouring, which in the past has led to juveniles and adults being classified as two different species. They are intolerant of poor water conditions and not always hardy, so they are expensive.

Centropyge spp.

C. argi (Cherubfish or Pygmy angel) comes from the Caribbean and tropical West Atlantic, and grows to only 8cm (3¼in). It has a beautiful violet or indigo body, with the head and forward part of the belly a bright chrome-yellow, and has a thin blue line around the eye. This fish is much hardier than other Angelfish, but is rather shy and easily bullied. It is generally very peaceful, and usually expensive.

C. bispinosus (Dusky angelfish) is another dwarf Angelfish. From the Indo-Pacific, it grows to 12cm (4¾in). It has a violet body flushed with magenta below and with dull orange vertical stripes on the sides. The fins are fringed with a thin blue line. It is fairly hardy and easy to sex, as males have more orange on their flanks. It may be possible to keep them as a pair.

C. fisheri (Flame-back angel or Fireball) is one of the prettiest Angelfish; it comes from the Indian Ocean and grows to only 8cm (3¼in). It has blue-grey sides and anal fin, while the head, back, dorsal fin and tail are all coloured brilliant orange-gold. There is a conspicuous black edge on the rear of the dorsal fin and on the top and bottom of the tail. This fish is very hardy and peaceful, except with its own species.

Holacanthus tricolor

Holacanthus tricolor
(Rock beauty)

This boldly coloured fish from the Caribbean and Western Atlantic grows to 45cm (17¾in). The body is bright yellow, and in young fish there is a bold black spot on the dorsal fin; as the fish grows this gradually spreads to cover the whole of the sides, leaving a yellow fringe to the dorsal and anal fins. With maturity, trailing points develop on the dorsal and anal fins. This fish is rather shy and delicate, but may fight other tankmates.

Holacanthus trimaculatus
(Three-spot angelfish)

A medium-sized Angelfish from the Indo-Pacific, growing to 20cm (7¾in), this is golden-yellow with a blue snout and a conspicuous black-and-white anal fin. There is a dark spot on each side behind the gills, and a single spot on the nape, above the eyes. This fish eats large amounts of plant foods.

Holacanthus trimaculatus

Pomacanthus annularis

Pomacanthus spp.

P. annularis (Blue-ringed angelfish) is a large species from the Indo-Pacific, growing to 35cm (13¾in). It is golden-brown with an orange-tipped white tail. Several wavy blue lines cross the sides and head diagonally, and there is a conspicuous blue ring on the shoulder — hence the popular name. In adults the dorsal fin carries a long trailing point. This Angelfish is relatively hardy, and easy to raise from the blue-and-white-striped juveniles.

Pomacanthus imperator

P. imperator (Emperor angelfish), probably the most spectacular member of the genus, comes from the Indo-Pacific, and grows to nearly 40cm (15¾in). Adults are bright blue, with many bright yellow lengthways stripes. The head and the edge of the dorsal are yellow, as is the tail. The belly is dusky. There is a conspicuous blue-edged black mask across the eyes and forehead, and a similarly coloured patch on the shoulder. Juveniles are patterned with concentric circles of dark blue and white. This species is very intolerant of nitrites and poor water conditions, which can result in large parts of the skin sloughing off.

Pomacanthus paru

Details of Angelfish, showing spine on gill cover.

P. paru (French angelfish), from the Atlantic, grows to about 14 inches. It is kept for the beauty of the juveniles, which are black with conspicuous vertical yellow stripes and a bright red eye. The colour fades in adults, each scale being black with a yellow edge to produce a net-like pattern. Adults have long trailing dorsal and anal fins. This is the hardiest Angelfish, and is not too aggressive.

Pygoplites diacanthus
(Regal angelfish)

A very boldly coloured fish from the Indo-Pacific, growing to 25cm (9¾in). In adults, the body is orange-yellow, crossed by nine pale blue vertical bands edged with black. The anal fin is striped in blue and orange, and the tail is bright yellow. It is difficult to acclimatize but, once established, is quite hardy. Unfortunately, it is a very aggressive fish.

CLOWNFISH

Clownfish resemble Damselfish, their fellow-members of the Pomacentridae family, in being generally plump, active fish with spiny dorsal fins. They are mostly brightly coloured, and are very popular in the aquarium. They are notable for their habit of living in symbiosis with very large Sea anemones of the Stoichactinidae family; these normally feed on small fish and invertebrates, but Clownfishes are able to live among their tentacles without damage, protected from predators by the stinging cells: the fish incorporate some of the anemone's slime into the mucus covering their scales, so that the anemone does not recognize them as potential prey. The anemones are thought to benefit from this arrangement by feeding on food particles dropped by the Clownfish. Some

Pygoplites diacanthus

species, such as *Amphiprion akallopisos*, do not fare well away from the anemones, but others seem to thrive alone.

Clownfish are not tolerant of poor water conditions, and appreciate frequent water changes. They are particularly prone to *Oodinium* infections. They breed easily in captivity, depositing up to 200 large eggs at the base of their anemone home. These hatch into large fry, which are at first a problem to feed, because they are nevertheless too small to eat newly hatched Brine shrimp. They may take specially prepared dried foods, but really require living plankton — difficult to provide unless you live near the sea.

Clownfish will inhabit anemones of the genera *Discosoma*, *Stoicactis* and *Radianthus*, which require very strong lighting and must be fed separately with chunks of Shrimp or fish. The anemones come in various colours, and great care must be taken to purchase only obviously healthy specimens. Frequent water changes are necessary.

Amphiprion akallopisos
(Orange skunk clown)

This Clownfish from the Indo-Pacific grow to 8cm (3¼in) and is highly dependent on its anemone host. It is orange-gold with a conspicuous white stripe along the back from the nose to the tail. A very peaceful fish, it seldom emerges from the cover of its anemone except to feed.

Amphiprion frenatus
(Tomato clown)

A hardy and popular Clownfish from the Indo-Pacific, growing to 10cm (4in), this fish is bright red with a conspicuous black-edged white stripe behind the eye. In young fish there is a similar stripe across the flanks, but this fades with age. In adults the rear part of the body becomes sooty. Not very dependent on its anemone host, this fish can be kept independently — preferably in a small shoal. It breeds very easily and is ideal for the beginning aquarist.

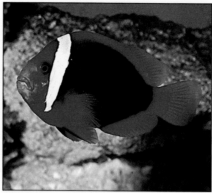

Amphiprion frenatus

Amphiprion percula
(Common clownfish)

The most commonly imported Clownfish, this comes from the Indo-Pacific and grows to 8cm (3¼in). The body is yellowish-orange, with three very broad white bands edged with black. A very active fish, this is not too dependent on an anemone as a home. It breeds easily, and many available fish are tank-reared. It can be rather sensitive to adverse water conditions and to disease.

Amphiprion percula

Amphiprion polymnus
(Saddle-back clown)

A. polymnus comes from the Indo-Pacific and grows to 15cm (6in). Its colouring is unusual for Clownfish: chocolate brown with, in males, some orange on the head. There is a bold white stripe behind the eye and a conspicuous white 'saddle' across the dorsal fin and back. This fish is unfortunately rather delicate, and needs an anemone host.

SURGEONFISH (TANGS)

The Surgeonfish, or Tangs, are members of the Acanthuridae family, a relatively small group of exclusively tropical fish. Most are rather large, and all have thick ovoid bodies and are very active swimmers. On each side of the tail they have a large erectile spine which is used in self-defence and, occasionally, to attack other fish — or, during handling, the aquarist. They have very small scales and bright colours, which are less liable to fade or change with mood than with other fish. Vegetable matter is a very important part of their diet: they become constipated and may die if given only meat- or fish-based foods. Surgeonfish swim by paddling swiftly with their pectoral fins, so that their motion is erratic. Although they shoal in the wild, they are very intolerant of their own kind in the aquarium. They are rather delicate and never bred in captivity.

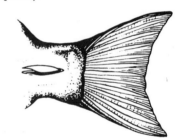

Detail of spine at the base of the Surgeonfish's tail.

Acanthurus spp.

A. coeruleus (Blue tang) is from the Caribbean and tropical Atlantic; it grows to 30cm (11¾in). Juveniles are deep-bodied and yellow with a bright blue eye. Adults are blue, with many light-blue lengthways lines, and a yellow tail. They are comparatively hardy and peaceful with fish of their own size.

A. glaucopareius (Lipstick surgeon, Gold-rimmed surgeonfish, or White-cheek surgeon), from the Indo-Pacific, grows to 35cm (13¾in). It has a grey-brown body, flushed with violet. Dorsal and anal fins are deep blue, with orange and white edges. The tail is pale

Acanthurus coeruleus

Acanthurus leucosternon

blue with a yellow bar, and there is a conspicuous wedge-shaped white bar on the face, below the eye. The lips are large and protuberant. It is fairly peaceful with large fish.

Acanthurus glaucopareius

A. leucosternon (Powder-blue surgeon) is a popular but aggressive fish from the Indo-Pacific and Red Sea; it grows to 30cm (11¾in). The body is a beautiful mid-blue, and the tail is barred vertically in blue and black. The dorsal fin and the tail root are yellow, and the anal fin blue and white. The head is velvety black, edged with a broad white band. A very hardy fish, it needs plenty of tank space for its active swimming. It is almost completely vegetarian.

Acanthurus lineatus

A. lineatus (Clown surgeonfish or Pyjama tang) comes from the Indo-Pacific and grows to 18cm (7in). Its body is orange-yellow, crossed with numerous pale-blue lines that are edged with black. The belly is purple and the tail is marked with a deep blue crescent. The tips of the tail fin are prolonged into points. Although very attractive, this is one of the most aggressive Surgeonfish, and must be treated with caution.

Paracanthurus hepatus

Zebrasoma veliferum

Paracanthurus hepatus
(Blue tang; Regal tang)

Known also as *P. teuthis*, this is a beautiful and rare import from the Indo-Pacific, growing to 25cm (9¾in). Its body is the brightest blue imaginable, and the sides are marked with a bold black lengthways stripe. The tail is bright yellow, edged top and bottom with black. The dorsal and anal fins are likewise edged with black. Unfortunately, the colour fades to a rather tedious yellow-grey as the fish grows to maturity. This fish is unusual in tolerating its own kind in the aquarium, and is hardy once acclimatized. Great care must be taken in introducing it to the tank, as it may go into a state of shock. Dim the lights and leave it well alone for several hours.

Zanclus canescens

Zanclus canescens
(Moorish idol)

Known also as *Z. cornutus*, this is sometimes placed in a separate family from the Acanthuridae; it comes from the Indo-Pacific, and grows to 25cm (9¾in). It looks bizarre, being immensely foreshortened and having a tremendously elongated dorsal fin which terminates in a long filament. The mouth is carried on a definite beak. The body is creamy yellow, with three broad black bands across the head, rear body, and tail. There is a yellow 'mask' just in front of the eyes. This fish is almost exclusively vegetarian, and is unfortunately both delicate and a finicky eater. Once established, it is very long-lived, and generally peaceful towards other fish

— although its long trailing dorsal pennant is often the victim of fin-nibblers. Buy only small specimens: these give the best chance of successful acclimatization to captivity.

Zebrasoma spp.

Z. veliferum (Sailfin tang) is an active fish from the Indo-Pacific and Red Sea which grows to 40cm (15¾in). It has an extremely deep, compressed body, with very large, rounded dorsal and anal fins and a pointed snout. The body is blue-grey, crossed by numerous vertical white-edged yellow lines. The head and belly are speckled with pale spots, and the fins are barred with yellow and blue. It is capable of quite extensive colour changes, and individuals often vary markedly. This fish is very aggressive and extremely active, and will not tolerate any overcrowding. It is almost exclusively vegetarian.

Z. xanthurum (Yellow-tailed tang) is a striking fish from the Indo-Pacific and Red Sea, growing to 40cm (15¾in). It is very variable in colouring, but those from the Red Sea are bright blue with dark speckles and a yellow tail; specimens from other regions are more brownish in colour, although the tail may be a brighter yellow. Very aggressive but quite hardy, this fish needs plenty of vegetable food.

TRIGGERFISH

Attractive and odd-looking fish of the Balistidae family, the Triggerfish are characterized by a huge head which accounts for a third of the body length. They have a very large spine in the dorsal fin, which can be erected and locked rigidly; this holds the fish immovably in caves and coral, and it is futile to attempt to remove them by force. Triggerfish have small mouths containing very strong beak-like teeth. Unfortunately, they use these freely, and can bite pieces clean out of other fish, the aquarist's hand or, when feeling particularly suicidal, out of the heater cable. They are therefore best kept in single-species tanks whose

Zebrasoma xanthurum

Balistes vetula

heater cable is protected by coral. Even then, they will try to shift the coral around so as to rearrange the tank to their own satisfaction. Any invertebrates are of course immediately eaten. Other odd habits are resting flat on their sides on the tank floor, and swimming by waving their anal and dorsal fins to and fro while holding their bodies stiff. They have bred on occasion in large public aquaria, making a nest in the gravel and guarding the eggs. Triggerfish are exclusively carnivorous and are best fed hard-shelled invertebrates such as Shrimp — complete with shells!

Balistes vetula
(Queen triggerfish)

From the Atlantic and Caribbean, this fish grows to 50cm (20in). Hardy and rapid-growing, it is less belligerent than most of the group, and can be trained to take food from the hands. It is yellowish, with two bright blue crescent-shaped lines at the sides of the head. The dorsal and anal fins and the tail are also striped with blue. The tips of the dorsal fin and the tail are elongated into long points.

Balistoides niger

Balistoides niger
(Clown triggerfish)

Also known as *B. conspicullum*, this attractive fish from the Indo-Pacific and Red Sea grows to 50cm (20in). It is sooty brown, and the underside is covered with large circular white spots. There is a black-spotted yellow 'saddle' on the back, and the lips are bright orange edged with white. The tail is barred in black and white. There is a yellowish 'mask' across the head, just

Rhinecanthus aculeatus

below the eyes. This fish becomes very tame with its owner, but is unpredictably vicious with its tankmates. It has a strong kamikaze instinct, and determinedly chews through heater cables and thermostats. It is uncommon even in its native haunts and is therefore expensive.

Chaetoderma penicilligera
(Prickly leatherjacket)

This very odd fish from the Indo-Pacific region grows to 25cm (9¾in). Its diamond-shaped body is golden brown with numerous dark lines and

Triggerfish wedged in coral, showing locked dorsal spine.

light speckles. The whole body is covered with small fleshy branched appendages shaped like little trees. Their function is unknown, and they may simply serve as camouflage. This fish is a very greedy feeder, but is quite peaceful and not aggressive even to small tankmates.

Rhinecanthus aculeatus
(Picasso fish; Humu-humu-nuku-
nuku-a-puaa)

An Indo-Pacific triggerfish which grows to 30cm (11¾in); its more cumbersome popular name is Hawaiian in origin. The head is disproportionately huge, even for a triggerfish. The body is whitish, with a bold yellow line from the mouth to the middle of the body. The sides are boldly marked with alternating light and dark lines, arranged in a V-shape. Blue and yellow stripes run from one eye to the other over the forehead. There are three rows of small black spines running along each side of the base of the tail. An aggressive fish, this may become tame with its owner.

BOXFISH, PUFFERS AND THEIR RELATIVES

These fish form several related families which share many characteristics and are best considered together. Their single most important common feature is the fusion of the teeth into a beak which is strong enough to bite into coral, invertebrates such as Shrimps, and, sometimes, other fish — although they are not usually aggressive except with their own kind. All have very fat bodies, and use the tail for steering, propelling themselves by rowing movements of the pectoral fins and the waving action of the dorsal and anal fins.

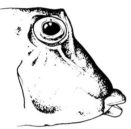

Detail of Boxfish.

The Ostraciontidae, known as Boxfish, Trunkfish or Cowfish, are the oddest. The entire body is encased in a rigid body box, with the fins, mouth and eyes protruding through apertures. These fish are very attractive, but are clumsy swimmers, easily bullied, and prone to skin diseases. One unfortunate property is their ability to release a lethal toxin when frightened, killing both the Trunkfish and its tankmates.

Porcupine fish (Diodontidae) are very similar to the Puffers (Tetraodontidae), differing significantly only in being covered with conspicuous spines. Both types can inflate themselves into a ball when frightened, but should never be encouraged to do this, as harm can result.

Canthigaster solandri

Almost without exception these fish are quite peaceful with their tankmates. They are all hardy and easy to feed, but have not been bred in the aquarium (although this has been achieved with the freshwater species of *Tetraodon*).

Canthigaster solandri
(Sharp-nosed puffer)

A common Puffer from the Indo-Pacific and Red Sea, sold also as *C. papua* (there are, too, numerous similar species). It is a slim-bodied Puffer with a long pointed snout. The body is golden-brown, covered with bluish dots that are edged with black; on the back, these coalesce to form lines. There is a conspicuous black 'eye spot', edged with blue, at the base of the dorsal fin. A timid but very hardy fish which is an effective scavenger and is quite peaceful.

Diodon holocanthus
(Porcupine fish)

A very common fish, found in most tropical seas, which grows to 40cm (15¾in). It is covered with fine spines which are inconspicuous when the fish is not inflated. Its colour is variable, but usually light brown on the back and white underneath. The back is speckled and barred with large brown marks, edged with pale blue or white. This fish is very peaceful, and may bury itself in the gravel at night. Eats almost anything.

D. hystrix (Porcupine fish) is very similar and also found in most tropical seas. It grows to 90cm (35in), but is much smaller in captivity. It is yellowish with small brown speckles and bars, and is very peaceful and extremely hardy. Recommended for beginners.

Lactoria cornuta
(Cowfish)

An odd and unmistakeable fish from the Indo-Pacific, growing to 45cm (17¾in), but usually much smaller. It is

Lactoria cornuta

a Boxfish, and its bony shell is prolonged into two long forward-pointing horns above the eyes, and two more horns pointing backwards near the anal fin. This makes the fish absolutely inedible even by large Groupers. It is yellowish with numerous pale blue spots. Very easily tamed, it eats most foods from the fingers. It is very active and bold, but should not be kept with aggressive fish like Damselfish, which pester it continually.

Ostracion tuberculatus

Ostracion tuberculatus
(Black-spotted trunkfish)

A large — 45cm (17¾in) — Boxfish from the Indo-Pacific. The hard shell of the body is very broad and is square in section. In young fish the body is bright yellow, covered with round black spots; in adults it becomes greyish, and the spots are blue-white. This fish is especially prone to release lethal toxins when frightened, but is otherwise very peaceful.

Tetrasomus gibbosus
(Hovercraft boxfish; Pyramid trunkfish)

An Indo-Pacific Boxfish growing to 30cm (11¾in), in which the bony shell is pyramid-shaped, with short horns pointing outwards in all directions.

Tetrasomus gibbosus

The colour is a nondescript brown. Extremely tame, peaceful and hardy, apart from a tendency to develop skin diseases, this fish, unlike many of its relatives, is not known to release toxins when frightened.

MISCELLANEOUS MARINE FISH

Amanses sandwichiensis
(Leopard filefish)

Filefish are found throughout most tropical seas and grow to 38cm(15in). They are closely related to Triggerfish, having the same erectile spine on the back. They have also an erectile spine on the lower surface of the body which, when extended, causes the outline of the body to become grotesquely enlarged. The body is covered with rough tubercles, and is mottled brown, although the colour can be varied almost at will. This is a quiet, inoffensive fish which eats anything and seldom bothers other fish. It will, however, eat may invertebrates — even Sea anemones.

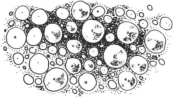

Detail of abrasive skin of Amanses sandwichiensis.

Apogon spp.

A. maculatus (Flamefish) is one of the large group of Cardinalfish, which are small shoaling fish; unusually for

Apogon maculatus

Apogon nematopterus

166

marine fish, they have a habit of hanging motionless in mid-water. This 12cm (4¾in) species comes from the Caribbean and Western Atlantic. It is brilliant red with a black spot at the base of the tail and on the sides. It is seminocturnal, and has very large eyes. Though hardy, it will usually eat only live food. It has bred in the aquarium, and is a mouth-breeder, the fry being cared for by the male.

A. nematopterus (Pyjama cardinal fish) is from the Indian Ocean and grows to only 8cm (3¼in). Very hardy and slow-moving, it has a short, plump, yellowish body with a broad black band extending across the midline into the sail-like dorsal fin. The rear of the body is speckled with reddish spots. The fins are held stiffly erect at all times. These fish should be kept in small groups, and have spawned in captivity several times; they usually take only live foods.

Dendrochirus brachypterus
(Dwarf lion fish)

A Lionfish from the Indo-Pacific and Red Sea which grows to 15cm (6in). Lionfish (which include *Pterois* spp. — see page 170) are short and stocky, with a very large mouth and immensely elongated spiny fin rays which are extremely poisonous should they penetrate the skin. In this small species, the body is pink, crossed with brown stripes. The fin rays, though long, are connected by membranes, and the pectoral fins are especially winglike. The fins are all barred in pink and white. These fish are slow swimmers, drifting about with fins extended. They are completely peaceful, gulping small fish but otherwise ignoring their tankmates. They can, with difficulty, be trained to eat freeze-dried food or strips of fish.

D. zebra (Spotfin lionfish) is a large version of *D. brachypterus*, growing to 20cm (7¾in). It is more brightly coloured, with red and black markings, and is extremely hardy.

If the spines of either species penetrate the hand, they cause agonizing pain. As the toxin is destroyed by heat, the affected part must at once be immersed in extremely hot water and

Dendrochirus zebra

held there for at least half an hour. Medical attention must then be sought promptly.

Equetus spp.

E. acuminatus (Cubbyu or High hat) is a small member of the Croaker family from the Western Atlantic and Caribbean, growing to 25cm (9¾in). The body is straight underneath, strongly arched above, and the large, black sail-like dorsal fin is held stiffly erect. The body is marked with lengthways brown-and-white stripes. A shy and partly nocturnal fish, *E. acuminatus* is very

active and quite hardy. It is generally peaceful. Has spawned in captivity, scattering its eggs like *Barbus*, but so far fry have not been reared.

E. lanceolatus (Ribbonfish or Jack-knife), from the Caribbean and Western Atlantic, grows to 25cm (9¾in). The body is greyish-pink, and the dorsal fin is extremely long and erect. A bold black stripe, edged with white, extends down the dorsal fin and back along the body to the tip of the tail; a similar stripe crosses the head, and another the forward part of the body. An attractive but delicate fish, best kept in small groups, *C. lanceolatus* is very difficult to acclimatize to a new tank, and often dies of shock. It

Gobiosoma (Elacatinus) oceanops

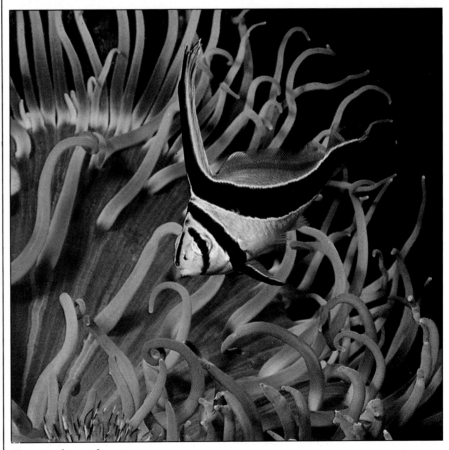
Equetus lanceolatus

167

may need to be tempted with live shrimp to start it feeding.

Gobiosoma oceanops
(Neon goby)

This small Caribbean Goby, growing to 8cm (3¼in), often acts as a cleaner fish. It has a long slender body, with a broad iridescent-blue lengthways band edged on either side with black. It is very peaceful, but so small as to be often eaten by tankmates. It is frequently bred, with eggs laid in small caves or shells: both parents guard the eggs, but should be removed after 10 days, just before hatching, in case they eat the fry. The young are difficult to raise until they are large enough to eat newly hatched Brine shrimps.

Hippocampus kuda
(Seahorse)

This interesting curiosity from the Indo-Pacific is not really suitable for the home aquarium. Golden-brown, with darker speckles, this seahorse grows to a length of 18cm (7in). It feeds only on live food, such as Brine shrimps, and, because it is unable to pursue its food, cannot be kept in a tank where the filters create a strong current. It must have plenty of coral or marine algae to which it can cling with its prehensile tail, waiting for food to drift past. It can be bred in the aquarium, provided a suitable source of live food can be found for both fry and adults. The eggs are transferred to a brood pouch in the male's belly, and are quite large when born. As it cannot compete for food, *Hippocampus kuda* cannot be kept with other fish, or it will starve.

Holocentrus ruber
(Red squirrelfish)

A spiny finned fish resembling the Perch and found in the Indo-Pacific and the Red Sea; it has strayed through the Suez Canal into the eastern Mediterranean. 28cm (11in)

Hippocampus kuda

long, it has a red body, with silvery lengthwise stripes. The upper part of the dorsal fin is black, as is the anal fin. The eye is very large, as this is a nocturnal fish. In the wild it seeks live food by night, but it can be trained to accept dead shrimps and pieces of fish. Although sociable with its own kind, it cannot be trusted with small fish. Do not expose it to very strong light or its eyes will be damaged.

Monodactylus argenteus
(Malay angel; Silver finger)

A shoaling fish from the Indo-Pacific, growing to 20cm (7¾in), this fish is found in fresh waters, brackish estuaries and open seas, and is therefore very tolerant of changing or adverse water conditions. The body is diamond-shaped and silvery, with stiffly erect dorsal and anal fins. A vertical black line crosses the eye, and another runs down the front of the dorsal fin, across the shoulder, and

along the anal fin. The dorsal and anal fins and the tail are yellow. It is a lively swimmer, doing well in small groups, and is quite peaceful. It must be given some vegetables. Being very hardy, it is an excellent fish for the beginner, and is useful for conditioning a newly set-up tank, tolerating high nitrite levels. It has not been bred in captivity.

M. sebae, a close relative, comes from the West African coast. It differs in being almost grotesquely deep-bodied; its depth is twice its body-length. It is silver with three conspicuous vertical bands. Although not quite as hardy as *M. argenteus*, it is generally a very good fish for the beginner.

Opistognathus aurifrons

Opistognathus aurifrons, *in burrow.*

Opistognathus aurifrons
(Yellow jawfish)

An interesting Caribbean fish, growing to 12cm (4¾in), *O. aurifrons* is elongated with a sky-blue body and a golden head, with very large eyes. It constructs a burrow for itself, surrounding the entrance with a barrier of stones, and guards this against all intruders; it must have at least 10cm (4in) of gravel in which to burrow. A mouthbreeder, it has been spawned in the aquarium, but the fry have not been raised successfully. Very hardy, it feeds readily on most foods: indeed, a mixed diet is essential, as otherwise it may suffer fatal ulceration of the throat.

Platax spp.

P. orbicularis (Round batfish) is a hardy shoaling fish from the Indo-Pacific and the Red Sea; it grows to

Platax orbicularis

60cm (2ft) in length and nearly 90cm (3ft) in depth! The body is rounded and compressed, and the dorsal and anal fins are immense and sail-like. The overall colour is tan, with a black band through the eye. The fish swims in a noticeably nose-down manner. This tough, hardy fish eats anything, but unfortunately grows very rapidly — up to 25cm (9¾in) per year — and so can be maintained only in very large tanks. It is easily bullied by other species. These fish are very peaceful but, to avoid squabbles, they should be kept either on their own or in groups of five or more.

P. pinnatus (Red-face batfish or Long-finned batfish), from the eastern Indian Ocean, has an even more extreme shape. While small, it is grotesquely elongated, although the dorsal and anal fins become proportionately smaller as the fish increases in size to its maximum 40cm (15¾in). It is chocolate brown with paler vertical stripes, and the whole outline is trimmed with bright orange. The colours are less intense with increasing size. Not as hardy as *P. orbicularis.*

Platax pinnatus

Plectorhynchus (Gaterin) spp.

P. albovittatus (Yellow-lined sweet-lips), a shoaling fish with a spiny dorsal fin, is from the Indo-Pacific. The young are attractively marked with lengthways black-and-orange stripes,

Plectorhynchus albovittatus

but these fade to dull brown in adults, which reach 60cm (2ft). *Plectorhynchus* are rather delicate and temperamental in general, but this is the toughest of the species available.

P. chaetodonoides (Clown sweet-lips or Polka-dot grunt) is a gaily coloured fish from the Malaysian region. It has a short, stout body, growing to 30cm (11¾in) in the aquarium. It is dark brown in youth, covered with numerous large irregular white patches which are bordered with black; the colouring fades to uniform mid-brown with darker spots in adults. A quiet, retiring and very peaceful fish, which must have plenty of hiding places, it is rather sensitive to water conditions, and needs a good, mixed diet.

P. orientalis (Oriental sweetlips) is very similar to *P. chaetodonoides*, but has yellow (not white) patches on a brown background. The adults are brighter than in *P. chaetodonoides*, however, with yellow lengthways stripes.

Plotosus anquillaris
(Coral catfish)

One of the very few Catfish found in saltwater, this fish comes from the Indo-Pacific. It grows to 30cm (11¾in) and is extremely hardy. It is tadpole-shaped, with a very broad flat head and

Plectorhynchus chaetodonoides

a wide mouth fringed with barbels. The body is eel-like, with long ribbon-like dorsal and anal fins. Body colour is dark brown, and the sides are marked with lengthwise stripes of bright yellow. Young fish swarm in a 'ball' which appears to roll along the bottom, but become more solitary as they mature. Eats absolutely anything, and is not to

be trusted with small fish. The pectoral and dorsal spines are sharp and carry an unpleasant toxin which produces very painful wounds if you handle the fish.

Pterois volitans
(Lionfish; Dragonfish; Turkeyfish)

A very popular fish from the Indo-Pacific and Red Sea, this grows to 35cm (13¾in) but is usually smaller. It is closely related to *Dendrochirus* (see page 167), but the spiny fin rays are not connected by a membrane: instead, all the fin rays stand out stiffly. It is gaily

Plectorhynchus orientalis

Pterois volitans

coloured in maroon, pink and white stripes over the whole body and the fins. Its fins carry dangerous toxins (see *Dendrochirus* for treatment of 'stings'). A very hardy fish which becomes extremely tame, it may need to be coaxed to take dead shrimps or pieces of fish. It has a very large mouth, and cannot be trusted with small fish, but is otherwise completely peaceful. Grows rapidly but, because it is relatively inactive, can live in a fairly small aquarium. It has not been bred in captivity.

Several very similar species are available, some with even longer fin rays.

Scatophagus argus
(Scat)

Usually sold as a freshwater fish, but actually much better as a marine fish, the Scat is found in the eastern Indian Ocean, in estuaries and the open sea. It has a deep, roughly square body, which is compressed but muscular, and grows to 30cm (11¾in). The body is silvery-olive, and is covered with large, round black spots. A common variety, *S. argus rubifrons*, has orange patches on the dorsal fins and upper back. Colours tend to fade as the fish

Scatophagus argus

matures. This fish is immensely hardy when kept in seawater, although prone to fungus diseases when in freshwater. It eats enormous amounts of food, and requires a lot of vegetable food if it is to remain healthy. Very peaceful, not yet bred in the aquarium, it is an ideal fish to condition a new tank, as it is highly tolerant of excess nitrite levels.

Siganus spp.

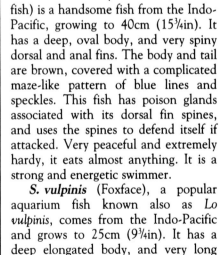

S. vermiculatus (Reticulated rabbit-fish) is a handsome fish from the Indo-Pacific, growing to 40cm (15¾in). It has a deep, oval body, and very spiny dorsal and anal fins. The body and tail are brown, covered with a complicated maze-like pattern of blue lines and speckles. This fish has poison glands associated with its dorsal fin spines, and uses the spines to defend itself if attacked. Very peaceful and extremely hardy, it eats almost anything. It is a strong and energetic swimmer.

S. vulpinis (Foxface), a popular aquarium fish known also as *Lo vulpinis*, comes from the Indo-Pacific and grows to 25cm (9¾in). It has a deep elongated body, and very long spines on its dorsal and anal fins: these can be moved to face an attacker, and carry a powerful toxin. The snout is prolonged, with a protruding beak. Body and fins are chrome yellow, and the head and shoulders are white with bold black markings. A highly desirable aquarium fish, very hardy and completely peaceful, except with its own kind, *S. vulpinis* eats anything, and needs large amounts of plant foods. It has not bred in the aquarium.

Siganus vermiculatus

INDEX

Page numbers in *italic* refer to illustrations

172

INDEX OF PLANTS

Page numbers in *italic*
refer to illustrations

ACKNOWLEDGEMENTS

The pictures on these pages were reproduced by courtesy of the following:

Keith Hampshire: 145(c,b).

Jan-Eric Larsson: 6, 8-9(tr,cr), 16(t), 24-25(b), 38-39, 46-47(b), 73(b), 75, 77(t), 78(b), 79, 81-84, 85(tr), 87, 88(t,b), 91, 92(tl,cl,bl), 93(b), 94(tr,b), 95(tr,br), 97(t), 98(t), 100(tr,bl), 101(t,b), 102(t,b), 104(t), 105(b), 106(cr), 107(b), 108-111, 112(t,bl), 113(b), 114-115, 117(t,cr), 118(t), 120(b), 121, 122(c), 123(b), 125(b), 126(b), 127(cl,br), 128, 129(bl,br), 165(tr), 167(ct,cr), 168(b).

Steven Preston: 144, 145(t).

Alan Rothwell: 80(tr), 88(c), 89(c), 95(tl), 96(cr), 107(t), 148(r), 149(tr,br), 151(c), 152(bl), 153(cl,bl,cr), 154(cl), 155(tl,cl), 157(bl), 158(cl), 159(cl,bl), 164(cl), 165(bl), 166(tl).

Spectrum Colour Library: 77(b), 80(bl), 85(cl), 90(cl), 104(b), 105(t), 106(tr), 160, 161(bl,tr,cr), 162(cr), 165(cr), 168(t), 169(bl), 170(br).

A. van den Nieuwenhuizen: 7, 8-9(tl,b), 10, 12-13, 16(b), 17-23, 24-25(tl,tr), 27, 28, 30, 33, 34, 43, 44-45, 46-47(t), 48-51, 54-57, 73(t), 74, 76, 78(t), 85(br), 86, 89(t,b), 90(tr,cr), 93(t), 94(tl), 96(tl), 97(b), 98(b), 99, 100(cl), 101(c), 102(c), 103, 106(bl), 112(br), 113(t), 116, 117(b), 118(b), 119, 120(t), 122(t), 123(t), 124, 125(t), 126(t), 127(t), 129(t), 130-134, 136-137, 140-141(c), 142-143, 148(l), 149(tl,cl), 150, 151(t,b), 152(tl,br), 153(t), 154(tl,br), 155(tr), 156, 157(tl,br), 158(tr,br), 159(br), 161(tl), 162(tl,bl), 163, 164(tr), 166(tr,br), 167(br), 169(tr,br), 170(bl,tr), 171.

All other photographs are the property of Quill Publishing Limited.

Key: (t) top; (b) bottom; (l) left; (r) right; (c) centre.

While every effort has been made to acknowledge all copyright holders, we apologize if any omissions have been made.